The Majority Press

BRAZIL: Mixture or Massacre?
Essays in the Genocide of a Black People

ABDIAS DO NASCIMENTO was born in Franca, São Paulo, Brazil, in 1914. In Rio de Janeiro, he founded the Black Experimental Theater in 1944 and the Museum of Black Art in 1968, as tools in his life's work, dedicated to advancing Black political and cultural consciousness. His play Sortilege (Black Mystery) revolutionized the concept of Black theater. From 1968 to 1982 he lived in the United States, in exile from political persecution. He is Professor Emeritus at the State University of New York at Buffalo, where he taught African Cultures in the New World at its Puerto Rican Studies and Research Center, which he directed from 1978-1980. He was Visiting Lecturer at the Wesleyan Center for the Humanities at Wesleyan University and, in 1976-77, Visiting Professor at the Department of African Languages and Literatures, University of Ife, Ile-Ife, Nigeria. As an artist, he has exhibited his Afro-Brazilian paintings all over the U.S. and Brazil. On the international scene, he was delegate to the Sixth Pan-African Congress (Dar-es-Salaam, 1974), Encounter on African World Alternatives (Dakar, 1976), participant in the Colloquium of the Second World Festival of Black and African Arts and Culture (Lagos, 1977), First Congress of Black Culture in the Americas (Cali, 1977) and the Seminar "Brazil at the Doorstep of the 1980's" (Stockholm, 1978). Returning to Brazil in 1981, he founded the Afro-Brazilian Studies and Research Institute (IPEAFRO) and the journal Afrodiaspora, a multilingual periodical on African world affairs. Nascimento was elected to the Brazilian national Congress in 1982. He served until 1986 as the first Afro-Brazilian Congressman working fulltime for the Black community's human and civil rights. In 1984, he founded the Afro-Brazilian Arts, Education and Culture Foundation, later renamed the Abdias Nascimento Cultural Foundation. Nascimento is a member of the International Bureau of the Pan-African Arts and Culture Festival (FESPAC) and of the national Commission for the Centennial of the Abolition of Slavery, Brazilian Ministry of Culture (1988).

Books by ABDIAS DO NASCIMENTO

Sortilégio (mistério negro). (Play.) Teatro Experimental do Negro: Rio de Janeiro, 1960.

Dramas para negros e prólogo para brancos. (Anthology of Afro-Brazilian dramatic works.) Teatro Experimental do Negro: Rio de Janeiro, 1966.

O Negro Revoltado, 2nd edition. Rio de Janeiro: Nova Fronteira, 1980. (1st edition GRD: Rio de Janeiro, 1968.)

"Racial Democracy" in Brazil: Myth or Reality?, translation by Elisa Larkin Nascimento. Ibadan: Sketch Publishing Co., 1977.

O Genocídio do Negro Brasileiro. Rio de Janeiro: Paz e Terra, 1978.

Sortilege (Black Mystery), translation by Peter Lownds. Chicago: Third World Press, 1978.

Sortilégio II: Mistério Negro de Zumbi Redivivo. Rio de Janeiro: Paz e Terra, 1979.

Sitiado em Lagos. (Under Siege in Lagos. Essay on author's experience at Festac '77.) Rio de Janeiro: Nova Fronteira, 1981.

Axés do Sangue e da Esperança. (Poetry.) Rio de Janeiro: Achiamé, 1982.

Combate ao Racismo. (Speeches and bills of law presented at the Brazilian Congress), Vols. 1-6. Brasilia: Camara do Deputados, 1983-86.

Afrodiaspora: Journal of Black World Thought, Nos. 1-6 (editor). Rio de Janeiro: IPEAFRO, 1982-86.

*Most of the books listed are available on a non-commercial basis through Afrodiaspora, Afro-Brazilian Studies and Research Institute (IPEAFRO), rua Benjamin Constant, 55/1104—Glória—20241 Rio de Janeiro, RJ—Brasil.

Abdias do Nascimento

BRAZIL
Mixture or Massacre?
Essays in the Genocide of a Black People

Second Edition

translated by
Elisa Larkin Nascimento

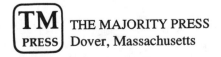

THE MAJORITY PRESS
Dover, Massachusetts

Library of Congress Cataloging-in-Publication Data

Nascimento, Abdias do, 1914-
Brazil, mixture or massacre?

Bibliography: p.
1. Blacks—Brazil.   2.Brazil—Race relations.
3. Brazil—Civilization—African influences.   I. Title.
II. Title: Mixture or massacre?
F2659.N4N3713   1988   981'.00496   88-8951
ISBN 0-912469-26-9

First published in 1979.

First Majority Press edition, 1989.

The Majority Press
P.O. Box 538
Dover, Massachusetts 02030

Printed in the United States of America

10 9 8 7 6 5 4 3 2 1

In remembrance of the hundreds of millions of Africans and their descendants assassinated by the slavers, oppressors, ravagers, racists, rapists and white supremacists -

I dedicate this book to the young Blacks in Brazil and in the world in the hope that they will continue the struggle for a world of justice and equality in which these disasters can never again repeat themselves .

In fraternal love

The slave that kills his master practices an act of legitimate self-defense.

Luis Gama
(words pronounced before a Court of Justice)

PREFACE TO THE SECOND EDITION

It is now almost ten years since this book was first published by Afrodiaspora. In the course of the decade, much has happened to alter Afro-Brazilian reality, adding to it new dimensions. Currently, the race question in Brazil is extremely dynamic, and its discussion is ever broader and more widespread. Considered until very recently the specific problem of one segment of Brazil's population, the Afro-Brazilian issue has gained the status of a national issue. No longer is it only the Black community vanguard and a few rare personalities in the academic world who are committed to questioning racism and racial discrimination against Blacks in Brazilian society. Afro-Brazilians' forceful denunciation of the racial contradiction has succeeded in awakening the attention of national political leaders and political parties, as well as other significant forces like churches, religious and community organizations, schools and educational systems, dance and recreational clubs and so on.

Until very recently, the norm was to nullify Black identity by placing Afro-Brazilians indiscriminately in the category of "Brazilian people" or "the working class," in order to avoid Black people's specific problems emerging as a serious social question. The attempt was to silence millions of Brazilians of African origin with the illusion that, by solving the dichotomy between rich and poor or between worker and employer, all racial problems would be automatically resolved. This position of the white Eurocentric ruling elite was taken to the extreme of elaborating an ideology called "racial democracy" whose goal was to proclaim the virtues of Brazilian race relations, presenting them as an example to be followed by the rest of the world.

However, this ideology was based on race mixture, the never-too-celebrated miscegenation syndrome, as the great proof of its anti-racist efficacy. According to this theory, Brazil is the only country formed by various races, amalgamating them into one, the mixed or mulatto race, by the works and grace of this miraculous "racial democracy" under the aegis of which took place the process of molding our people and nation.

The incredible part is that this obvious racial aggression perpetrated by the political, economic, cultural, religious and social elite should be shared by all its segments, from those defined as liberals, leftists and rightists to the Marxists and the reactionaries. Behold the most outrageous and scandalous of all unanimities: in Brazil there are no race problems. In the empire of racial democracy all are compulsorily Brazilian and equal before the law. This myth has become one of the most deeply ingrained elements of the Brazilian social consciousness, since the entire educational system, mass communications media, system of justice and other agents influencing public opinion all work to sustain it.

Since 1979, when this work was first published, the data on race discrimination in Brazil have confirmed the falsehood of the racial democracy myth. According to underestimated official statistics, 44.34% of Brazilians represent in the 1980 census the sum of the two categories *preto* (Black) and *pardo* (roughly the equivalent of "Brown," except that many browns classify themselves as whites). For purposes of statistical analysis, we will define the sum of these two categories as the Afro-Brazilian population, although we are aware that these official data greatly underestimate the true dimension of the Afro-Brazilian demographic presence. Only 5.89% classify themselves as *pretos*. But statistics on employment and education show that the 38.45% who call themselves *pardos* suffer the same kinds of discrimination. Among men classified as *pretos*, for instance, 46.7% have one year of schooling or less, while about half that percentage (24.3%) applies to whites. And *pardos*? Their situation is worse that that of *pretos*: 48.2% had one year's schooling or less. On the other hand, 5.6% of white men had 12 years' education or more, while that percentage was 0.5% for *pretos* and 0.9% for *pardos*. In other words, whites have 6 times more chance to complete 12 years' education or more.

In terms of income, the situation is not much different. Among white men, 17.8% earn the minimum wage (about US$30.00

monthly) or less, while among *pretos* the percentage is 33% and among *pardos,* 32.5%. White men earning more than ten times the minimum are 6.5% of the total, while only 0.4% of *pretos* and 1.1% of *pardos* earn that much. Among women, the situation of double discrimination is evident. 14.6% of white women earn the minimum wage or less, while twice that many *pretas* (28.5%) and 19.8% of *pardas* are in that situation. These data reflect the only significant advantage held by mixed bloods. The vast majority of *pretas* (Black women) are to this day exploited as domestic servants at less than poverty wages. Some mulatto women have a greater chance of escaping this trap. On the other hand, they do not do much better than *pretas* on the high end of the income scale: 0.8% of white women earn more than ten times the minimum wage, while 0.03% of *pretas* and 0.09% of *pardas* are in that bracket.

These statistics, as a whole, render useless the "mulatto escape hatch" theory in which some sociologists posit that greater social status conferred upon mixed-bloods creates an outlet through which potential protest is neutralized by the possibility of social climbing through miscegenation (Degler 1971). I can attest, as a Black militant, that a very large portion of our colleagues in the struggle against racism are "mulattoes" who identify themselves as Afro-Brazilian.

In contrast to the image of "racial democracy," the data cited show a clear racial hierarchy in terms of income and educational opportunity. At the top are white men; next, white women; third, Black men, and lastly Black women. Between 1980 and 1982, this situation tended to worsen (PNAD 1982).

Nonetheless, to this day, Africans who raise the question of racism in public as a political issue are dismissed with the allegation "That's not race discrimination, it's a class question. Here we have poor whites and poor Blacks, but not racism." This in a country where, even according to distorted official statistics, about 50% of whites as opposed to more than 75% of Blacks live on or below the poverty line.

The most sinister effect of this racial ideology is that the victims themselves become convinced that racism does not exist. Thus, the Black movement expends enormous energies trying to "prove" to its own people that their situation is due to race discrimination. Continuously, we must answer the question "Does racism really exist in Brazil?," turning our energies away from the real questions facing us in struggle. Indeed, if Brazilian racism is effective from the statistical point of view, keeping Africans well "in their place" socio-economically, its real achievement lies in this capacity to curb the growth of African consciousness and the community's protagonism on its own behalf.

This is not to say that Afro-Brazilian resistance abated after abolition. On the contrary, the present century has witnessed from the start an active vanguard of Black consciousness. Most often, it is expressed in non-political forms such as religious brotherhoods, African religious organizations, mutual aid societies, recreational clubs, samba schools and so on. Even at the turn of the century and into the teens, there existed a proliferation of these organizations with the name "Quilombo" or "Palmares," in direct reference to the military struggle carried out by our ancestors. An active Black press also existed, with foreseeable problems and lack of continuity due to the community's destitution. In the 1930's, the Brazilian Black Front, led by José Correia Leite and others, sponsored mass demonstrations against discrimination in São Paulo state, where Jim Crow policies were common. The Front grew into a political force of national scope, but was dissolved by the New State dictatorship in 1937.

The focus on African identity and cultural values was introduced by the Black Experimental Theater (TEN), founded by this author in Rio de Janeiro, in 1944. Among many other similar events, the TEN organized the National Black Conventions (Rio de Janeiro, 1946 and São Paulo, 1945) and the First Congress of Brazilian Blacks (Rio de Janeiro, 1950). The National Black Convention of São Paulo, which took place in 1945, was responsible for presenting to the National Constituent Assembly a series of measures which were, predictably, rejected by the writers of that constitution under the allegation that no discrimination existed in Brazil. Characteristic of Brazilian power relations and Black alienation is the fact that among more than 300 members of that Assembly, only one was African: Claudino José da Silva of the Brazilian Communist Party. Following the Party's orders, he voted against the Afro-Brazilian community's proposal. It seems the Party feared the measures would somehow prejudice working class solidarity.

During the military dictatorship of the sixties and seventies, mere discussion of race questions was banned by the National Security Law. Nevertheless, the Black movement grew, particularly during the latter half of the seventies. In 1978, a major demonstration against racism was held in São Paulo. Black organizations, in various forms and branches of activity, appeared all over the country.

Today, myths and falsehoods like racial democracy are no longer able to dope the consciousness of the Black community. At the moment I write this Preface, Black women and men of this country are well aware of the fraud embodied in the slogan "all are equal before the law." The law is white, made by whites in their interests. For this reason, Afro-Brazilians are increasingly organizing to participate in the legislative and political process, attempting to make real and significant changes.

During the 1982 state and congressional elections, several Afro-Brazilians ran for legislative office. While few of these were successful, the political weight of the movement did increase. For the first time in the nation's history, an Afro-Brazilian, this author, took office in the federal Congress with the explicit commitment to defend the Black community's specific interests. In Rio de Janeiro, three Africans were appointed to first-line posts in Leonel Brizola's state government. In São Paulo, the state government headed by Governor Franco Montoro created its Council for Black Community Development and Participation. With the civilian federal government of Tancredo Neves (substituted, before actually taking office, by José Sarney) inaugurated in March 1985, an Afro-Brazilian advisory council was created in the federal government's Ministry of Culture.

Currently, two historical moments have converged to create a unique crossroads in Afro-Brazilian experience. The Brazilian Congress is writing a new constitution for the nation, promulgation of which will coincide with the centennial of slavery's abolition.

While only three Afro-Brazilian representatives were elected to the current Constitutional Assembly, the process of drafting the document has illustrated the extent to which the Afro-Brazilian movement, organized in almost every State, is making its political weight felt. Among the articles included in the draft document prepared by various subcommittees and submitted to the Systematization Committee responsible for the final draft, we find the following, specifically addressing questions affecting Africans and their community.

Article 86. Everyone, male or female, is equal before the law, which will punish as crime without recourse to bail any discrimination offending human rights or rights here established. It is considered a form of discrimination to underrate, stereotype or degrade ethnic, racial or color groups, or persons belonging to such groups, through words, images or representations in any means of communication.

Article 87. Application by the State of compensatory measures designed to implement the constitutional principle of equality before the law in relation to groups or persons victimized by documented discrimination does not constitute privilege. Compensatory measures are those designed to give preference to certain citizens or groups of citizens, in order to guarantee their equal participation in and access to employment, education health care and other social rights.

Article 88. Education will emphasize juridical equality among the sexes, affirm the multicultural and pluriethnic characteristics of the Brazilian people and condemn racism and all forms of discrimination.

Article 106. At all educational levels, the government will reformulate the teaching of Brazilian History, with the goal of contemplating on an equal basis the contributions of different ethnic groups to the Brazilian people's multicultural and pluriethnic formation. The law will provide for fixation of commemorative dates important to the different national ethnic segments.

Article 89. Brazil will not maintain diplomatic relations nor sign treaties, agreements or pacts with countries which adopt official policies of race discrimination, nor permit in its territory the activities of these countries' corporations.

These are not the only draft dispositions presented by the Afro-Brazilian movement to the Constituent Assembly for consideration by its subcommittees. Nonetheless, debate of these propositions and acceptance of some of them by the subcommittees represents a considerable advance in Afro-Brazilian political struggle.

Indeed, during the 1982-86 legislative term, when I participated in the Congress as the first and only Afro-Brazilian legislator working specifically to defend the human and civil rights of the Black community, this advance began to be palpable. While other Afro-Brazilian legislators have existed, they do not identify themselves with the Black cause, and often do not even identify themselves as Black. The idea of raising the race question as an issue before the Brazilian Congress was patently absurd to a ruling elite convinced of the "racial democracy" theory's absolute truth. Reaction by the House of Deputies to my first speeches and legislative proposals was, for the most part, governed by the traditional Brazilian elite's attitude of irony or disdain: "Imagine the Brazilian Congress wasting time and energy on this nonsense!"

During the course of the term, however, it became clear that many colleagues were rethinking the question. I presented several bills of law, including among others one considering racism a crime against humanity with severe penalties, another establishing programs for integration of Blacks in the labor force and in education through quota systems, and one establishing November 20, National Black Consciousness Day, as a national holiday (Nascimento 1983-86). Most of these were approved in the various committees of the House of Deputies, but did not come to vote for bureaucratic reasons. One was approved in committee and by the House plenary, but rejected by the more conservative Senate as a result of one senator's objection. The influence of this early activity can be seen in the fact that several of the draft articles presented to the Constituent Assembly use language taken directly from these bills of law.

It is not likely that the Constituent Assembly will approve the measures cited, since the process of voting in the plenary will alter the draft text almost in its entirety. Conservative forces are dominant in the plenary to a greater extent than in the subcommittees and the committee which drafted the working text. We have no illusions: the new Constitution probably will not contribute to solving the emergent problems facing the Black community in Brazil. But the movement's victory is clear even if only to the extent that these questions have been addressed and debated seriously on a national level.

One index to the prevalence of this change in attitude is the position of the leftist forces like the Communist Party and its various splinter groups, and socialist parties as well. Previously they were, perhaps, more reluctant to deal with race issues than other political forces. Invocation of the "unity of the working class" and other slogans sufficed to render them entirely insensitive to Afro-Brazilians' specific problems. Today, these parties are sympathetic and actively seek to recruit and develop Afro-Brazilian militants in their ranks. Our goal, of course, is to consolidate the Black movement's autonomy, rejecting its cooptation by any political party. Nevertheless, this fact reflects the gaining of support and sympathy for our cause in society in general and in political circles in particular.

The 1988 centennial has brought about a motive for consideration, by the nation as a whole, of the state of Afro-Brazilian community. Debates, seminars, and many other activities are scheduled, and in almost every university, high school and community group the race question is being discussed. The Afro-Brazilian movement is at the forefront of these activities. It is worth noting, for example, that the Christian church in Brazil, both Catholic and Protestant, has Black consciousness groups, and that most universities have some kind of Afro-Brazilian student organization. Beyond this, there exist myriad Afro-Brazilian organizations independent of other contexts.

The Centennial activities are channelled partly through the National Commission for the Centennial of the Abolition of Slavery, created by the Ministry of Culture through its Advisory Council on Afro-Brazilian Affairs. This commission takes suggestions and supports activities presented and carried out by the Afro-Brazilian community itself. In a recent national meeting in Salvador, Bahia, the community's position was stated very clearly. While recognizing the relative historical importance of the date of slavery's abolition, it decided that the date deserves no celebration, but that it provides an occasion for reflection on and denunciation of the injustice and racist oppression still weighing upon the Afro-Brazilian people after a century of so-called freedom. This position is coherent with the same attitude announced by the Black movement in various demonstrations in recent years, in which May 13 has been symbolically buried as a protest against the falseness of this supposed abolition. The date has been designated National Day of Denunciation of Racism in Brazil, while November 20, National Black Consciousness Day, has been successfully instated as the true date commemorating Black liberation struggle.

I would like to end these considerations by citing a recent document approved by vote of the participants in the First National Encounter of the Abolition Centennial, held in Bahia in late November 1987. After examining the nature of the various crises shaking the country (economic-financial crisis, social crisis, cultural crisis, political crisis), Afro-Brazilian men and women concluded that

> The elites of Brazil have one face only: white, rich, university-educated and egotistic; the Nation has many faces. . . . Racism in its multiple forms—disguised or outright—is a basic tool of domination used by the State over the Nation. This means that, for us, the solution to the Brazilian crisis lies in the fight against racism and depends on us, those who have been fighting it in an organized way for at least 50 years.

The document ends with the following recommendations directed to "all those who wish to walk with us."

> 1) Redouble efforts toward the final liberation of Namibia and South Africa.

> 2) Continue the struggle to gain space in the formal political arena, such as party organizations and elections, without allowing, by any means, any dilution of the racial question, seen as an essential aspect of the Brazilian crisis.

> 3) Strengthen alliances with other social movements, especially those which represent living forces in Brazilian society and, like us, are struggling to reverse domination by the elites.

Afro-Brazilians will continue to organize and fight against racism as long as the realities depicted in this book do not change in substantial and significant ways. I do not hesitate to republish the text as it came out in 1979, for while a few minor details may be outdated, in essence the situation it examines remains the same. Until the country takes radical steps to change that situation, the outcry of the Afro-Brazilian people will not be stilled.

Rio de Janeiro, 1 January 1988
Abdias do Nascimento

BIBLIOGRAPHY

Degler, Carl (1971). *Neither Black nor White*. New York: Macmillan.

Nascimento, Abdias (1983-86). *Combate ao Racismo: Discursos e Projetos de Lei*. Brasília: Câmara do Deputados.

PNAD 1982 (National Survey of Domicile Samples). Rio de Janeiro: Brazilian Institute of Geography and Statistics.

TABLE OF CONTENTS

INTRODUCTION

For various reasons I have hesitated before making the decision to publish these studies as a book. One reason: they were written in different situations and with different intended destinies in time and space, and therefore they lack formal and expository unity. There were also problems with the translation of the essays. But the major reason was that I had doubts with respect to the ultimate usefulness of this book. One thing I was certain of: its basic coherence in the objective of revealing the experience of Africans in Brazil and in the attempt to relate our experience to the efforts of Black men and women in any part of the world to conquer our liberty, equality and human dignity in the exercise of our own historical protagonism.

Wondering to what extent I would really be contributing to the reciprocity of historical experience between the Afro-Brazilian and his brothers in the African world, the factor that weighed most in the scales of decision was the clamorous absence of information about Brazilian Black people, both here in the U.S. and among English-speaking Africans generally. Various scholars from the U.S., almost all of them white, have published works focalizing on the Black Brazilian; the same can be said of a few Brazilians, also white social scientists or literati. But: when and which Black person of my country has transmitted to the North American reader directly, without intermediaries or interpreters, the Afro-Brazilian version of our history, our vicissitudes, our creative efforts or our economic and socio-political battles? As far as I know, not one Black Brazilian has ever published a work of this sort in English. On the other hand, in Brazil several books by Africans from the U.S. have been published in translation in Portuese. Offhand I can recall, for example, the autobiography of Booker T. Washington, which I read with interest, with anxiety, back in the thirties. I remember reading, also long ago and very moved, *The Big Sea* by Langston Hughes, with whom I came to exchange sparse and fraternal correspondence. Another unforgettable was Richard Wright with *Native Son* and *Black Boy;* I also remember *The Street* by Ann Petry and, more recently, *Giovanni's Room, Another Land,* and *The Fire Next Time* by

1

James Baldwin, *The Blues People* by Leroi Jones, *Soul On Ice* by Eldridge Cleaver, and probably *The Invisible Man,* by Ralph Ellison (which I know was translated into Spanish). Certainly the latest has been *Roots,* by Alex Haley. There are probably many more books by Black authors from the U.S. that have come out in Portuguese, which I don't know of or don't recall. What I want to point out is that the Black Brazilian writer is completely absent here in the U.S., and not only here: in our own country we are almost inexistent, not counting the few exceptions that confirm the rule. The reason: racism. A very special type of racism, an exclusive Luso-Brazilian creation, subtle, diffuse, evasive, asymmetrical, but so persistent and so implacable that it is liquidating completely what is left of the Black race in Brazil. This type of racism has managed to deceive the world by masking itself in an ideology of racial utopia called "racial democracy," whose entrenchment has the power of confusing the Afro-Brazilian people, doping them, numbing them inside, frustrating them or barring almost definitively any possibility of their self-affirmation, integrity or identity.

Even some astute observers, alert in the African world, sometimes do not escape the "racial democracy" trap. The distortion of information and the informational sleight of hand perpetrated and perpetuated by Brazil have produced deplorable damage. For example, we have even a competent and reliable historian such as John Henrik Clarke, who has stated twice that

> In South America and the West Indies, the slave masters did not outlaw the African drum, African ornamentations, African religions, or other things dear to the African remembered from his former way of life. [...] Families were, in the main, kept together. (1974: 118 and 1977: 9)

In the course of the reading of these pages one will see that the opposite corresponds better to historical truth. African cultural expression, especially religion, has been outlawed not only in colonial times, but even today suffers harassment and restriction.

The history of Brazil is a history that has been written by whites, for whites, just as all of her economic, socio-cultural, military and political structures have been usurped by whites for

2

whites. We have to consider that the information current in the United States leads to this kind of confusion. I will cite as illustrations Donald Pierson's *Negroes in Brazil* and Gilberto Freyre's *Mansions and Shanties.* Both of these furnish a soothing, sugar-coated vision of the relations between Blacks and whites in Brazil. As for the Caribbean, I recall at the Second World Festival of Black Arts and Culture in Lagos last year, that the performers of the steel band from, I think, Trinidad, in their introduction stated that the steel band, the most original creation of Black Caribbean music, originated because African drums and instruments were outlawed in colonial times, and the Africans therefore drummed on whatever tin cans or canisters they could find rather than submit to the criminalization of their music. In any case, the false image of a mild or even pleasant form of slavery is attributed not only to Brazil, but to Latin America in general, with the common justification that "interbreeding" took place between the races -- as if there were no mulattoes in the United States -- and analogously, among the cultures, of Africa and Europe. The cultural tenacity of the Africans in South America, however, cannot reasonably be attributed to a supposed benevolence on the part of Latin Aryans, nor to their character and culture being any the less racist. Africans were not "allowed" to practice their customs and traditions; they forced the whites to succomb to the fact of their cultural integrity, through their own ingenuity and steadfastness, and, of course, by virtue of certain historical circumstances that differed, such as lower slave prices resulting in huge concentrations of Africans, the differing strategies of divide and rule used by the oppressors, the varying conditions of rural versus urban life, etc.

The common struggle of Black people requires a mutual reciprocal understanding that has been denied to us by the different languages which the white oppressors imposed upon us, their monopoly of media and channels of communication, their exlusive control of economic resources and educational and cultural institutions. The publication of these essays has the objective of penetrating this blockade; helping to understand the processes and the diverse strategies of the forces that exploit, alienate and oppress us. To re-establish our family, ideological and cultural bonds is a necessary condition to our success, for we know that the struggle transcends the borders of our respective countries -- the suffering of Black men, women and children is an international phenomenon. President Julius Nyerere of Tanzania put the question on its true terms when he said,

> ...men and women of Africa, and of African descent, have had one thing in common -- an experience of discrimination and humiliation imposed upon them because of their African origins. Their colour was made into both a badge, and a cause of their poverty, their humiliation and their oppression. (1974: 18-19)

An iron, rigid monopoly of power has remained, in Brazil, in the hands of the white ruling strata, from colonial times to the present, as if it were a question of "natural" or even "democratic" right. "Racial democracy" is founded on this premise. Throughout all the socio-economic and political changes that the country has gone through from 1500 to 1978, the structure of race relations has remained inalterable and unaltered: the race factor has continued irreducibly to be one of the fundamental contradictions in Brazilian society. And here we remember the powerful words of Maulana Ron Karenga,

> ...it is social contradictions which are basic to life and struggle and it is these we should and must study and understand. [...] They are particular in their motion and essence, particular to given societies. [...] Different contradictions demand different solutions and we make a serious mistake not to understand this and act accordingly. (1975: 28)

The racial concentration of income and power exclusively in the hands of the whites was and is a privilege considered "just" and "necessary" by the dominant classes and also by the cultural elites. (Fernandes 1972: 265) This phenomenon reaches the point where the class regime in Brazil did not succeed in altering, in Black/white relations, the fact referred to by Molefi K. Asante with relation to the U.S. -- that "race is a fundamental category of class". (1978: 4)

4

There are theoreticians who, like Carl N. Degler, white social scientist from the U.S., cited in an article by Marcelo Beraba in the prominent Brazilian newspaper *O Globo* (July 6, 1976: 41) entitled "Sociologists Analyse the Racial Question in Brazil," espouse the "...argument that the barriers that Blacks confront in Brazil are of socio-economic character and not racial." Such statements are shown to be false by the facts. In the same report it is verified that even among the hungry and miserable population of the Northeast the race factor prevails. Another social scientist, Carlos Alfredo Hasenbalg, after informing us that 80 percent of the Black population lives in the rural zones, affirms: "... discrimination and inequality are maintained in the most accentuated form in the poorest regions, *where the Black population is in the majority.*" (emphasis mine) In the text of this volume I will deal with this problem from several angles, including in the last chapter, a look at the relations between Marxists in Brazil and the liberation efforts of the Black Brazilian people. This problem has also been central to the Black movement in the U.S., as Ron Walters notes in his article "Marxist-Leninism and the Black Revolution" in *Black Books Bulletin:*

> Perhaps the most dangerous lesson from the 1930's was that of white cooptation of Black organizations, individuals and goals. One simply cannot come away from a reading of Harold Cruse's *Crisis of the Negro Intellectual,* or the last 100 pages of George Padmore's *Pan Africanism or Communism,* or Wilson Record's *Race and Radicalism* without an overwhelming understanding of the betrayal and exploitation of the Black community by the white left. (1977: 15)

I myself have come to these truths not through scholastic education or book-learning, but by walking the roads of the reality of my people in Brazil. During my entire childhood and adolescence I participated in and witnessed a major phenomenon that had been occuring since the end of the nineteenth century: the invasion of the country by white workers from Europe, who came with the support of their governments of origin, financed by the Brazilian government, while the huge Black work force was rejected by those who embodied the "economic system." The "system" and the Aryan immigrant-workers excluded Black people in callous and cruel ways from any significant opportunity for work; both the "system" and the immigrant-proletariat benefitting immensely from the total plunder of the African descendant.

Evoking my distant childhood, I can see my father permanently anxious and distressed, trying to find precarious jobs in shoe factories, and escaping the unrelenting pressures by playing the guitar in small local groups. My mother making candy, sewing, wet nursing the children of rural landowners, the coffee dons. We were six brothers and one sister -- a family Black and poor, and from early childhood, without even shoes on our feet, we tried to make some contribution to help our parents. Before going to classes in elementary school at 8 a.m., by dawn I would be out earning some pennies delivering meat and milk to the doors of the local bourgeoisie. After classes, in the afternoon, I would clean a doctor's office, or wash flasks in a pharmacy and deliver medicine... My mother usually spent the nights stirring big vats of guava jelly or some other sweet. The pulp of the fruit and sugar would form a boiling paste, red and good-smelling, that would spurt frequently and explode in igneous balls onto my mother's arms. Countless times I accompanied her through the night, so I was able to share life intimately with her, learn from her energy, her goodness and her compassion. She had inherited the ancient African wisdom of herbs and patience, and she was constantly involved in the preparation of medicine for some sick person. But also, one time I saw my mother defend a little Black orphan, my schoolmate, who was being whipped by a white neighbor. My mother went in and fought physically. This scene from my childhood, from the little city in the interior of the state of São Paulo, Franca, where I was born, constituted my first lesson in racial solidarity and Pan-African struggle. Already at that time I had seen many concrete examples of the difficulties of being Black, even in a country whose majority are African descendants...

I have no basis, neither in my biographical experience nor in my witnessing of Afro-Brazilian life, for trying to mollify or soften the true image of the violent cruelty that Africans and

6

their descendants have suffered for centuries in Brazil. Without any intent to glorify the idea of self-sacrifice, I consider it indispensable to evoke and always have in mind this process of collective massacre of the race. Shawna Maglangbayan is one of the few non-Brazilian Black sisters who knows and recognizes facts like this one:

> In Brazil, it is the white minority which rules; that is, from the *class, racial, cultural* and *historical* standpoint, it is the whites who are the dominant and exploitative element. (emphasis in the original. (1972: 87)

We have forgotten for too long. We must shout and clamor without hesitation or timidness. Why should we submit to the call for us to keep quiet and forgive the holocaust of the countless millions -- one hundred, two hundred, three hundred? -- of African men, women and children murderously assassinated, tortured and ravished by European criminals during slavery? Because it was a "necessary step" in the development of capitalism, the stage leading to a future paradise? A "necessary step" so that Aryo-Euro-North-American supremacy could consummate itself and impose upon us, with iron, fire and hunger, its economic, socio-cultural, ideological and political dictates?

I say that the Black masses in Brazil have only one option: to disappear. Whether it be through compulsory miscegenation/assimilation or, when they escape from this, through direct elimination -- death pure and simple. This has been going on for four centuries. Meanwhile, though, on the slippery terrain where Black Brazilians have to move, they have taken advantage of the smallest breach in order to try to recapture the threads of their own history, and begin, again and again, the task of dignifying and enriching their original culture on the level of a national institution, with total consciousness of the fact that they will only have a future when there occurs a transformation of all the economic, socio-cultural and political structures of the country. The Afro-Brazilian people also know that their participation on all levels of power is an imperative for collective survival. On this point the struggle differs from that of our brothers in the U.S., who are a minority surrounded by a racist society of majority whites. In the various gradations of color, the masses of African descendants constitute the majority of the Brazilian people. And aside from the specific styles of the respective dominant groups, Brazil executes, in South American form, a racial policy of racist content, segregationist and discriminatory, based on white-minority exclusivism, analogous to that practiced by white settlers in South Africa. We have no need, for example, to solve the land problem, which I note is a pivotal one for Blacks in the U.S. Like South African Blacks, we have only to take control of what is ours, along with the few Brazilian Indians who survived, since Africans and their descendants built the entire country with our singlehanded labor while the white settlers basked in the shade, slaughtered Indians, tortured slaves, raped Black women, or murdered those free Africans who fought for their liberty.

The fear of a possible takeover of power by Blacks has been a nightmare frightening the ruling classes of the country in the entire course of our history. This is a fundamental aspect in the conception of a technique and a strategy for the complete eradication of Blacks from Brazil. Although it remains clear in fact, there are no written testimonies to this policy currently; but the documentation from the early 1800's to the middle of this century is irrefutably clear, as we examine in Chapter II. And over all that time, the mindset dictating these policies became so ingrained that it no longer needed explicit statement; it became unwritten law, the given of national policy. In fact it became evident that it would be much more effective to deny that racism exists, despite reams of writings which belie it, and create a new fictitious history in which Brazil became the ultimate paradise of race harmony. But denial does not change reality.

Among the mechanisms of the social lynching of Black people are forced miscegenation, color prejudice, racial discrimination, and an immigration policy designed for the explicit purpose of whitening the country and taking the means of survival away from Africans. Historian Clovis Moura reminds us:

> There entered more Italian immigrants in the 30 years after abolition than the number of slaves who were benefitted by emancipation. With the abolition law, the

marginalization of the Black people was instituted.
(1977: 27)

In this immigrant wave there were also Spaniards, Germans, Jews, Syrians, Portuguese, Poles, Lebanese, and others, the latest group to enter being the Japanese. Most recently, racist exiles from Angola and Mozambique and leftover fascists from the fall of Salazarism have been welcomed by the Brazilian government. This is the artificial proletariat introduced steadily since a century ago to displace Black people from the job market. Black people were *excluded* from the working class. Plantation owners, coffee, cotton, sugar and rubber barons, businessmen, industrialists, bankers, and the ruling military caste -- all of Brazil's aristocracy and capitalists are Aryo-European, either of old colonial Portuguese stock or new immigrant tenor. They always have been, from the beginning of the colony to today. For four centuries Blacks have stayed at the bottom, while whites who arrived a matter of decades or days ago climb the ladders of power.

The white supremacy that for centuries has manipulated the racial ideology of utopia in Brazil called "racial democracy" has also held the tools of social control over the Black people and has done its best to brainwash them and castrate their reasoning faculties, a task which is not obstructed by the starvation, degradation and misery of our people. This contributes immensely to the efficacy of their strategy of annihilation, creating what Florestan Fernandes calls

...the "complex" as a psychodynamic and sociodynamic reactive development, by means of which the white invades the deep personality of the Black person and debilitates his psychic equilibrium, his character and his will. (1972: 273)

What is the consequence of this? In São Paulo, the largest industrial center of the country, as in all major urban centers, rates of suicide, mental illness, infant mortality, abandoned children, child delinquency, unemployment, and crime of a socio-economic nature (theft, robbery, prostitution) are all highly disproportionate among Black people. With this quality of life imposed on our community, how can we forget or forgive?

9

The white minority in Brazil has never hesitated to demonstrate and exercise loyalty and solidarity with its ethnic, cultural and politico-military European origin. Its links with Portugal during the bloody years of Salazarist fascism testify to this with profound implications. It is a collusion that has more in the way of mental subservience than of honest or dignified loyalty. We shall investigate some of the most significant expressions of this Aryan solidarity in the final chapter of this volume. Never has the so-called "Brazilian national conscience" questioned these spurious commitments. Europeans' solidarity and racial cohesion with their white counterparts in the Americas has earned great benefits and consolidated power on both sides.

For us this is also potentially true, and the Black majority should not have to invoke the precedent in order to act on its legitimate right to be loyal and faithful, to exercise solidarity with, its African origins, to feel and consider ourselves brothers of Africans on the Continent or outside of it. On the contrary, Black Brazilians must assert their ancestral Africanity on the level of power, in consort and fraternity with all Black people of the world. Institutionalize Black Brazil, which is a real fact, substituting the existent power, which is a fiction, a metaphor of Aryo-capitalist power, a servile imitator of Euro-United States. Institutionalize a power based on the self-determination of the Black people and inspired by the example of Palmares and of the traditional democratic communalism of Africa, in which there is no room for exploiters and exploited. To adopt African communalism, situate it in the context of the practical and conceptual exigencies of today, means nothing more than to be in favor of ourselves. It is to opt for a definition of socialism, which was practiced in Africa many centuries before the European theoreticians articulated their socialism "scientifically". And it is the African leader, Amilcar Cabral, who teaches us, referring to the "positive cultural values" of Africa, that

> ...the liberation struggle is, above all, a struggle both for the preservation and survival of the cultural values of the people and for harmonization and development of these values within a national framework. (1973: 48)

10

Institutionalizing the human being as a base of power, the African majority in Brazil will eliminate, with this updated communalism, white privilege on all levels of economy, polity, society and culture.

And let it be clear to the age-old accusers that by emphasizing this aspect we are not proposing vengeful racism in reverse. Haki Madhubuti put it well when he said:

> Yet it must be clear that one *is not against white people because they are white* -- one is against white people because of the *irrefutable documentation of their continuous war on Black people.* We are *for* Black people. (emphasis in the original. 1977: 242)

All of these essays have undergone revision, correction, editing and additions, which has altered their length or style, but has not modified the meaning of their original content. The first chapter transcribes the paper that I wrote for the Sixth Pan-African Congress in Dar-es-Salaam, Tanzania, 1974. I received a request to write it from the Minister of Foreign Relations of that country, Mr. John Malecela, chairman of the steering committee of the Congress. I was already in New York at the time, having come from Buffalo on the way to Tanzania, to participate as a delegate. I received Mr. Malecela's telegram simultaneously with (but independently of) the information that the delegation of Guyana and the coordinator of the Caribbean-South American region, Brother Eusi Kwayana, had been excluded from the Congress. After some moments of deep perplexity, vacillating between not attending the Congress in solidarity with the Guyanese delegation (the course chosen by leading Pan-Africanist C.L.R. James), and being present to protest against such discrimination, I decided for the latter course of action. As I delivered the speech, there were three or four warnings from the chairman, Mr. Aboud Jumbe, that I should cut it short, supposedly because of the time problem. However, I had heard many delegates from certain other countries speak frequently and at great length without being disturbed. (The strict political line imposed rigidly upon the Congress by certain factions has been discussed elsewhere, and the harassment of my speech was only part of this general aura.)

11

I did not abandon the microphone, but read the speech to its end. It was ironic to remember that the inspiring force and original organizer of the Sixth Pan-African Congress, C.L.R. James, during the preparative stages, had met with me in Washington D.C., a meeting arranged by Brother Roosevelt Brown. At that meeting he expressed to me his intention to dedicate an entire day in the Congress to sessions on the Brazilian situation: with all reason, Mr. James considered the awakening of the consciousness of the Afro-Brazilian contingent to be of decisive importance for the Pan-African cause, Brazil being the largest Black country outside the African continent, with only Nigeria on the continent itself having a population larger than that of the 70 million or more Afro-Brazilians. Yet here I was, the only delegate from the entire *continent* of South America, reading a speech that had been requested from me -- and attempts were being made to silence me!

In another preparatory session, the Conference held in Jamaica in 1973, in which I participated, I was able to meet and exchange experiences with Amy Jacques Garvey, widow of Marcus Garvey and author of two books on Garveyism. A formidable Black woman, strong and dedicated, whatever the disagreements we might have had.

On the second morning of the Congress itself in Dar-es-Salaam, President Julius Nyerere received me in a private interview in the State House, which lasted almost two hours. The conversation with him was frank and productive, and I came out of it more enriched and strengthened in my position of Afro-Brazilian resistance. Although I was limited by the rules adopted by the Congress, at the end of my speech I registered my protest against the exclusion policy that had been sponsored by reactionary governments of whatever ideological color.

The major problem inherent in any Afro-Brazilian's participation in international congresses of this sort is the linguistic exclusivism which dictates that Portuguese-speaking Africans, who represent a very significant contingent in the African world, including Brazil, Angola, Mozambique and Guinea-Bissau, must speak French or English -- a double colonization in terms of language! The need for special

12

translations, since the translation facilities provided did not include Portuguese, meant that it took me twice the time to make a statement. I was assisted by the courageous efforts of a French woman, member of the official corps of translators provided by the OAU, who although she was not a translator of Portuguese, did her best to provide a running translation of my speech into French, which could then be run through the normal channels. With my sincere apologies to her for not being able to record her name, I wish to express special thanks for her unforgettable dedication and graciousness.

Chapter II contains my speech to the Encounter: African World Alternatives, held in Dakar in early 1976, organized by the valiant efforts of Wole Soyinka, wielding weapons forged by Ogun, in his never-ending transitional leap through the existential chasm to African liberty. Distinct from the Congress at Dar-es-Salaam, whose final document sounds like the obituary of the idea of the Pan-African movement, the meeting in Dakar, without the interference of governmental powers and official delegates sounding their own horns, was conducted in a climate of constructiveness. At the end a motion of solidarity with the armed struggle of the MPLA in Angola, and the founding of the Association of Researchers of the African World under the presidency of Cheikh Anta Diop, represented without doubt concrete steps in our international organization toward complete liberation. The Union of Writers of the African People, the parent organization of the conference, adopted its constitution and made decisive steps toward the promotion of the adoption of one African language (Swahili) in which all Africans, ultimately, may communicate among ourselves. The need for the elimination of the necessity for complicated and expensive translation technology purely in the interest of efficiency was clear to me: once again, I had to be translated outside the apparatus and was thereby hamstrung under the necessary exigencies of time.

The third chapter, divided into two parts, constitutes the two seminars that I gave in the Department of African Languages and Literatures at the University of Ife, in Nigeria. This department, at that time directed by Professor Wande

Abimbola, exercises an extremely relevant role in the eradication of the evils provoked by mental and cultural colonization. With its work the African values of culture, religion, language, philosophy, arts, customs -- negated or underestimated during the centuries of English colonial control -- are being recuperated from marginalization, degradation and shame, and restored to their relevant socio-cultural function in a Nigerian society that progressively is asserting its originality and sovereignty. This university has also a sector denominated the Project of African Cultures in the Diaspora (Professors Abimbola, Soremekun and Akintoye are its co-chairmen) which is implicitly engaged in all movements, efforts, achievements that involve cultures of African origin in the Americas. It would be a wise and politically pivotal act on the part of the University if it were to emphasize this Project within its academic structure, furnishing the resources and means for it to fulfill the necessary and urgent objective which it has so auspiciously initiated, of meaningful study and exchange between Africa the continent and Africa the Diaspora. The Faculty Seminar, sponsored by the Department of African Languages and Literatures, was a stimulating and highly informative forum for academic and personal exchange (my own contributions, however, being those of an avowed non-scholar and non-academic). My sincerest congratulations to the Department for having created such an opportunity for learning and teaching.

To close the volume, in Chapter IV, is my intervention in the First Congress of Black Cultures in the Americas, which took place in Cali, Colombia in August of 1977, and at which I represented the Project of African Cultures in the Diaspora of the University of Ife. I was elected President of Working Group D:Ethnicity and Miscegenation. At the end of the Introduction I will transcribe excerpts from the Conclusions and Approved Recommendations of that Group. Unfortunately, the complete recommendations of the Congress are not available, but these were approved by the full assembly as well as by the Working Group itself. (Originally they were written in Spanish.)

This Congress was a landmark in African history, because it was the first reunion in which Black people of all the Americas met together in the four hundred years we have been in the New World. The reader in the U.S. may have noticed that I avoid using the term "Black American" to mean Blacks in the U.S.A. -- this is in an effort to affirm and establish the fact that the U.S. is not the only America: Black Americans can be found from Canada to the southern tip of Argentina, and the monopoly of the term by those in the U.S. tends to obscure your remembrance of those of us in the rest of the continent. The First Congress of Black Cultures in the Americas was a solid step toward the bonding of our unity as Black people in *all* of America. There was a fruitful climate of discussion and a productive rhythm of work, and the Congress was conducted without the intervention or influence of governments.

The Brazilian government, however, by means of bureaucratic manipulations typical of the traditional reactionarism of the country, prevented the Afro-Brazilian delegation, headed by historian Clovis Moura, from attending. It was to have been the strongest contingent at the Congress, in due proportion to the Afro-Brazilian presence in the Black population of the Americas, by far the largest Black community in any country of the new world -- a fact which may surprise Africans in the U.S.

Among the recommendations adopted by the plenary was one which I presented in an effort to support and add continuity to the decision adopted by the Union of African Writers at Dakar: to teach an African language in all universities in the Americas, so that ultimately, in coordination with the efforts on the Continent, all Africans could converse without intermediaries. I also wish to mention that, between these two events, at the Second World Festival of Black and African Arts and Cultures, which took place in Lagos, Nigeria in January-February of 1977, my proposal to include Portuguese as one of the official languages of all future international meetings of the African world, was adopted by the Colloquium, under the urging and espousal of it by eminent North American struggler Maulana Ron Karenga. The full story of my adventurous activity at the Colloquium, plagued by the constant efforts of official Brazil to silence me, is told in my book *"Racial Democracy" in Brazil: Myth or Reality?* (1977).

At the end of the plenary functions of the Congress in Cali, the decision to hold a Second Congress of Black Cultures in the Americas, in 1979 in Panama, ensured the continuity of this vital link among Black people in all the Americas. Let us hope that next time Brazilian Blacks will be permitted to participate in full and without harassment.

Finally, I would like to make public my sentiments of gratefulness to the Puerto Rican Studies and Research Center of the State University of New York at Buffalo, for the support that it has given me for more than seven years. My colleagues and *hermanos* Francisco Pabón and Alfredo Matilla, as well as our Puerto Rican students, have been sources of inspiration, energy and courage in our common struggle for decolonization, liberty, equality and dignity of the Black people of Puerto Rico and Brazil. My thanks also to the Department of African Languages and Literatures at the University of Ife for the support and stimulus it provided me during my year as Visiting Professor in Ile-Ife. My recognition also extends to all those who in one way or another contributed to the existence of this book, by discussing with the author the ideas contained herein, by collaborating in translation of speeches or typing texts. Among these are Clovis Brigagão, Kathryn Taverna, Vera Beato, Maximo Soriano, Erica Fritz and my wife Elisa, to whom this book owes much. Last but not least, Larry Chisolm, whose friendship and support were constant throughout.

A.N.

Buffalo, N.Y.
May 13, 1978

16

BIBLIOGRAPHY

Asante, Molefi Kete (1978) *Systematic Nationalism and Language Liberation*. Buffalo: New Horizons.

Cabral, Amilcar (1973) *Return to the Source: Selected Speeches of Amilcar Cabral* (ed. by Africa Information Service). New York and London: Monthly Review Press and Africa Information Service.

Clarke, John Henrik (1974) *Marcus Garvey and the Vision of Africa*. New York: Random House.

-- (1977) "The Development of Pan-Africanist Ideas in the Americas and Africa before 1900". Lagos: Festac '77 Colloquium. (Unpublished)

Fernandes, Florestan (1972) *O Negro no Mundo dos Brancos*. São Paulo: Difusão Européia do Livro.

Karenga, Maulana Ron (1975) "Ideology and Struggle: Some Preliminary Notes", *Black Scholar*. Sausalito: January-February (Vol. VI, no. 5) pp. 23-30.

Madhubuti, Haki (1977) *Enemies: the Clash of Races*. Chicago: Third World Press.

Maglangbayan, Shawna (1972) *Garvey, Lumumba, Malcolm: Black Nationalist Separatists*. Chicago: Third World Press.

Moura, Clovis (1977) "Negro: A Abolicão de uma Raça", interview in *Folha de São Paulo*. São Paulo: May 13, p. 27.

Nascimento, Abdias do (1977) *"Racial Democracy" in Brazil: Myth or Reality?* Ibadan: Sketch Publishing Co.

Nyerere, Julius K. (1974) "Speech to the Congress", *Black Scholar*. Sausalito: July-August (Vol. V, no. 10), pp. 16-22.

Walters, Ronald (1977) "Marxist-Leninism and the Black Revolution", *Black Books Bulletin*. Chicago: Fall (Vol. V, no. 3), pp. 12-17, 63.

17

Excerpts from the
CONCLUSIONS AND RECOMMENDATIONS OF WORKING GROUP D, ADOPTED BY FIRST CONGRESS OF BLACK CULTURES IN THE AMERICAS

Conclusions

Although in the United States certain particular laws of racism have been abolished, currently racial discrimination is exercised on a private and institutional level in a way which intends to be disguised, and which continues to be protected by law.

In Latin America, racial discrimination is practiced in a hidden, subtle, open or disguised form.

This discrimination uses the different tonalities of epidermic color of the Black people as a mechanism to see that the Black man disappears through the ideology of whitening as the search for the ideal man, in order to obtain better conditions of life, and with this same mechanism is destroyed the political, economic, religious and family solidarity of Black Groups.

The continuous repetition of the treatment given by whites to Blacks in the past, with no emphasis on their creative accomplishments, and their participation in the construction of America, is another form of discrimination.

The attitude adopted by intellectuals of certain political orientations which denies the existence of the racial question as an element which participates in the creation of social problems, maintaining that the situation is one of rich and poor, oppressed and oppressors only, is a form of racial discrimination.

Recommendations Approved

II.   Debating the racial situation in Colombia, we focalized the absence of just participation of the Black in the economy and politics of the country, as well as the causes of the same. A proposal was approved having in mind the fact that beyond the economic-social background there exists the element *race* used to deny to Black people a due participation in all levels of the life of the country.

-- Creation of a political and social consciousness for the authentic participation of the Black in Colombia and in other countries of America. And to that effect, discredit the homogeneous political schemes that group together the white, Black and Indian lumpen, or white, Black and Indian proletariat in a way that does not take into account the internalization of dominion that the white groups hold toward the non-white.

III. Mindful of the imminent danger of Brazil, Argentina and Chile, who by inspiration of the U.S. are in negotiations in collaboration with South Africa, toward the signing of a South Atlantic Treaty which would integrate South Africa into the defense perimeter of the U.S. and the Western world, which would effectively constitute an offensive military pact against the Black African people of Southern Africa

-- The Congress addresses itself to the governments of the U.S., Brazil, Argentina, and Chile, and to the United Nations, the Organization of American States, and the Organization of African Unity, manifesting our repulsion and our energetic opposition to all maneouvres and conversations, diplomatic or military, or any type of act which could lead to the realization of an Alliance or Treaty of the South Atlantic or to the creation of any other organization under any denomination, masking the objective of collaborating with the racist criminals who head the governments of the white supremacist states of Southern Africa.

IV. Confronting the question of how to resolve the problems of discrimination and racism that Black people suffer, and recognizing that they arise from an institutionalized system which is complex and vast, we affirm that

-- African descendants in the Americas must be aware that their problems will not be solved with small modifications of a topical nature, but that a basic structural change will be necessary in the society and the economic-political system in force. Therefore, we shall not limit ourselves to activity on an elitist intellectual plane, but will address the working people, and the marginalized and illiterate masses, to work with them toward true revolution of economic, social, political and cultural character which will permit neither exploitation nor racism.

VI.   Considering the necessity for instruments with which to concretize the ideals and the objectives of study, interchange of ideas, and strategies of struggle, we propose:

-- The creation of dynamic organisms in each country charged with investigating, directing, developing and supporting all activities which tend to transform economic and social structures toward the liberation of the Blacks in the Americas. There shall be a confederated central body in which each country's institution shall have a delegate. This organ should include these sections:

    a) Political and strategic activity (Action)
    b) Cultural activity (Science, Arts, Economics)
    c) Technological development.

VII.   Discussing the problem of communication of African descendants of the Americas with their brothers on the Continent, and considering that we must eradicate all forms of colonialism including linguistic forms,

-- It has been proposed to educational organs of the countries of America that there be taught an African language which on a long-range basis could be used as a universal medium of education and communication among Blacks of all the world.

IX.   In the discussion of the concept that the Black has been co-colonizer in different countries of the Americas, there arose the proposition:

-- That having in mind that in many writings the Black has been portrayed as a co-colonizer of America and that colonization was an act of physical and cultural genocide carried out by Europeans against both Africans and the native Indians of America, we demand that this notion be rectified, making it clear that on the contrary the Black was forced against his will to participate as one of the builders of America.

XI. In all countries of America are observed phenomena of dispersion and division among deprived peoples as a mechanism of manipulation of the dominant socio-political and economic power.

   -- This proposal and denunciation exhorts those who are victims of such manoeuvres to impede with their good judgment that the division and confrontation fomented among Black groups be stimulated, since it only favors their exploiters.

CHAPTER 1

CULTURAL REVOLUTION
AND
THE FUTURE OF PAN-AFRICANISM

speech delivered to
the Sixth Pan-African Congress
June 23, 1974
Dar-es-Salaam
Tanzania

... a true racial democratic revolution [in Brazil], in our era, can only happen under one condition: the Black man and the mulatto must become the *anti-white* man in order to embody the purest democratic radicalism and to demonstrate to whites the true sense of the democratic revolution of personality, of society and of culture.

Florestan Fernandes
O Negro no Mundo dos Brancos

First, I wish to thank President Julius Nyerere, the party of TANU and the people of Tanzania for the warm and fraternal reception received by this representative of the Black people of Brazil. I would also like to express the unconditional solidarity of my Black brothers in Brazil for the armed movements for national liberation of our brothers in Africa.

Brothers and Sisters:

The contemporary aspirations of Pan-Africanism were a reality for our forefathers. They lived in a land which was their own, having their own cultures, languages, life-styles and civilizations; they and only they enjoyed the fruits of their labor. This harmony -- man, labor and culture -- on the continent was disrupted by exploitation and a colonial invasion.

This Sixth Pan-African Congress is realized in the spirit which shone and continues to shine over the entire Pan-African struggle. This is the Congress of a ruptured unity, which not only the peoples of Africa but all of the Black peoples of the world wish to recuperate and enrich.

These are the historical circumstances of Africa and of the international scenario which preside over and make meaningful the Sixth Pan-African Congress. We have traversed a long and arduous road from the first of these Congresses up to the one in which we are now participating.

From the beginning of colonial domination the African people have developed an acute consciousness of the tragedy of their occupied continent, and now we progress toward what today confirms and reveals the Pan-African liberation process: from being invaded, raped and plundered --

the land of Africa occupied and her kidnapped sons valued only for their serviceability; her natural and cultural resources diverted from their rightful destination to the accumulation of the material wealth of the West --

from this we now march toward its opposite: that process which gestates self-government and promotes sovereignty. What was spirit in Africa, has been turned into capital in the West. What was a human being in Africa has been reified by capitalism, or

25

"nativized" in his own homeland by racist colonial attitudes and abuse.

The restitution to Africans of that which was originally theirs, in this historic moment when the crisis of capitalism takes place, necessarily has an ecumenical function.

Once again the redemption of the oppressed, in their full historic consciousness, comes to liberate the oppressor from the prisons to which he was led by the illusion of conquest.

Culture: A Creative Unity

Western culture has reached the point of historic exhaustion. Its validity has been extinguished and its quenching has produced a crossroads at which humanity must confront itself. An empire is perplexed. It seems that those societies which are most intrinsically westernized are the least able to deter the accelerating process of their own deterioration. Thus a role, not only an important, but an urgent role, is opened to the creative potential of all men and nations. At this point there emerges in another place, an unsuspected place, something: perhaps an historic mystery. The culture of a specific area, hitherto marginalized, projects itself toward the area of ecumenical expansion.

We are speaking of African culture and of Black cultures -- the cultures of Africans and their descendants in the Diaspora, which may or may not be entirely African or African-inspired, but which are specific to the Black communities of their homelands -- those cultures which sustain and support a Pan-African culture.

In this Sixth Pan-African Congress we may not be united in terms of the details of our various contributions and of our visions of the path to be taken. But it is the concept of African unity which is essential here. For what is culture if not the *creative unity* of forces which would only be dispersed in their singularity?

Tanzania understands our historic position. She is absorbed in self-questioning, interrogating the future; but, in a simultaneous movement, she incorporates those of her past experiences which have shown themselves valid to her existence of today and

26

tomorrow. Her culture becomes significant. Her global perspective of society -- Ujamaa, for example -- is a symbol upon which international attention and the hopes of the Black peoples have converged. This is why President Nyerere speaks for all of us when he affirms that we must

> Regain our former attitude of mind -- our traditional African socialism -- and apply it to the new societies we are building today. (1974: 8)

And thus, clearly and explicitly, it is said that we do not need to borrow either the concept or the appellative, since Ujamaa

> ...describes our socialism. It is opposed to capitalism, which seeks to build a happy society on the basis of the exploitation of man by man; and it is equally opposed to doctrinaire socialism which seeks to build its happy society on a philosophy of inevitable conflict between man and man. (1974: 12)

From my own perspective, the notion of self-reliance finds its champion in mythopoetics: as President Nyerere has stated, the land and the power of artistic creativity, both divine gifts, are instruments of similar importance in the building of the Pan-African revolution. (1974: 2)

Let us define our goal. It is not a matter of introducing new and unstudied knowledge into a supposed vaccuum, but of renewing, criticizing and amplifying our already existent knowledge.

Let us try to visualize the elements necessary for a Pan-African revolution. One is the possibility and the promise of the liberation of the human personality -- without the abdication of its responsibility as an historic being. Thus men and women must demonstrate to themselves that they are capable of transforming the circumstances in which they live; that, having been a people who were led, they can and will lead themselves; their history having been stolen, they can and will regain and retain sovereignty over their own collective legacy; that they can and will liberate themselves from those foreign elements of domination which in the past conquered them; that they can and will forcefully reject all forms of oppression and exploitation.

On the one hand, it is necessary to reaffirm our traditional integrity, in the egalitarian values of our Pan-African society: cooperation, creativity and collective wealth. Simultaneously, it is imperative that we transform this tradition into an active, timely and viable social being, criticize its anachronistic elements, update and modernize it. The contemporaneization of African and Black cultures in a Pan-African world is a primary goal of our vision.

There are those who say that the African traditions of communalism belong to a pre-capitalist phase of economic development, and therefore that they are archaic and must be rejected. Such people often claim that African economic forms are "primitive" and "unscientific".

But we reject these ideas as erroneous and dogmatic. We believe that it is not the nature of traditional African culture to be static and/or non-progressive, but that this condition was imposed upon them by the force of the arms of conquest. African cultures are in fact what we make them: they are flexible and creative enough to incorporate those "scientific" and "progressive" values that will serve them well. But they also contain their own intrinsic and valuable science, they also offer a wealth of needed wisdom that is pertinent to our organic existence. We must not reject out of hand the valid fundaments of our ancestral cultures, for they will be the spirit and the substance of a tomorrow for which the tired mechanical platitudes of Europe and the U.S. have failed to prepare us.

The Example of Palmares

... In early 1595, some of the enslaved Africans in Brazil broke the shackles of slavery and fled to the jungle between the states of Pernambuco and Alagoas. Initially it was a small band of escapees. But this group grew little by little until it became a community of nearly thirty thousand "rebel" Africans. They established the first government of free Africans in the New World, indisputably a true African State, known as the Republic of Palmares.

At more or less the same time it happened that, very close to our meeting place today, in Angola, the African Queen N'zingha was valiantly resisting, in armed struggle,

28

the invasion of her territories by the Portuguese.

These are only two historic examples out of the long history of resistance and struggle against foreign domination that is an integral part of our African heritage both in the continent and the Diaspora.

The Republic of Palmares, with its immense population by the standards of the epoch, dominated a territorial area more or less one third the size of Portugal. This land was the property of all. The fruits of collective labor were the property of all. The free Africans planted and harvested a wide variety of products and bartered with their white and indigenous Brazilian neighbors. They were very effectively organized, both socially and politically, in their African manner and tradition, and were highly skilled in the art of war.

Palmares put into question the entire colonial structure: the army, the land tenure system of the Portuguese patriarchs -- the *latifundio* -- and the Catholic Church. It withstood some twenty-seven wars of destruction, waged by both the Portuguese and the Dutch colonial military structures established in Pernambuco. Palmares resisted for more than half a century: from 1634 to 1694.

Zumbi, the last king of Palmares, is celebrated in the Pan-African experience of Brazil as the first hero of Pan-Africanism. We hope that he and his people of Palmares will be recognized and remembered by the rest of the Pan-African world as exemplary militants and forefathers of Pan-Africanism itself.

Language: an Obstacle to Unity

We all know of the visible means as well as the subterfuge utilized by colonialism to impede, hinder and prevent the furtherance of the struggle of Africans and Blacks against oppression, exploitation and racism. Dividing us, separating us, and undermining our physical strength and spiritual resistance -- these have been some of the continual strategies directed against our unity and our strength. In the systems of imposed barriers we must understand the fatiguing forcefulness of the fact that we mutually understand one another using the languages of our oppressors. The principal reason for the absence of Black Brazilians from previous Pan-African Congresses is one tragic instance of separation imposed upon us by language barriers constructed by colonialism.

Because of the socio-economic conditions of Afro-Brazilians, who occupy a place so low on the ladder of society that they cannot even reach the rungs of social mobility, opportunity for education -- and especially for exposure to foreign languages -- is almost entirely closed to them. But the international meetings of the Pan-African world have restricted themselves almost exclusively to French and English; Portuguese has never been used as an official or even *de facto* language of such encounters. The result: Black Brazilians have been, for all practical purposes, unable to participate in the affairs of Pan-Africanism and its history.

Who does participate? Those Brazilians, almost exclusively white, who belong to the higher socio-economic strata and thereby have the linguistic flexibility (education) necessary to participate. And such people, until now, have been those "scholars" of Afro-Brazilian "ethnography" or "anthropology", who study Black Brazilians and their culture from an alien, static and Euro-centric academic vantage point. When these people are the only ones to "represent" the Afro-Brazilian community to the rest of the Pan-African world, it is almost inevitable that our brothers will obtain a highly distorted picture of us and of our situation: for such people, whatever their intentions, do not live, experience or concern themselves with our emergent existential problems as Afro-Brazilians.

It is because of this problem of linguistic elitism that we Africans of Brazil have been absent from the stage of international struggle; and worse, we have been misrepresented on that stage by presumptuous others who arrogantly present a version of our life in whose elaboration we did not participate. Physical absence, however, is no indication of neglectfulness on our part during this period of incessant struggle, of battles and of suffering in the African world.

Brazil: From Slave To Pariah

Although the date is not known precisely, slavery began soon after the arrival of Pedro Alvares Cabral on the coast of Brazil. The history of our country records his name as the "discoverer" of a land which had been inhabited for centuries, indeed millenia, by the Brazilian indigenous people. The year 1500 is recorded as the year of "discovery"; very soon thereafter Africans began to plant sugar cane and to run the sugar mills under the regime of forced labor and commercial kidnap called slavery. For the first two centuries of the nascent colony's existence, sugar was the main export product in a mono-culture economy producing for the colonial metropolis in Europe. Sugar production was concentrated in the coastal Northeastern region of Brazil -- the states of Pernambuco and Bahia primarily. Therefore these were the focal points of the African slave trade. In the eighteenth century there began a heavy mining production, centered primarily in the interior state of Minas Gerais to the south; therefore, a slave population began to develop and grow in greater proportions there. With the industrial revolution in Britain and the creation of great demand for cotton for her textile factories, there appeared a rash of cotton production in the Northeast, concentrated in the state of Maranhão. By 1817, when sugar production reached its peak in Bahia and Pernambuco, Maranhão was already exporting an equivalent amount of cotton in value. Thus a heavy concentration of Africans was created in Maranhão and in Minas by the new demands of the market. Finally, in the nineteenth century, the country entered into a "coffee cycle", beginning a new phase of the mono-culture economy and once again shifting the focus of the African slave presence: this time to the southern states of Rio de Janeiro and São Paulo, which later was to become the industrial capital of Brazil. These, then, became the main loci of the Black populations in Brazil -- determined by the vicissitudes of the colonial export economy which was in turn dependent upon the economic events of the European metropolis.

Throughout all these stages of production, on all these various levels of economic development of the nation, the African

31

remained continually the sole laborer and the only producer. He built a nation for others: whites.

The indigenous people of Brazil cannot be included in the concept of "others" here, since they were rapidly disappearing, either as a result of direct violence committed against them by the white ruling elite or by virtue of the grace and "benevolence" of the "civilizing force" of imposed Western culture. And, as the destruction of the indigenous populations occurred, so did the simultaneous slaughter of African populations that rose up against slavery. These movements of armed revolt aiming at liberation and the fall of the slave system were found in all the territorial extension in which there existed a significant captive African population. They quite often took the form of *quilombos* like that of Palmares: organized communities of free Africans refusing to submit to slavery. These communities were to be found throughout the territory of Brazil during the entire period of slavery, and often were organized along the efficient agrarian economic and social forms of Africa.

The repression of these *quilombos,* and other types of slave uprisings and revolts, took on an extremely violent and murderous character. It was in fact a perfect policy of collective extermination of the Black population. Here I will cite only a few of the many examples registered in our history of the genocide of Africans in Brazil (as studied extensively in Clovis Moura's book *Rebeliões da Senzala).*

Quilombos, Insurrections and Guerrillas

A rash of slave revolts occurred in Bahia in 1807, 1808 and 1809. Slaves formed a secret society entitled OGBONI, of powerful influence in the struggle against slavery. In February of 1813, six hundred slaves revolted and attempted to occupy the Capital of Bahia. The uprising quelled by iron and fire, some slaves died in combat, others committed suicide and others fell prisoner. But by the end of May of the same year, a new revolt was being planned, which did not get underway because it was betrayed to the authorities by an informer. The Count of Arcos dealt with its instigators with extreme severity. Of the thirty-nine

32

prisoners, twelve died in prison, undoubtedly tortured; four were condemned to death and executed -- ironically, the executions took place in the *Praça da Piedade* or Mercy Square on the 18th of November, 1814; others were whipped or banished. While these and other insurrections took place in the capital city, the interior of the state was also being agitated by slave unrest, as the revolt of Cachoeira, an important cultural and economic center, in 1814, testifies.

In the year 1826, slaves established a *quilombo* in the jungles of Urubu, near the Capital of Bahia, which, owing to its aggressive activities against the dominant structure, was destroyed and a great number of prisoners taken, among them the slave Zeferina, who valiantly brandished bow and arrows, fighting bravely before being captured. An enormous quantity of religious material and ritual objects was also seized.

A new movement emerged in 1830, which was repressed drastically and violently: beatings in the streets, lynchings, stonings. Innumerable slaves were assassinated, in a veritable "jubilee of blood", in the words of Clovis Moura (1972: 150).

However, the most important insurrection occurred in 1835, directed primarily by Yoruba and Islamized slaves. A revolt planned in its most minor details, with identification signs (e.g. a ring). The participants dressed all in white on the day of the action. Among the revolutionaries was a teacher, the slave Tomás, who taught his companions in arms to write. The revolt included not only the groups from the various parts of the Bahian capital city, but also from Recôncavo Baiano, from Santo Amaro, Itaparica, and other areas. The careful military plan was prepared, and financial provisions taken care of. Despite stool pidgeons, the authorities were not able to prevent the military scheme of the slaves from being implemented and completed. The revolt exploded in the night of January 24, 1835. The repression took the character of a true bloodbath. The slaves involved were destroyed by infantry, cavalry and even naval forces -- the *Fragata Baiana,* which was in the port of Salvador at the time. Against such superior arms and troops, the slaves, despite small tactical victories gained during the fighting, suffered a clamorous defeat. Between freemen and slaves, 281 were taken prisoner. Luisa Mahin, African woman and mother of Luis Gama, took an active part in the revolt. Cited as leaders were the slaves Diogo, Ramil, James, João, Carlos, all of them imprisoned. Condemned to death for refusing to be enslaved, and shot on May 14, 1835: Gonçalo, Joaquim and Pedro, slaves; and the freemen Jorge da Cunha Barbosa and José Francisco Gonçalves. Many suffered rigorous punishments of whippings and many others died under torture in the prisons.

Still in the Bahian capital, another insurrection took place in 1844, which is seldom mentioned, perhaps for lack of documentation. It is known, however, that this revolt was denounced by Maria, lover of freeman Francisco Lisboa, one of the organizers of the movement.

In the city of Rio de Janeiro, then capital of the nation, and the state of São Paulo -- *quilombos* were organized in the entire extent of Brazilian territory. One of them, the *Quilombo de Jabaquara,* in the region of Santos, became a famous bastion of slaves who abandoned the coffee plantations of São Paulo state.

In the state of Rio de Janeiro, on a plantation called *Fazenda Freguesia,* in 1838, slaves rose up in arms, executing and expelling foremen. They invaded other rural properties, and fled immediately to the forests. The slave leader Manuel Congo was acclaimed king by his companions in struggle. They defeated the troops of the government. But, on December 11, 1838, they were overcome at last and murdered mercilessly by the Imperial troops commanded by Lima Silva, Duke of Caxias. Manuel Congo was executed by hanging on September 6, 1839.

In the state of Minas Gerais there occurred the phenomenon of an African who became legend. Isidoro, the Martyr, at the front of the *quilombo* warriors of Garimpeiros who united under his leadership, was never vanquished. After a long persecution, he was finally wounded by bullets, taken prisoner, and beaten and tortured barbarously. He died with his body torn, blood gushing from the open wounds, in 1809. After his death his people venerated him as a saint.

In the same state there were also the *Quilombo do Ambrósio* (1746-1747), and *Quilombo de Sapucaí,* which were long considered impregnable.

In the *Quilombo de Campo Grande,* also in the state of Minas Gerais, in 1726, a community of 20,000, an enormous population at that time, were living their African agricultural and communitarian tradition. In 1759 this peaceful group was destroyed, by *bandeirante* Bartolomeu Bueno do Prado, from São Paulo. He later exhibited his war trophies: 3,900 ears taken from the bodies of the Blacks he assassinated in this brutal massacre. *Bandeirantes* are historic figures from the ranks of the white settlers of São Paulo, who went down in the nation's history as heroes of the expansion of its territory. In fact, they were simply common thieves and assassins. Another criminal of the same species was *bandeirante* Domingo Jorge Velho. He passed into history as the bloody destroyer of the Republic of Palmares.

In the state of Maranhão in 1839, slaves led by Prêto Cosme and Manuel Balaio unleashed a guerrilla struggle involving 3,000 *quilombo* dwellers in collaboration with other political forces also opposed to the imperial government. In the streets of the city of Caxias, the most important town in the interior of the territory, the slaves could be heard singing:

O Balaio chegou!	Balaio has come!
O Balaio chegou!	Balaio has come!
Cadê branco?	Where's whitey?
Não há mais branco	No more whitey
Não ha mais sinhô.	No more master.

(Moura 1977: 139)

The famous slave-slaughterer, Caxias, now patron of the Brazilian Army, once more commanded the crushing of the rebellious slaves. Prêto Cosme was hanged in São Luis, capital of the Province.

In this movement of Balaio, the slaves were allied with the *Bem-te-vis,* a white opposition group which also fought against the Empire. When their movement was defeated, these white forces turned against their former "allies" and joined the Imperial forces to hunt and murder the slaves as part of their surrender pact.

In the province of Ceará, with a weak demographic index of Africans, on October 22, 1839, the slave Constantino and five

35

others were condemned to hang and were executed in Fortaleza, the capital city. They had mutinied in the boat *Laura Segunda,* demanding better conditions and treatment on board for the 23 crew members of the launch.

In Recife, in 1824, a military unit of mulattoes revolted and groups of insurgent slaves adhered to their cause. The leader of the revolt, Emiliano Mandacaru, issued a manifesto in verse where he said:

Qual eu imito Cristovão	As I imitate Christophe
Esse imortal haitiano,	The immortal Haitian
Eia! Imitar o seu povo,	Hey! Imitate his people
O'meu povo soberano!	O my sovereign people!

(Moura 1977: 116)

In this verse is verified the inspiration Brazilian Blacks took from the victorious struggles of Toussaint-L'Ouverture, Dessalines and Henri Christophe to liberate Haiti from the white dominion of the French and to establish a sovereign state governed by Blacks.

In Alagoas the *quilombolas* (members of *quilombos*) participated in the revolutionary movement called *Cabano* which left a legendary fame in the region. The struggle lasted more or less from 1833 to 1841. Likewise, various *quilombos* are cited in Sergipe, which used with great efficacy the tactic of guerrilla warfare. Indeed, in Sergipe, before 1690, the colonial government was already fighting against the *quilombo* warriors, having invited Fernão Carrilho to take charge of destroying these insurgent slaves in the territory. The army of the Africans used horses so fleet and audacious "that they enter the towns and villages, ten or twelve, armed and well mounted, shooting their rifles into the doors of some authorities." (Moura 1972: 123)

In 1839, in the southernmost territory of Rio Grande do Sul, the *Revolução Farroupilha* (Ragged Revolution) had in the slaves a combative ally, since the Revolution demanded the abolition of slavery. The authorities of the so-called *Republic dos Farrapos* (Republic of Rags) in retaliation to the pro-slavery Imperial Government, decreed:

36

Only Article:
From the moment in which any coloured man in the service of the Republic has been whipped by the authorities of the Government of Brazil, the Commander-General, Head of the Army or Commander of the various divisions thereof [of the Rag Republic] shall draw lots among the officials of whatever rank of the Imperial troops our prisoners and shall send before the firing squad he whom the lots shall designate. (Moura 1972: 83)

This movement made a policy of buying the liberty of slaves who enlisted in the rebel forces; an exception to the general practice of forcing slaves to fight on one side or the other according to the master's whim. An interesting detail: when the Ragged movement was defeated, one of the clauses of the document of surrender was the following: "The slaves who served in the Revolution are free and recognized as such." (Moura 1972: 84) This was an event without precedent in the history of the slave participation in the political and/or military skirmishes of the country. For the rule was always the merciless murder of the Africans who revolted against the dominant powers, in whatever context. We have no evidence, of course, that this condition was honored by the authorities.

The Pernambucan revolution of 1817, which envisaged a non-slaveholding independent Republic, was repressed by Count Arcos; many slaves were killed participating in the uprising. In Paraiba, twenty-three slaves went to the gallows: the movement had spread widely enough to cover the entire Northeast region, Ceará, Rio Grande do Norte, Paraiba, etc. In 1823 an armed rebellion in Recife had as its leader the mulatto Captain Pedro da Silva Pedroso, with the fundamental participation of Blacks sacrificing their lives for the end of slavery.

In the territory of Mato Grosso there were various *quilombos,* among them the *Quilombo do Piolho,* later named *Quilombo da Carlota,* which flourished in the last decade of the eighteenth century. The city of Vila Bela, former capital of the region, became a haven for fugitive slaves. Today it comprises a curious city inhabited exclusively by Blacks, who live a way of life reminiscent of traditional styles of Africa.

It would hardly be necessary to describe to this audience the hideous nature of the slave system against which these martyrs of African liberty were revolting, except for the fact that the white "scholars" of my country -- those who have the means and the voice to articulate their views outside Brazil -- have made it their business to construct a fictitious "history" which they peddle as fact on the international market. Thus Brazil has acquired an image of innocence, a countenance of kindness and humanitarianism in its slave regime, a reputation as "unique" in the utopian tropical perfection of its Lusitanian splendor: qualities it is supposed to share with the Portuguese colonies in Africa. The Africans of Brazil, Guinea-Bissau, Mozambique and Angola know better.

The truth is that the Portuguese colonial aristocracy in Brazil was as utterly racist, cruel and inhuman in its treatment of Africans as any other white slaveholding elite of the Americas. Slaves were continually and systematically tortured, murdered, abused and maltreated. Since trade routes to Africa from Brazil and back were shorter and more direct, prices were lower than in North America. Slaves were so cheap in Brazil that it was more economical to buy new replacements than to care for them -- especially old or sick people, children, or the many who were deformed or crippled from torture or overwork. The concentration of slaves on a single plantation was greater. Thus for purely economic reasons, living conditions for slaves in Brazil were far worse in general than in other colonies, where replacements were more expensive.

Here we have characterized another form of the genocide practiced against Africans in Brazil: the decimation of their population by prevention of normal births and by maintenance of such horrible living conditions that only a minimal number could survive their servitude. In 1830, for example, it is calculated that there were 1,930,000 slaves. At about that time the annual number of deaths was 87,308, and of births, 78, 336. At this slow rate, Aryan scientists lamented, it would take three centuries for Blacks to disappear!

Nearly a century before the so-called Abolition of slavery, in 1798, a group of Blacks, mulattoes and whites held a series of meetings in Bahia. They founded a revolutionary movement for Independence, their principal demands being: 1) the Independence of the territory of Bahia; 2) Republican government; 3) Liberty of trade and the opening of all ports "especially to France;" 4) Each soldier would earn a salary of 200 *reis* daily; 5) the emancipation of slaves. They were strongly influenced by the ideals of the French revolution. (Moura 1972: 66) This movement, called the Revolt of the Tailors, included four Black men: Luis Gonzaga das Virgens, 36 years old; Lucas Dantas, 24; João de Deus Nascimento, 24; Manuel Faustino dos Santos Lira, 23. These four were the only conspirators who, upon being convicted for participation in the revolt, were condemned to be hanged and quartered, their bodies hung on public posts as an example to other "uppity niggers," and their sons declared damned forever. (Andrade 1971) The fate of these four Black men who gave their lives for the independence of Brazil has never been given a place in the forefront of our history. They remain unsung heroes. But a white man who suffered the same fate for his part in the struggle for the same ideals, Tiradentes, who was a slaveowner (Moura 1972: 60) has passed into history with the glory and the praises of a nation. Such cases are innumerable, since the Black martyrs of our independence have been largely forgotten by a Brazilian society that finds it more natural to sing the praises of white men. When it does remember a Black historical figure, it is only those who did nothing for the freedom or improvement of the plight of their own people, but who contributed to their oppression by supporting their enemies -- such as Henrique Dias (seventeenth century). At the service of the Portuguese he fought the Dutch invaders of Pernambuco. He also participated in the repression of Africans in the *quilombos* of Bahia (Moura 1972: 168.) Another example is that of Marcilio Dias of the nineteenth century, who served the white imperialist army of Brazil against Paraguay.

Several decades after the Revolt of the Tailors, there occurred an extraordinary historic event: the son of the Portuguese king Dom João VI, Prince Dom Pedro, in collusion with the rural oligarchy of Brazil, declared Brazil independent. This incident, called the Cry of Ipiranga, took place on September 7, 1822, and might be considered something of a paradox if it did not so clearly reveal the roots of Portuguese neo-colonialism. But even the milestone of independence in Brazil had no effect on the enslavement of Africans and their descendants.

Independence having been proclaimed, when Dom Pedro was travelling from Rio de Janeiro to São Paulo, the Governor of Arms in Bahia, General Madeira de Melo, rejected the proclamation, and the Portuguese aristocracy opposed the independence movement in armed resistance. Inevitably, the position of the slaves was confused in such a politically charged and complicated situation. Some slaves took advantage of the situation and escaped to the forests; others, hoping to win their freedom, joined the actions for liberty; while others were forced to fight for the Portuguese troops, purely in obedience to their masters' orders. Of these, in a company of about two hundred, after being vanquished by Labatut, fifty were shot by firing squad and the rest suffered the punishment of the whip.

This experience of "independence" might serve as a warning for our brothers of Mozambique, Angola and Guinea-Bissau. But there is no need for such a warning, because my African brothers know -- in their very flesh, weapons in hand -- of the greed, violence, hypocrisy and cruelty of Portuguese colonialism. As a result of its "virtues" and "discoveries," Portugal succeeded in becoming the colonialist paradigm: the first to invade Africa, to begin the pillage and rape of her land and people -- and the last to leave. And she would be there still if it were not for the valiant struggle of the people of Angola, Guinea Bissau and Mozambique, who are taking up armed resistance, continuing in the militant tradition of our African ancestors N'zingha, Zumbi, Shaka and others.

Brazil had no such experience. The Independence of our country was purely a manipulation on the level of superstructure by the white settler aristocracy itself. The masses of the Brazilian people -- and especially Afro-Brazilians -- did not participate consciously in the winning of Independence nor in its fruits and benefits. They were simply the pawns of the Portuguese ruling classes, the political material -- objects, not subjects -- in a superficial juridical proclamation of little or no real significance in changing the nature of Brazil. And this Brazil, proudly following the footsteps of its mother Portugal, was among the very first in the New World to enslave Africans on its soil, and the last to "liberate" them from captivity...

Chico-Rei: History turned Legend

Throughout the great expanse of Brazil during the entire epoch of slavery, free African men and women organized in *quilombos* struggled against slavery. Another form and style of resistance was used by an African king, who was enslaved along with his family and his tribe. In the middle of the Atlantic Ocean his wife and one of his two sons died. The slaveholders baptized him compulsorily with the name "Francisco." He and his tribe were sold to a gold mine owner in the Town of Vila Rica, today called Ouro Preto, in the state of Minas Gerais. All of these slaves, considered of excellent stock and behavior, were given one day per week in which they were allowed to work for their own benefit. Francisco took full advantage of the opportunity. He labored during these free days, dearly saving what he earned, until he had enough to buy the liberty of his son. He continued to work and save his earnings, now with the help of his free son; and in a short while the time came to purchase the liberty of Francisco himself. They continued their arduous struggle, both working and liberating more members of their tribe. These then joined Francisco and his son, freeing more and more until they had freed the entire tribe. Francisco, above and beyond being an indefatigable worker, proved himself also to have exceptional political talents. They were thus able to gather enough money to purchase one of the gold mines -- the mine of Encardideira -- which had belonged to their old owner. The Encardideira mine prospered. It was the collective property of the entire tribe. Francisco remarried and also built a Catholic Church for his people. (Catholicism was the official religion of the State in Brazil.) The prestige and power of Francisco grew; he became virtually a Head of State within the state of Minas

41

Gerais, and came to be known as Chico-Rei. His community and their mine attained the greatest splendor that the Gold Age in Brazil was capable of producing, until it was finally completely destroyed. Few documents remain to tell of its fabulous existence. Chico-Rei attained the legendary immortality of mytho-poetry. This occurred in the eighteenth century.

"Abolition:" of Whom?

The formal abolition of slavery took place in 1888. The enslaved African became a "citizen" as stated under the law, but he also became a nigger: cornered from all sides. If slavery had been a crime, even more monstrous and cruel a crime was the manner in which the African was "liberated." As other historians, researchers and scholars have stated: abolition was simply a business transaction carried out by whites, for the benefit of whites.

This legal Abolition had no roots in the true struggles of the slaves against bondage. Ever since the sixteenth century slaves had engaged in the struggle to the death to abolish the slave regime. We have seen only a few of the heroic examples that fill the unwritten, unsung history of Brazil: the Republic of Palmares, the Revolt of the Tailors, Balaio, Preto Cosme, Manuel Congo. The valiant efforts of these leaders and their hundreds of thousands of followers resulted in no legal Abolition; yet *they* were the legitimate expressions of the refusal of Africans to submit to the dehumanizing regime of slavery.

What, then, was the nature of this belated "emancipation" decreed by elements that had no relation to the aspirations of the slaves themselves?

With the industrial revolution in England and the rise of capitalist production based on "free" labor, Britain had proceeded to prohibit the practice of slavery: not for humanitarian reasons, but simply because it was no longer to her economic advantage, and threatened the wage-labor economy. Britain policing the high seas, Brazil's legal slave traffic stopped in 1850. It was only when the Brazilian ruling classes recognized that it was also in their own economic interest to abolish slavery that they decreed "emancipation" in 1888: long after every other slaveowning country in the Americas had already done so.

And what did this "abolition" mean to the Africans and their descendants themselves? Even before 1888, there were "free" Blacks: the ill, the crippled, the aged, the helpless were "freed" to fend for themselves when the masters considered them too expensive to justify supporting. "Freedom" meant abandonment to a slow death in the street. "Abolition" was simply a massive extension of this treatment: slaves were cast into a freedom without employment, no shelter, no means of subsistence or support. Many were forced to stay with their masters and continued working under much the same conditions. Others who ventured out found only hunger and misery in their "liberty". From shackled victim of the racist regime of forced labor, the slave passed to the state of true pariah.

In the following year, 1889, a Marshall proclaimed Brazil a Republic, and Emperor Pedro II was sent into exile. Through this and all the other landmarks of Brazilian history, the fate of the ex-slaves remained the same. There inevitably followed a period of starvation, disease, prostitution and criminality in the Black population, destitute as it was of economic possibility.

At about this time, the economy began to undergo a radical process of industrialization. With the accelerating expansion of urban industrial production, it might be expected that free Blacks would find a welcome source of employment. But this potential for progress was also denied to them, for the ruling classes and the government, ashamed of the "black stain" that the Black population constituted on its Aryan aspirations, was subsidizing a massive influx of white European immigration: in order, explicitly, to "whiten" the country. (Skidmore 1974) These Europeans, naturally, were preferred almost exclusively by the white employers in the industrial and agricultural sectors, because of their "superior ethnic stock." Racial discrimination and prejudice arose as yet one more barrier to a necessary reorganization and survival of the Black personality and family. Although the conventional texts deny the existence of racial discrimination, there are many episodes and facts which have incontrovertibly proved that such discrimination is common practice in my country (see Fernandes 1972; Nascimento et. al. 1968; Nascimento 1968 and 1977.)

Heroic Black Men

It was during the campaign to abolish slavery in Brazil that two Black men distinguished themselves. One, José do Patrocínio, was the son of a white Catholic priest and a Black woman; he was born in Campos, a town in the State of Rio de Janeiro. Later he went to the then capital of the nation, Rio de Janeiro. This town was the arena where his journalistic and oratorical battles against slavery took place. The other was Luis Gama, son of a free African woman and a Portuguese aristocrat who sold his son as a slave in Bahia to pay off a gambling debt. As a slave, Luis Gama was sent to São Paulo. In spite of his bondage, he managed to study and became a brilliant lawyer. His eloquent oratory effectively confronted all the pomp and arrogant pretentiousness of the rural aristocracy. The money which he earned as an attorney was destined to purchase the liberty of his Black brothers. He also wrote poetry satirizing mulattoes who aspired to be white, and singing the beauty of Black woman. He was a model of dignity, generosity, integrity and greatness.

After Abolition, on the 22 of November 1910, the Navy of War (Brazilian Armada) rebelled under the leadership of sailor João Candido, whom I have had the opportunity to know personally. The objective of the revolt was the extinction of the *chibata,* that is, the corporal punishment, remnant of the slavery regime, that was commonly applied by white officials on Black sailors. These were truly "anti-human relations existing between seamen and officials" (Moura 1977: 148) -- along definitely racial lines. The rebellious sailors had full military control of the situation for a time in the revolt; they were able to make demands. But they unfortunately were naive enough to enter into an agreement with the Government of the Republic which had been conceived simply as a stratagem to unarm and finally massacre them. This is a page in our history which remains veiled and vetoed from public knowledge, but the physical

44

extermination of this group of Black sailors must remain forever as a chapter of the bloody and unmerciful genocide suffered by the Black masses of Brazil.

These seeds of non-conformity, dissent and revolt, of persistence in the struggle for freedom, bore fruit between 1920 and 1937. A protest movement began in São Paulo. The Black press voiced dissatisfaction, condemned discrimination against Blacks in employment, denounced the racism which prohibited Blacks from entering certain commercial establishments, schools, housing, hotels, military organizations, diplomatic circles, etc.

This protest movement which began in São Paulo, an industrial center in the south of Brazil, and spread to all of the principal urban centers of the nation, such as Rio de Janeiro, Pernambuco, Porto Alegre, Bahia, Belo Horizonte, etc., took the form of a mass movement under the name *Frente Negra Brasileira* (Black Brazilian Front.) Just as it truly began to grow and evolve into a meaningful movement, the Front was eradicated by the dictatorship of the *Estado Novo* (New State) of Getúlio Vargas in 1937.

The Black Experimental Theater

When, in 1944, I founded the *Teatro Experimental do Negro* (Black Experimental Theater), or TEN, in Rio de Janeiro, the battle for the freedom of Blacks once again regained its force. What was this "Black Experimental Theater?" In terms of its purpose, quite a complex organization. It existed, fundamentally, as a project designed to redeem Black African values, oppressed and relegated to an inferior place within Brazilian culture. A laboratory of artistic and cultural experimentation. The Black Experimental Theater was conceived as an instrument to counter the domination and supremacy of white European culture, and as a systematic unmasking of the hypocritical racial ideology ruling the nation. For there was, and still is, a philosophy of race relations which underlies Brazilian society. Paradoxically, it is called "Racial Democracy." In reality it merely supports the privileges of the white strata of society at the expense of African descendants.

45

Marginalization of the Black community accompanied the abolition of slavery, while miserable living conditions made the Black man a "declassified" citizen. All non-Black workers benefitted from this precarious state of existence of the Black population. Some of these non-Black workers became members of the middle classes, while others even aspired to the national bourgeoisie, their upward social mobility based firmly on the misery and disgrace of the Black people.

"Racial democracy" in Brazil continues to denote the oppression of Blacks, the degradation and proscription of their cultural values, and the insensitive and cruel exploitation of them by all sectors of white society, rich and poor alike. The country has thus developed a culture based on racist values, institutionalizing a situation which may be called the "pathology of whiteness." Sociologically, this framework of race relations represents a form of genocide.

As a consequence of the immutability of the structure of Black and white relationships, all efforts of Blacks to change their situation and attain a decent standard of existence have been futile. All of the Black people's efforts to develop a consuetudinary and effective racial democracy have only earned them the white man's domination of the country, the disinterest or disdain of whites, threats and violence. The white man has been arbitrarily dictating what Christianity, justice, beauty and civilization mean since the beginning of Brazil's existence. Monopolizing economic, social and political power, whites are driving the Black population to extinction, already having tried to wipe us out of the history books.

The population of Brazil exceeds 120 million inhabitants. Over fifty percent of these are Black -- including both the very dark and those considered lighter. Brazil is therefore the second largest Black country in the world. But Blacks do not even pose a threat to the system - only perhaps potentially, in the purely abstract sense of numbers, a potential far from being realized. The majority of Blacks continue to be semi-slaves hardly able to survive, incapable, by virtue of their socio-economic position of closed opportunities, of developing the critical consciousness necessary to perceive the gravity of their plight and to understand the underpinnings of the context molding their existence. They are utterly plundered: both physically and in spirit.

The Black Experimental Theater, carrying out its revolutionary purpose, introduced the Black hero and his formidable dramatic and lyrical potential to the Brazilian stage. The Black Experimental Theater transformed many typical Black women, often humble domestic servants, cooks, or maids, and many modest Black workers, some of them illiterate, into actors and dramatic interpreters of the highest quality. The existence of Black dramatic actors and actresses of quality demonstrated the artistic precariousness of the customary practice of blackfacing white actors to play Black roles when they involved any artistic responsibility. It also made the traditionally dominant image of the Black person as a caricature or domesticated servant obsolete. A dramatic literature and an aesthetic of performance, founded on the values of African culture in Brazil, emerged as a result of the scrutiny, reflection, criticism and realizations of TEN. By organizing and sponsoring national conferences and congresses, which gave Blacks the chance to analyse, discuss, and exchange information and experience, TEN encouraged a critical revision of the prevailing trends in studies of the Black people and their culture. We exposed as totally distorted the purely descriptive historical or ethnographic focus, and blissful conclusions, of many research studies conducted by whites who had used Blacks as objects of their pseudo-scientific studies. (Ramos 1957: 162)

Self-Reliance and Pan-African Culture

Isolated efforts such as the one just described have occurred in almost all African nations and also among Blacks in most non-African countries where they form a community. Our isolation from each other has been a burden imposed upon us by colonialism, imperialism and racism. But the dream of a Pan-African unity is still alive in all of us wherever we may be. The independence of so many African nations emerges as the first victory of the dream and of the struggle. If each nationhood was

47

and still is a necessary step in the dismantling of colonialism, then this represents a tactic of necessity. New steps must be resolutely taken toward a strategy of progress and complete liberation, taking into consideration the objectives of the communion between our brotherly peoples.

All strategy, every struggle, presupposes a very clear ideology, if the actions resulting from it, that is, from the unity of the dream, are not to be sabotaged or destroyed along the arduous road to reality, and if struggle is to be possible among brothers. The presence here today of governments which support this political, economic and cultural Pan-African unity, gives us hope that conflicting positions between actual sovereign units can be solved rapidly.

It is clear then that the building of transcultural mechanisms in the heart of the Pan-African community is the fundamental step which will guarantee the realization of Pan-Africanism. Future steps on the pragmatic path, must search for means of emphasizing and developing Pan-African culture, rather than merely promote Black-Brazilian, Yoruba, Haitian, or any other single culture.

The notion of self-reliance is implicit in the unfolding of this process. This goal of necessary unity requires us to traverse the long road of self-emancipation in our singular capacities. We must immediately begin to recognize our dependence upon ourselves, explore our potential strength, study and know our circumstances, control our energies and resources -- these are the ways in which we will be able to systematically build our own unity.

The terms we have referred to, this cultural policy, should be appropriate to the concrete reality of each unit -- be it individual, partisan or national -- but neither should it exhaust itself in the practice of its own singular experience. In this dialectic of vocation for self-reliance and reciprocal cooperation, long sought unity will be consolidated. Autonomy and self-reliance must not be synonyms for isolation. The example on the continental scale of the OAU has demonstrated in some instances the efficacy of this strategy. It is an obligation of this Congress to develop new aspects, new perspectives towards the concretization of these ends. In this unity, the Pan-African movement will consolidate and amplify its potential, obtaining thereby the conditions necessary to the fulfillment of its historic destiny on the international level.

Concerning Science and Technology

The same opinion applies with respect to technology and science. The same principles should prevail. The initial appeal is for the encouragement of investigation, the consecration of autocthonous knowledge, in the sense of building a national being, spiritually and materially. We believe in a pedagogy which frees technology of its current tendency to enslave the human being. On the contrary, this technology ought to exist as a buttress to the consecration of Man/Woman in their condition of being. Self-reliance in the building up of technology and in scientific development must occur simultaneously with the development of nations, with their functional adjustments to their environmental and human realities. This is why in the structure of the present phase of "technical aid," advanced forms of technology of industrial capitalism not only do not cooperate in building, but actually instigate and promote the alienation of national self-knowledge. This technological and scientific "aid" will be able to take the direction of liberation only when the values which rule and regulate their mechanisms are not used to deter the development of the consciousness of the people and of national independence. As the late President Nkrumah said, capitalist technology is the producer of colonized "noble servants" of the structure of colonial knowledge.

One consequence of our reasoning is that nations first must develop their own conceptual, organizational and technological apparatus; only then may they also realize their technological liberation. Secondly, technical/scientific cooperation within the Pan-African world has a pedagogical significance: a productive efficacy, an administrative "economicity," its own practices, and convenience and facility of use in the social sense.

The transmission of technology should not constitute a means of accentuating the gap between producer and consumer, but something which respects the structures and individual needs as well as the customs of different regional and developmental units or entities. Scientific and technical cooperation must also imply a system of values articulated in the realization of the objectives of Pan-African unity. To promote unity as a value is to give it a sense of liberation, rather than one of dependency. And scientific and technological dependency, equivalent to strangulation, is created by systems that are oppressive because they are based on the value of ambition for profit. Or, as stated by President Nyerere, the system where money is *King*. For us, the *King* is the principle of sovereignty-consciousness, knowledge, technological projections, all interwoven, moving directly toward our emancipation.

A cultural revolution, based on technological and scientific autonomy, is not only the foundation of social justice and human dignity, but also a prerequisite for the economic international progress of mankind and the sovereignty of peoples.

There exists in the Pan-African world the need for scientific and technological cooperation in order to accelerate and further the global development of our culture. However, this necessity must not allow the acceptance of "foreign aid" with colonialist or imperialist motivations. "Aid" is not a synonym for exploitation but implies a free association between he who offers and he who receives, and it should be a catalyst of collective efforts.

Capitalism versus Communalism

We have attempted to say up to now, that capitalism is in direct contradiction to the traditional communalism of our African cultures. That the mechanical notions which have been proposed to understand Africa and Pan-Africanism under criteria which apply to capitalism, can lead to grave errors. We must understand, radically, the novelty of the African experience, in a timely sense.

Emerging directly from colonialism, we are a people in the process of self-analysis and reflection, searching for the means to situate ourselves effectively for further development and the best of lives for our people. In a certain sense we are the weakest link of the iron chain of capitalism; meanwhile we hold the conviction that it is through Pan-African communalism that this iron chain will be made forever unable to mend itself. We enter into the construction of our own path with the purest of heart and hands. We are beings who remain open in the face of unexpected events.

We must view as enemies all those who, if perhaps unconsciously, clamor for a "modernity" which is already past: we are contemporary beings poised for a new life.

The span of our project demands a permanent cultural revolution. We all know that a revolution cannot consist of substituting one person for another, or even in the exchange of one system for another. At best, on the contrary, a revolution *creates* both persons and systems. The system of values is the backbone of all cultures. Values impregnate our creative spirit, thus forming the complex of inaugural myths: the mytho-poetry of a culture.

As quintessential images of experience, these myths constitute a matrix which reproduces our daily actions. They embody the most original aspects of our ontology.

Our historic being is of mythic origin. It is a lesson in our art. Our art, contrary to that of the West, is, for us, a most natural and creative experience.

As the nourishment of our beliefs and values, we realize that art is a most powerful instrument in our social communication, in the dialogue with our deepest roots.

In the African cultures, art is our grasp of all life experience, and because of this, the Black man is integral in his rhythm, in his mystery. Neither European rationalism, nor North American mechanics; art is that other eye of Ifa which inspires, organizes and gives meaning to our daily lives.

Pan-African culture is the form and the exegesis of mytho-poetry.

The adventure of mytho-poetics is concomitant with our existence while at the same time far anterior to it. Part of the subject and part of the object, it is capable of inducing and of being reflected. Our reason is poetic as well as forged -- an instrument to detect our prospective visions.

One of the basic pillars of the Pan-African revolution is the capacity for struggle of the Black woman. We in Brazil celebrate the name of Luisa Mahin, mother of Luis Gama. Between 1825 and 1835, during various slave revolts and uprisings, Luisa Mahin combatted slavery without respite. She was finally thrown into jail. Yemanja, Goddess of the waters, Mother of Gods and men. Heroine of African history and martyr of the history of the West. The Black woman does not have to revindicate: she already conquered the right to exercise responsibility on all levels of life a long time ago. Thus through strength and suffering the race has survived. Embodied in the Black woman, mytho-poetry maintains itself and becomes permanent as a ritual of love continually renewed.

Pan-Africanists in Action

In 1938, six Blacks, young men between the ages of 18 and 25, got together and organized an Afro-Campineiro Congress in the city of Campinas, in the state of São Paulo in Brazil. They were Aguinaldo Camargo, Geraldo Campos, Agur Sampaio, José Alberto Ferreira, Jerônimo and Abdias do Nascimento. It was a private session, and they swore one day to return to Africa to contribute what they could to the liberation of Blacks and of the African continent. Life separated them, dispersed them in the immense geography of the nation. However, it happened that one of them was able to fulfill the oath. For the first time I walk the soil of my ancestors, in the free land of Tanzania. And this happened in an exceptional moment. I have the happy opportunity to testify to something truly marvelous. It has to do with prophets.

Once upon a time a prophet isolated himself on the peak of a mountain and remained there for some time, praying and meditating. When the prophet descended from the hills, he carried in his hand a tablet of laws needed to lead his people to salvation.

An inverse motion is now taking place. The prophet, and his people, together, are climbing the mountain. He carries in his heart a lighted candle which is planted on the peak of Mount Kilimanjaro: it is the light of Pan-Africanism. This light radiates all over Africa and reaches beyond to the rest of the world. It illuminates all people and all races, bringing to all "hope where there was despair, love where before there was hate, and dignity where before there was only humiliation." (Nyerere 1959)

Evocation of the Absent; The Silenced and the Imprisoned

My brothers and my sisters:
We all know why, today, Blacks in Brazil remain silent.
Yet yesterday all of us here heard the Representative of Tanzania, the Honorable Joseph Rwegasira, insisting, against objections from certain factions, on the validity of the expression "Black people." There seems to have been established, throughout the world, a new category of crime: the crime of being Black. The Black race has suffered, and suffers, solely by virtue of its epidermic condition, all sorts of aggression. Not only physical injury, but also continuous attacks on our spirit and intelligence. This is why we wish to evoke, in this historic Congress, the voices which have been silenced; at this time we call forth the Black people who were intimidated and threatened, even here in the very venue of this Congress; the voices which have been thwarted from being present here by the Congress organizers as well as the governments, dictatorial or "democratic," black or white; those who are now in prison because of their militancy on behalf of a Pan-African and/or Black revolution. We vehemently condemn anti-Black intolerance, including not only capitalist style governments and military dictatorships, but also the countries whose socialism should constitute an effective guarantee for the exercise of our integral and full realization as Human Beings.

The escapism of "humanity without color" leads simply to the endorsement of our ethnic alienation, so persistently advocated by the ideas and ideals of Eurocentric supremacy. Millenia before the Europeans attempted to deny Africa and Africans through the dehumanization of slavery and of colonial invasion -- with the simultaneous negation of their history and culture -- Black Africans recognized themselves as Blacks and were not ashamed of their concrete indentity. The Pan-African cultural revolution must assume, as a priority, the responsibility of guaranteeing the ransom of this blackness that has been violated, distorted, and in so many ways attacked, but which does not surrender because it emerges as much from the wounds of its historic vicissitudes as from the spiritual forces that sustain the vitality of the race.

BIBLIOGRAPHY

Andrade, Jorge (1971) "Quatro Tiradentes Baianos," *Realidade*. São Paulo: November, pp. 34-53.

Fernandes, Florestan (1972) *O Negro no Mundo dos Brancos*. São Paulo: Difusão Européia do Livro.

Moura, Clovis (1972) *Rebeliões da Senzala - Quilombos, Insurreições, Guerrilhas*. Rio de Janeiro: Editôra Conquista.

-- (1977) *O Negro - de Bom Escravo a Mau Cidadão?*. Rio de Janeiro: Editôra Conquista.

Nabuco, Joaquim (1949) *O Abolicionismo*. São Paulo: Instituto Progresso Editorial.

Nascimento, Abdias do (1968) *O Negro Revoltado*. Rio de Janeiro: Edições GRD.

-- (1977) *"Racial Democracy" in Brazil: Myth or Reality?*. Ibadan: Sketch Publishing Co., Ltd.

Nascimento, et. al. (1968) *80 Anos de Abolição*. Rio de Janeiro: Cadernos Brasileiros.

Nyerere, Julius (1974) *Ujamaa - Essays on Socialism*. London/New York: Oxford University Press.

-- (1959) Hansard, 35th Session, October 22.

Ramos, Guerreiro (1957) *Introdução Crítica à Sociologia Brasileira*. Rio de Janeiro: Editorial Andes.

Skidmore, Thomas E. (1974) *Black into White: Race and Nationality in Brazilian Thought*. New York: Oxford University Press.

CHAPTER 2

GENOCIDE:
THE SOCIAL LYNCHING OF AFRICANS
AND THEIR DESCENDANTS IN BRAZIL

THE IDEAS AND PROBLEMS IN THIS CHAPTER WERE
DEVELOPED AND DISCUSSED IN BOTH:

<table>
<tr><td>speech delivered at
Seminar for African World
Alternatives
February 4-6, 1976
Dakar
Senegal</td><td>and</td><td>paper delivered to
Faculty Seminar
University of Ife, Depart-
ment of African Languages
and Literatures
February 14, 1977
Ile-Ife, Nigeria</td></tr>
</table>

-- Who can say that the Black race has not the right to protest before the world and before history against the behavior of Brazil?

Joaquim Nabuco
O Abolicionismo

-- To this day, the Black has been judged by the white man, a judge completely biased on his own behalf, certainly more than partial and unjust, when not flagrantly criminal.

A. Silva Mello
Estudos sobre o Negro

B razil as a nation proclaims herself the only racial democracy in the world, and much of the world views and accepts her as such. But an examination of the historical development of my country reveals the true nature of her social, cultural, political and economic anatomy: it is essentially racist and vitally threatening to Black people.

Throughout the era of slavery from 1530 to 1888, Brazil carried out a policy of systematic liquidation of the African. From the legal abolition of slavery in 1888 to the present, this scheme has been continued by means of various well-defined mechanisms of oppression and extermination, leaving white supremacy unthreatened in Brazil.

During the era of Western colonial expansion, the African people were considered non-human and bestial. The tradition of European racism which uniquely informed the system of enslavement of Africans by Aryans differentiated it from all other forms of slavery known to human history. Slaves were forced to live the filth, misery and degradation of their "scientifically determined" social status. This meant medical and hygienic neglect, malnutrition and subjection to physical torture and sexual abuse. These tribulations led to the mental, emotional and cultural deprivation of the Black people with which we are all, I think, familiar.

After "abolition," the masters, especially owners of coffee plantations in the Southern states, refused to employ "freed" Black people as workers and gave preference instead to Aryan immigrants from Europe. They denied former slaves the most basic element of subsistence, then accused them of laziness and indolence or of having no interest in leading productive lives. They ignored the basic fact that it was they themselves who had turned the African slave into "little more than a brute and little less than a child" by their infamous exploitation of him and of his family. Then they turned the result of this process of dehumanization into an "argument" against any possibility of his becoming a free man.

During and since slave times, the most effective tool of physical and spiritual genocide of Black people has been the manipulative mystique of whitening the Brazilian population.

The testimonies to the predominantly and often explicitly racist orientation of Brazilian immigration policies are many and varied. They attest to a prevalent attitude that the Brazilian population was ugly and genetically inferior because of the presence of African blood, and that it needed to "... fortify itself through joining with the higher value of the European race." (Skidmore 1974: 30)

This attitude was endorsed by supposedly scientific and sociological theory, which provided vital intellectual support for the white supremacist ploys. In the words of leading intellectual Sílvio Romero: "My argument is that future victory in the life struggle among us will belong to the white race." (Skidmore 1974: 36) Writer Jose Veríssimo also remarked:

> As ethnographers assure us, and as can be confirmed at first glance, race mixture is facilitating the prevalence of the superior race here. Sooner or later it will eliminate the black race. Here this obviously already is happening. (Skidmore 1974: 73)

Religious endorsement of these concepts was also obtained: even the Catholic church held that the Black people suffered "infected blood." (Degler 1971: 214)

The aggressively racist nature of the official policies of immigration is not difficult to discern: as late as the administration of Getúlio Vargas, on 18 September 1945, by Law Decree 7967, the government regulated the entry of immigrants according to

> ...the necessity to preserve and develop in the ethnic composition of the population the more desirable characteristics of its European ancestry. (Skidmore 1974: 199)

The support of the intellectual and religious sectors allowed the governing strata to exercise these policies over almost all the aspects of Brazilian society. Various strategies of domination developed in the cultural composition of the society, one of them being religious repression. Aryan western cultural imperialism masks itself in a movement of apparent exchange of influences labelled among conventional scholars as *religious syncretism*. This expression, however, ignores the fact that such a term is legitimate only if "exchange" occurs in an atmosphere of living spontaneity. In the case of Afro-Brazilian culture, on the contrary, we are dealing with the more or less violent *imposition* or *superimposition* of white Western cultural norms and values in a systematic attempt to undermine the African spiritual and philosophical modes. Such a process can only be described as *forced* syncretization.

Another deadly tool in this scheme of immobilizing and fossilizing the vital dynamic elements of African culture can be found in its marginalization as simple folklore: a subtle form of ethnocide. All of these processes take place in an aura of subterfuge and mystification in order to mask and dilute their significance or make them seem ostensibily superficial. But despite such attempts at deceit, the fact remains that the concepts of white Western culture reign in this supposedly ecumenical culture in a country of Blacks, marginalizing and undervaluing our heritage of Africa in the process. For this white-identified culture, the "folkloric man" is the *natural man,* destitute of history, projects and problems. He has only a profound alienation from his African identity. Since raw material is non-entity waiting to take form, for this conventional culture "folklore" is the raw material that the white man manipulates, manufactures and profits from.

On the whole, in this pretentious concept of "racial democracy," there lies deliberately buried the true face of Brazilian society: only one of the racial elements has any rights or power -- whites. They control the means of dissemination of information, educational curriculum and institutions, conceptual definitions, aesthetic norms, and all other forms of social/cultural values. This control accounts for the widespread and rather innocent belief of the Brazilian people in "racial democracy" itself.

Slavery and Sexual Abuse Of African Women

The role of the African slave was crucial to the early history and political economy of a country founded, as was Brazil, on

61

colonial-imperialist parasitism. Without the slave the economic system could never have existed. The slave constructed the foundations of the new society with the bend and break of his backbone, backbone of the very colony. He nurtured and gathered the wealth of the land, only to see the fruits of his labor reaped forcibly by the white aristocracy. In plantations of sugar cane and coffee, in mines, and in cities, Africans were the hands and the feet of a white settler elite that would not degrade itself with work of any kind. The genteel occupations of the colonial aristrocracy were cultivation of ignorance, prejudice, and lasciviousness.

There is an erroneous notion that has been spread by the beneficiaries of slavery in Brazil and the rest of Latin America. It says that in the Spanish and Portuguese colonies of South and Central America and the Carribbean, slavery was less harsh than in the English colonies, especially the United States. Many authors have tried to buttress this argument by referring to the fact that there was more interbreeding -- often erroneously called "intermarriage" among Portuguese and Spanish masters and their slave women than there was in English-dominated slave societies. This fact is supposed to prove a greater "respect" for Africans as human beings on the part of the Latin American white slaveholders. Such a conception is, historically, a total falsity: yet it is propounded continually both inside and outside Brazil.

In the United States, for example, in his book *Negroes in Brazil* Donald Pierson says that slavery there "... was ordinarily a mild form of servitude." Unfolding his analysis, the North American sociologist continues:

> In general, slavery in Brazil was characterized by the gradual and continuous growth of intimate, personal relations between master and slave which tended to humanize the institution and undermine its formal character.
> (1942: 45)

Later Pierson expounds upon the phenomenon of ethnic cross-breeding, the Brazilian strategy of liquidating the Black African, in this tenor:

Thus miscegenation has gone on in Brazil in an unobtrusive way over a long period of time. In few places in the world perhaps, has the interpenetration of peoples of divergent racial stocks proceeded so continuously and on so extensive a scale. (1942: 119)

Contrary to this benign image of the slave regime depicted by such descriptions, the cruelty inflicted on African families by slave owners and traders in Brazil was as appalling as anything to be encountered in the New World. The interbreeding of white masters with African women, far from being a result of absence of race prejudice, can be explained at least in part as an outcome of the nature of the colonial situation. The difference was that the Portuguese had come to the New World to make a fortune and return to Europe. They left their women home. English settlers had come to stay, so they brought their wives with them. The use of African women to satisfy slaveowners in the absence of white women was outright rape. It had nothing to do with "respect" for the victims as human beings.

Since the motive for importing slaves was purely one of profit, Africans were treated to an ideology which considered them subhuman. They were not considered human beings with families. Therefore the proportion of women to men imported was close to 1:5, and even the few women imported were prevented from establishing any stable childrearing structure.

In dealing with the misconception that "intermarriage" characterized harmonious relations among white masters and their Black slaves, we should not forget that the laws of the colony explicity specified that

Concubinage between master and slave woman does not diminish the latter's condition of slave, nor are the very sons of the master free. (Moura 1972: 58)

This law was rooted in the social realities of the colony. Concubinage was frequent, intermarriage unheard of. What was prevalent was the practice among white slaveowners of holding Black women as prostitutes for profit. It is no exaggeration to say that these Portuguese colonials as a group were not only lechers but common, if aristocratic, pimps.

This social reality is diametrically opposed to the miscegenation ideology, which portrays Brazil's development as an unbiased process of integration. The password of this credo is "intermarriage," a term which is hardly appropriate. An old saying, as popular today as it was a century ago, gives an accurate picture of the real nature of sexual interaction among the races, as the Brazilian people see it:

Branca para casar,	White lady for marrying,
Negra p'ra trabalhar,	Black woman for working,
Mulata p'ra fornicar.	Mulatto woman for fornicating.

Another trademark of the ideology of race mixture is the evocation of sentimental images of interracial affection, nurtured by such immortal stereotypes as the Black Mammy/Aunt Jemima figure or the Uncle Tom and pickanninny syndromes. Pierre Verger supplies us with a prime example:

> Especially during the period of slavery, one could rarely find a white child that had not been reared by a black nurse who suckled it, lulled it to sleep in her arms or in a hammock, and taught it its first words in clumsy Portuguese. When a child learned to speak, it was undoubtedly more often with its nurse or chamber-maid than with its parents. (1977: 9)

This is exactly the same cheap emotional appeal that the slave era produced in the United States, and its image still stares at Black people from boxes of powdered pancake mix and Uncle Ben's rice. Brazil is far from unique for the Black Mammy: white women of the colonial aristocracies were universally parasitic, neglectful of their own children, leaving their maternal responsibilities to slave women whose very milk was drained from the mouths of their Black sons and daughters. The contention that such circumstances constitute the grounds of a "racial democracy" can only be classed as patently absurd.

The entire premise of the Brazilian "racial democracy" myth is destroyed by a realistic evaluation of the experience of the United States. Brazilians insist upon comparing their country's race and slavery relations favorably with those of the U.S., pointing to miscegenation as final proof of the superiority of Brazilian racial harmony. The assumption, apparently, is that here in the North of the Americas there was no cross-breeding, both races remaining biologically pure. Such thinking can only be a result of massive ignorance or maliciousness on the part of our "scientists," who persist in deifying race misture as an exlusively Brazilian experience. But, as Thomas E. Skidmore, social scientist from the U.S., appropriately shows:

> ...no slave society in the Americas failed to produce a vast mulatto population. [...] In 1850, for example, [in the U.S.] the black population was 11 percent mulatto; and around 1910 the percentage of mulattoes grew to 21 percent. (1976: 87)

What Brazilian (and French) "scientists" need is to avoid confusing a system of legal and social segregation with purity of race. Langston Hughes, the notable Black North American poet, wrote a play entitled *Mulatto,* which treats the tragic situation of the child of the white master and Black woman in the United States.

The fallacy of the notion that the Portuguese showed an "innate tendency" to interbreed with Black women is easily exposed on examination of Portuguese behavior in Africa. José Honório Rodrigues, in his study of race relations in African colonies, concludes:

> If we examine Portuguese acts in Africa we will see that the proclaimed lack of prejudice did not lead to miscegenation. Because, as we have already accentuated, at the end of the last century when colonization really commenced there, there was no *slavery,* which would permit, with or without prejudice, the use and abuse of slaves on a purely material and sexual plane. (1961: 41)

The process of sexual exploitation of Black women resulted in simple genocide. With the growth of the mulatto population, the Black race began to disappear. This development was turned into an explicit and intentional policy of the governing strata. Additionally, maltreatment and abuse of Africans and their descendants, including torture, starvation and overwork, resulted in an extremely high rate of infant mortality. The decimation of the African people in Brazil can be clearly seen. In 1870 in Rio de Janeiro, the city where the slave population was treated with more care than anywhere else in Brazil, because it was the capital of the nation, the infant mortality rate was an appalling 88 percent.

The crime of sexual violence committed against Black women by the white male was perpetuated through generations by her own mulatto sons, who inherited a precarious prestige from their fathers and continued to exploit the Black woman. In an attempt to assuage their guilt in this aggression, the Aryan male dominant forces heralded the mulatto as the key to the solution of the "racial problem:" the beginning of the liquidation of the Black race and the whitening of the Brazilian population. But despite any apparent advantage in social status as the racial bridge between Black and white, the mulatto's position is in essence equivalent to that of the Black. He suffers much the same discrimination, prejudice and disdain in white society. His only choice is to pretend and aspire to be white.

Foremost among illustrations of this fact is the social position of the mulatto woman in Brazil. She is frequently held up to the world as the symbol of racial democracy because she is considered desirable by the "unprejudiced" Brazilian white male. But her social and economic status eloquently testifies to the reality of her historical origins. She is the product of the systematic prostitution of the Black race, and she remains, because of her poverty and lack of social status, the easily accessible and vulnerable victim of aggression and control by white men. Listen to the words of Black Brazilian women in their public manifesto issued at the Women's Congress held in the *Associação Brasileira de Imprensa* (Brazilian Association of the Press) in Rio de Janeiro on July 2, 1975:

...the Black Brazilian woman received a cruel inheritance: to be the object of the pleasure of the colonizers. The fruit of this cowardly interbreeding is what is now acclaimed and proclaimed as "the only national product fit to be exported: the Brazilian mulatto woman." But if the quality of the "product" is said to be high, the treatment she receives is extremely degrading, dirty and disrespectful.

The claim to racial democracy made by Brazil on the basis of the supposed "tendency of the races to intermarry" is greatly discredited by recent statistical work. The social reality is that the mulatto continues to be a product of prostitution and concubinage of Black and mulatto women, and not of legitimate marital unions. Sociologist Octávio Ianni, in a study published in 1972, surveyed a statistically significant group of randomly selected Brazilians. His question was "Would you approve of the marriage of your friend, brother or sister, or yourself with a Black or a mulatto?" His results are as follows (in percentages):

	Black	Mulatto	
Would not like friend to marry	35	29	
Would not like brother to marry	74	70	
Would not like sister to marry	76	72	
I would not like to marry	89	87	(124)

As the author concludes,

...we note clearly the progressive rejection, of the Black woman as well as the mulatto, as the manifestations come closer to the social world of the informant himself. [...] the white eliminates Blacks and mulattoes from his most intimate circle of social life: the family. This is how he dissimulates the rigid barriers imposed on the former. (124)

The Catholic Church

Another theory which is widely promoted regarding the slave regime of Brazil is that the harshness of slavery was mitigated by the humanist influence of the Catholic church as opposed to the Protestant English church in other colonies, particularly the United States. This myth attempts to exonerate the Catholic church from implication in the violent racism upon which slavery was based during European colonial expansion. An examination of the religious teachings of Catholicism, however, quickly reveals the true nature of the Church's attitudes toward Black Africans. The famous Jesuit of Bahia, Antônio Vieira, pronounced the following in one of his sermons in Lisbon in 1662:

An Ethiopian who bathes in the waters of Zaire, becomes clean, but does not become white; however, in those of baptism, yes, one thing and the other (1940: 399)

Meaning that the waters of baptism possess the diverse virtues of Christly justifying the servitude of Africans and also of eradicating their race -- of turning them physically and spiritually *white*. In 1633 the same priest sang the praises of black bondage in a sermon directed to the enslaved African people of Bahia:

> You should give infinite thanks to God for giving you the knowledge of yourselves, and for having taken you away from your lands, where your parents and you lived as heathen, and having brought you to this one, where, instructed in the faith, you live as Christians and save yourselves. (1940: 23-24)

Vieira further counselled:

> Slaves, you are subjects and obedient in everything to your master, not only to the good and modest one, but also the the bad and unjust ... because in this state in which God has put you, it is your vocation similar to that of his Son, who died for us, leaving you the example that you must imitate. (1940: 399-400)

It is curious that Vieira did not preach the inverse; if the Christian is to aspire to salvation through an emulation of Christ, why does this pious priest not advocate the martyrdom of slavery for white Europeans? This would at least inject some integrity and coherence in his religious morals. But such incoherence -- or better, oppressor ideology -- is not the privilege only of the Catholics. With almost the same words the Protestant pastor of English America, Morgan Goldwin, dogmatized:

> Christianity established the authority of masters over their servants and slaves in as great a measure as the very masters themselves could have prescribed it ... demanding that they serve them with a pure heart as if they served God and not men ... And it is far from fomenting resistance that He does not permit the slaves the liberty to contradict or to reply in undue form to their masters. And He permits them future compensation in Heaven for the loyal services they have given on Earth. (Davis 1968: 187)

Such is the mitigation that the Catholic as well as the Protestant Churches exercised on slavery. It is evident that the Catholic ideology expressed by Vieira, which urges slaves to accept meekly the abuses of "the bad and the unjust," makes no more concession to the harshness of everyday life for the slave than does that of the Protestant pastor. Christianity in all its forms constituted nothing but a condonement and rationalization of the very barbarousness of the white master toward his slaves. It aptly demonstrated its own racism in such concepts as the baptism that turns the African white, a state which the Church obviously sees as superior to being Black.

Mystification of African Cultural Survivals

There is a tradition of Brazilian historical thought, whose most well-known proponent is Gilberto Freyre, which alleges that the presence of African cultural forms, especially in the field of religion, bespeaks a history of amiable relations between master and slave and between Blacks and whites in Brazil. Here again, Brazilians point to the U.S., where African religions did not flourish, as a departure for the conclusion that the contrast in these historical situations verifies the superiority of Brazilian race relations. Songs, dances, foods and religious rituals of African origin are seen as "proof" of the absence of racial prejudice or discrimination in Brazil. We will give this school of thought its proper name: the *mystification of African cultural survivals*. It is part and parcel of the miscegenation ideology we examined earlier, and most dangerous because its appeal has been seductive enough to capture the enthusiastic platform of "scholars" in Brazil and abroad. The idea has lately been expounded in Africa by Pierre Verger in the paper cited earlier. Quoting from several authorities of this tradition of scholarship, most notably Gilberto Freyre and Luiz Vianna Filho, Verger points out the following phenomena:

> ... [in colonial times] a most frequent entertainment engaged in by guests at private parties were dances of African origin. The onlookers seemed to be delighted with these choreographic demonstrations and cheered on the dancers with hearty applause.

> ... when the Africans were frolicking in their spare time, black Creoles and mulattoes would join them, and all would dance in the same fashion, which led [Koster] to believe that these dances were as representative of Brazil as they were of Africa. (1977: 11)

69

The gist of these examples is to show that

> ... if it is true that the slaves were Europeanized through
> the contact with their masters, it is equally true that the
> same Portuguese masters in turn underwent a process of
> Africanization through the contact with their slaves.
> (1977: 9)

What is treacherous here is not the simple exposition of such
situations, but the generalizations and conclusions which are
extrapolated from them:

> This concern with accepting all contributions *without any
> distinction,* be they European, Amerindian, or African, is
> certainly worthy of praise. (emphasis added. 1977: 13)

> The outstanding role played by African religions in giving
> African descendants an *acceptable social status in Brazil*
> cannot be overemphasized. (emphasis added. 1977: 15)

This is the classical line of reasoning of this school of thought.
From the existence of religious and other manifestations of
African culture, they jump to a postulation of an "acceptable
social status" of African descendants in Brazil. They take the
step with all the blithe facility of self-evidence, as if one were the
logical, necessary and sufficient premise for the other. No
examination of the conditions under which these African
cultural traits persisted is deemed necessary: probably because
such an examination would destroy the very premise of the
thesis. For the African forms of worship and celebration
survived *despite* constant police persecution, legal restrictions
and manipulation by the white European elite. They survive in
an atmosphere of extreme derision and marginality. The only
legitimation granted them is their commercial value as tourist
commodity.

Whatever the cultural influence of Africa in Brazil, it does not
constitute a demonstration or proof of anything about race
relations in my country today. In the apt phrase of Florestan
Fernandes:

> All of those who have read Gilberto Freyre will know
> about the double interaction which established itself in
> both directions [between master and slave]. However, at
> no time did these reciprocal influences change the

70

character of social progress. The Black remained forever condemned to a world that did not bring itself to treat him as a human being or as an equal. (1972: 15)

Gilberto Freyre himself, the patron of this ideology, carried it to the extreme of absurdity recently in an article published by the Federal Ministry of Education and Culture (1976) for circulation in Africa on the occasion of the Second World Festival of Black and African Arts and Culture. A special talent of Freyre has been his coinage of euphemisms in the attempt to paint Brazilian racial harmony in the rosiest hues possible. The first of these is *morenidade* (brunettism), which he uses to describe the "democratic" objectives of race mixture. As we shall see shortly, this invention does little to obscure the true nature of a racial mystique whose target from the start has been the definitive disappearance of the African descendant, physically and spiritually, through the insidious process of whitening the ethnic and cultural composition of Brazilian society.

Freyre, fertile creator of mirages, does not stop with *morenidade*. He goes on to attempt to harness Africans to the lost sinking ship of colonialist illusions:

> Here we can justify the neologism created by the Brazilian socio-anthropologist: *co-colonization*. A concept which would correspond to the characterization of the Black African, despite his condition of slave, as a co-colonizer of Brazil with considerable acculturative influence over the Amerindian who was less developed in his culture than the African Negro. (1976: 8)

Blind to the preposterousness of the suggestion that a people who were conquered, hunted, captured and kidnapped from their home in chains of bondage, could be called "colonizers" of a land where they were held in captivity, Freyre implies here that Africans share the responsibility for the extermination of the Brazilian indigenous peoples! A process which, having reduced their population from two million at the beginning of colonization to fewer than two hundred thousand today, remains an explicit objective of the Brazilian government. In the words of Rangel Reis, Minister of the Interior, the Department which presides over Indian affairs through the National Foundation of the Indian (FUNAI):

Let us seek to fulfill the objectives fixed by President Geisel, so that, through concentrated work among various Ministries, within ten years, we can reduce to twenty thousand the 220 thousand Indians existing today in Brazil, and within thirty years, all of them shall be duly integrated into the national society. (1976)

But the ideological fecundity of Gilberto Freyre surpasses even this stage. Not content merely to implicate Africans in the genocide of Indians in Brazil, Freyre continues to nourish Brazilian fantasy with the coinage of a new euphemism: the *metarraça* (metarace). The metarace, the beyond-race, that ephemeral goal of cafe-au-lait universalism, is, according to Gilberto Freyre, the basis of Brazilian consciousness. And from this we arrive at *morenidade metarracial* (metaracial brunettism) which Freyre proceeds to eulogize as against Aryanism and Negritude, both of which he labels racist. (1976: 19) In doing so, he conveniently neglects to deal with the racist fundaments of the miscegenation *(morenidade)* ideology, which we shall see in ample detail.

Afro-Brazilian Soldiery: "Integration" in War?

One of the supreme ironies of Brazilian history is the way it has treated the subject of the participation of Africans and their descendants in the military exploits of the country. A good example of the distortion used in this area can be found in an official publication of the Brazilian government's delegation to Festac '77, by Manuel Diegues Junior. Referring to the War of Expulsion of the Dutch from Pernambuco in 1630-1654 he states:

... the negro participated in this reaction against Dutch dominion, giving proof in this way of his already Brazilian spirit, integrated into the direction of our formation with its essentially Lusitanian base. (1977: 137)

In general, slaves were herded together and forced to fight a war which had no meaning or consequence for them. They simply were used as a corpus of dispensable soldiers to carry the brunt of war's destruction for the whites. This force of Black soldiers was sometimes obtained by granting Africans "freedom" on their conscription for military service. Slaves "enlisted" in order to win their liberty: liberty to die in the white man's war or to be left to starve in the street if they managed to survive. Henrique Dias, the famous Black commander in this war, upon victory had to humiliate himself and beg for favors promised by the Portuguese crown he had served so well. The cowardice of this process was poignantly illustrated by the white sons of the colonial masters, who, when they themselves were conscripted, often sent their slaves to war instead of risking their own lives. This technique of substituting African blood for Portuguese or Brazilian also was used in 1865-69 when Brazil attacked the legal government of Solano Lopez in Paraguay.

Whatever the contribution of these Blacks to the preservation and security of the country, it did not earn them emancipation from the bonds of slavery. Throughout all these wars, Africans and their descendants remained enslaved.

"Free" Africans

During colonial times slaveowners took "legal" steps to ensure the permanent security of the supply of slave labor. The entire judicial and legislative structure was geared to this objective. The prisons of Brazil before abolition were filled with "free Africans." Often these were exemplaries, to intimidate Blacks with any desire to return to Africa or to live a free life. The slave, not recognized legally as a person, had no legal access to redress of grievance. The *Acordão da Relação do Rio* (Decision of the Court -- organ of Federal Justice) of April 1, 1879, proclaimed

> The slave cannot make complaint against any person, even if it be against he who seeks to lead him into slavery. (Moura 1972: 58)

Thus even a legally free African had no means of redress against being taken back into captivity by a white, and we have the following scene in Ouro Preto, 1835, described in the newspaper *O Universal* on April 10:

> Just a few days ago it is confirmed that there passed, in the direction of *Ponte Nova* one Manuel de Santa Ana, a

> criminal murderer, convicted in the Courts of the city of
> Mariana, conducting nineteen Africans, of whom we are
> well convinced that more than two thirds are free.
> (Sena 1977: 109)

A white man, convicted murderer, publically kidnaps free Blacks
with impunity: they have no right of complaint.

And so the just and deserved response of ex-slave and
attorney Luis Gama to the slaveowners who in the courts were
accusing him of hiding escaped slaves:

> The slave whose rights are violated, and who assassinates
> his master, is practicing an act of legitimate self-defense.
> (Moura 1972: 47)

After their years of labor, the old and the sick, no longer
productive, were "freed:" cast into the street to fend for
themselves with no resources. This "freedom" was multiplied
into a form of collective assassination in 1888 with the
"abolition" of slavery. They cast us out of society. At that point
the responsibility of master, state and church -- of the entire
Christian world -- toward the African "savage" and his
descendant, was terminated. Carl Degler, in the face of this
clamorous injustice, asks: "What can we expect of a society
founded in the fatal hunt of the Indian, in slavery, in the
degradation of women?" (1971: 214)

To add insult to injury, the white dominant society, having
disposed of the "burden" of slavery, proceeded to accuse Black
people, who had been brought from Africa in shackles and
chains, of being the cause of "the problem." Influential writer
Monteiro Lobato expounded:

> What terrible problems the poor African Negro created
> for us by his unintentional revenge [miscegenation]. Per-
> haps our salvation will come from São Paulo and other
> areas which have had a heavy influx of European blood.
> (Skidmore 1974: 180)

The Whitening of the Race: A Strategy of Genocide

The abolition of slavery on May 13, 1888 did present a
severe cultural, social and economic problem for the white elite
in the new "free society." But they did not view this problem in

terms of how to integrate a new group of citizens into the socio-economic, political or cultural fabric of the country; or how to ensure this group the means and liberty to assert and develop its own institutions or traditions. For them, the racial problem was simply *how to save the white race from the threat of inferiorization posed by the presence of black blood.* The racist ideology of the time was so unabashed that the stated objective of government projects was the eradication of the Black race through the "salvation" of European immigration and the infusion of massive quantities of Aryan blood into the national stock. Declared politician João Pandiá Calógeras:

> The black stain is destined to disappear in a relatively short space of time because of the influx of white immigration in which the heritage of Ham is dissolving. [Theodore] Roosevelt rightly pointed out that the future has reserved for us a great boon: the happy solution of a problem fraught with tremendous, even mortal, dangers -- the problem of a possible conflict between the races.
> (Skidmore 1974: 205)

By virtue of its finality in enforcement, the law is perhaps the most visible tool of genocide. And it is undeniable that the immigration laws promulgated in post-abolition times were calculated to one end: the disappearance of the "black stain" from the Brazilian population. A decree of June 28, 1890 conceded "free entry by persons healthy and able to work, except natives of Asia and of Africa, who can be admitted only by authorization of the National Congress." (Skidmore 1974: 139) On various occasions the *Câmara de Deputados* (House of Representatives) of Brazil considered and discussed bills which would have outrightly prohibited any entry by "human beings of the black race." (Skidmore 1974: 193) The previously cited decree of 1945, Law-Decree 7967, made explicit the objective of preserving and "upgrading" the superior -- i.e., white European -- character of Brazil's ethnic make-up. Most recently, the government has taken steps to encourage the immigration of racist white exiles from recently liberated African colonies: Belgians from the former Congo, Portuguese from Mozambique and Angola. Afro-American writer Angela Gilliam has had occasion to observe that Brazil's official policy "... exhorts whites running away from independent African nations to choose Brazil." (1975: 24)

Intellectual convention, through its collusion in the construction of these programs throughout the history of Brazil as a nation, has been pivotal to their acceptance and practice. In the 1920's, Brazil was subsidizing by law the immigration of European whites (Celts and Nordic races, Iberians, Slavs, Germans, Portuguese, Austrians, Spanish, Russians and Italians) who flooded the labor market and took jobs from Blacks. Ample "scientific" validation of the procedure and its objective was available. Oliveira Viana, influential scientist and writer, commented, in his praise of immigration politics,

> ... the ethnic group that contributes the largest portion to the "melting pot" has the potential to dominate the make-up of the population, not only in its morphological type, but also in its psychological and cultural type. (1938: 126)

Prominent writer Paulo Prado affirmed:

> ... in the continuous mixture of our life since the colonial era the Negro is slowly disappearing, being transformed into the deceptive appearance of a pure Aryan. (Skidmore 1974: 204)

Arthur Neiva, another outspoken intellectual, lauded the policies of immigration in this manner: "Within a century the nation will be white!" (Skidmore 1974: 193) João Batista de Lacerda, the only Latin American delegate to the first Universal Races Congress in London in 1911, predicted that by 2012 the Black race would have disappeared from Brazil:

> In virtue of this process of ethnic reduction it is logical to expect that in the course of another century the *mètis* (half-breeds) will have disappeared from Brazil. This will coincide with the parallel extraction of the black race from our midst. (Skidmore 1974: 66)

Lacerda and Neiva's thesis was widely criticized, however, by worried Brazilians who were outraged by their estimate of the time it would take. They felt a century was far too long. (Skidmore 1976: 83) There was no mistaking the true objective of the body of political programs being formulated in the epoch. Their goal was unequivocally the disappearance of the Black people, a calculated strategy of extermination. This is corroborated by the suggestion of João Batista de Lacerda that Afro-Brazilians be intentionally rendered defenseless, "exposed to all types of agents of destruction, and without sufficient recourse to maintain themselves." (Skidmore 1976: 83)

One revealing incident in the history of Brazilian racial ideology came in 1921, when the President of the State of Mato Grosso made a series of land concessions to pioneers and settlers willing to brave the wilds of his state. It was divulged in the press that among the prospective settlers was a group of Black people from the United States. Upon learning of this disastrous possibility, the President of Mato Grosso immediately closed down the concessions and, in a tone of panic, notified the Federal Ministry of Foreign Relations. At this point Afrânio Peixoto, a prestigious physician and writer, joined in the general clamor against the perilous implications of a potential influx of 15 million Negroes from the North, exclaiming "Will we have enough albumin to refine all this scum? God help us, if he is Brazilian!" (Skidmore 1976: 212, 215)

Population statistics will clarify the mechanics of this social lynching of Blacks. According to the estimate of 1600 the population of the colony consisted of:

Indians	35,000
Whites	10,000
Africans and their descendants	20,000

(Viana Filho 1946: 45)

A demographic survey completed in 1798 resulted in the following data:

Civilized Indians	250,000
Whites	1,010,000
Slaves	1,582,000
Free Blacks	406,000

(Azevedo 1973: 67)

The famous politician Rio Branco shows that in 1822 there was a population of 3,800,000, distributed as follows:

Whites	1,043,000
Blacks	1,930,000
Mulattoes	526,000

(Nascimento 1968: 31)

According to the Brazilian Institute of Geography and Statistics the population developed from 1872 to 1950 in the following manner:

	1872	1890	1940	1950
Whites	3,787,289	6,308,198	26,171,778	32,027,661
Blacks	1,954,542	2,097,426	6,035,869	5,692,657
Pardos	4,188,737	5,934,291	8,744,365	13,786,742

(Pardo: brown, a euphemism for mulatto, i.e. Black)

(Nascimento 1968: 31)

From these statistics the decline of the Black population is evident along with an increasing whitening of the country; the percentage of each group in the population is:

	1872	1890	1940	1950
Blacks	19.68	14.63	14.64	10.96
Pardos	42.18	41.40	21.20	26.54
Whites	38.14	43.97	63.47	61.66

(Nascimento 1968: 31)

The figures certainly substantiate the observation of Clayton Cooper, visiting statesman from the U.S., who in 1917 reported:

> An honest attempt is being made here [in Brazil] to eliminate the Negros and mulattoes through the infusion of white blood. (Skidmore 1976: 91)

They also present a heavily distorted picture of the population, since the social pressures on the Blacks in Brazil produce a white-identified Black subculture. Lighter mulattoes (and even some who are not so light) describe themselves as whites. Blacks often identify themselves as mulatto, or *mestiço* or *pardo* or some other euphemism. This trend has taken place over many years. French writer João Maurício Rugendas observed in 1862:

> It is true that the law does not confer upon Negroes the right to vote or hold office; but the more or less dark-skinned officials make no difficulty recognizing as whites all those who wish to so style themselves, and provide them with the necessary documentation to establish the purity of their origins. (Skidmore 1974: 193)

Giorgio Mortara, recognized leader in the field of demographics in Brazil, concords:

> Those born from unions between brown-skinned and black-skinned people are classified as white: and through the reclassifications the black group loses a great deal and gains but little, the brown group gains much more than it loses, and the white group gains a great deal and loses nothing. (1970: 458)

Under these circumstances, it is clear that the distortion in such statistical data tends to weigh heavily on the side of the racist ideology of whitening the Brazilian population. This fact is well exploited by "social scientists" who serve the dominant powers by "objectively" bearing out the "facts" of ethnicity in Brazil. One such ideologue, in this case a servant of the current military dictatorship, Manuel Diegues Junior, in his paper distributed by the official Brazilian delegation at Festac '77, claims:

> The total of the Brazilian population in 1970, the year of the most recent census, is distributed over the territory with greater or lesser intensity of one of the groups, the predominance of the white element being evident, since in Brazil, even a *mestiço* who might have some quantity, small or large, of negro or Indian blood, is still considered white. Which testifies to the absence of any discrimination of racial nature regarding the ethnic origin of the person. (1977: 121)

The assumption, typical of this line of unreasoning, is that people of Indian or African origin prefer to be labelled white. The benevolent gesture of granting them the "privilege" of being so categorized is considered proof of the *absence* of racial prejudice! At the same time that he demonstrates the very artificiality of the inflation of statistics in the "white" category, Diegues enthusiastically accepts the conclusion construed from them: the "predominance of the white element."

The most recent demographic censuses have eliminated any reference at all to racial or ethnic origin or color -- a fact strangely ignored by Diegues in direct contradiction of two of his colleagues. Fernando Mourão of the University of São Paulo and Thomas E. Skidmore, social historian from the U.S., both confirm that the 1970 census in particular contained no data on racial distribution. Mourão states, "In the 1970 census, the criterion of color was no longer applied." (1977: 6) Skidmore, whose demographic information is thoroughly documented,

79

remarks: "In the census of 1970, for example, data on race was not collected." (1976: 238)

The fact is that since 1950 race and color data have been omitted from census information in Brazil on the assumption that an act of "white magic" can eliminate ethnicity by decree. This process occurs under the rationale that it is founded on a precept of social justice -- everyone is a Brazilian, be he Black, white, Indian or Asian. But its real significance is that it provides another instrument of social control. The reality of race relations is masked, and any information that Blacks could use in their struggle for social justice is withheld. The situation also leaves ample room for manipulation and interpretation of "data" by the agents and spokesmen of the ruling classes. More importantly, it represents the attitude that any movement by Afro-Brazilians toward consciousness of our own situation, any desire to clarify our understanding of our own history and experience, is seen as a "threat to national security," an "attempt to disintegrate Brazilian society and national unity," or worse, as retaliatory aggression and a call for imposition of a supposed Black superiority: reverse racism. Thus every effort is made to obstruct informational channels, isolating and marginalizing us as a group. For the outcome of such practices is to negate any racial, ethnic or cultural definition of the Black people, denying us any collective identity.

Although in social reality Black people are discriminated against precisely because of our race and color, we are denied by fundaments of law the right to self-defense. The Constitution recognizes no racial entities; everyone is just a Brazilian. This means that to this day the law of the slave era remains in force. Black people have no access to redress of grievance or to any form of "complaint" against the white man. As such, this ideology of "racial equality" is a double standard, a tool used conveniently to the interest of the power structure and to the detriment of Black people's dignity, self-respect and survival.

The Brazilian Reality of Discrimination

Legal convention in Brazil has constantly endorsed economic discrimination on the basis of color. Up until 1951 the practice of racial selection in employment and hiring policies was legal, flagrant and pervasive. Help-wanted ads were openly published with the qualification "Blacks and colored persons not acceptable." In that year the Afonso Arinos law was passed, ostensibly prohibiting racial discrimination. But in practice the Arinos legislation was entirely ineffectual, and it has never been enforced. Today, the same help-wanted ads read "persons of good appearance preferred." "Good appearance" means what precisely? We can easily infer that it does not mean Black...

This so-called "anti-discrimination" law was not a gratuitous or spontaneous gesture of unbiased or benevolent law-makers. It grew out of a demand made by organized Blacks at the *Convenção Nacional do Negro* (National Black Convention) which had taken place in São Paulo in 1945, with myself as president. The following year, 1946, as a result of our pressures, Senator Hamilton Nogueira proposed an anti-discrimination bill in the National Constituent Assembly. This body rejected it on the pretext of an "absence of concrete facts" to demonstrate the need. In 1951, when the bill was introduced again by Representative Afonso Arinos, it was passed into law because of the barring of Katherine Dunham from a São Paulo hotel.

So effective is the process of marginalization of the Black people in Brazil that even where Blacks are a majority of the population they exist as a minority in economic, cultural and political reality. The state of Bahia is an excellent example. According to the official census of 1950, a population of 4,822,024 in Bahia is distributed ethnically in the following way:

Whites.............................1,428,685 - 30%
Blacks and mulattoes ....3,393,183 - 70%
Asians.................................156 - 0.003%

Occupationally, however, the distribution is quite different:

Employees
Whites...................................23.01%
Blacks and mulattoes.....................76.98%

81

Employers

Whites................................51.90%

Blacks and mulattoes...... 48.11% (less economic
significance)

(Fernandes 1972: 60)

These figures are misleading, since the miniscule "businesses" which account for the vast majority of Black "employers" do not often go beyond street hawking. They have virtually no economic significance. The true "employers," those who command the means of production, finance and almost all the weight of the market, are whites.

Participation in education in Bahia, with its strong majority of Blacks, is distributed in this manner: (percentages)

	Elementary	*Intermediate*	*University*
Whites	54.46	82.56	88.21
Blacks	45.52	17.43	11.64

(Fernandes 1972: 60)

Once again, it is important to remember that these data are distorted by the ideological bias of Black people who have been conditioned to want to be white. But even taking into account the artificial inflation of the "white" category, it is clear that whites' participation in education is all out of proportion to their part in the population. As the educational level advances, the racial balance becomes more disproportionate.

Another manifestation of economic and social control is the creation and maintenance of Black slums and ghettoes. In the Northeast of the country, Blacks lives in *mocambos:* filth-infested structures in the stagnant, polluted ponds of the slums of Recife and other Northeastern cities. In São Paulo, the prominent residence of Black people is the *porão* (basement) in the shabby sections of the city. In Rio de Janeiro, it is the *favela,* the hillside slums of mud, filth and degradation so famous throughout the world. The newspaper *O Estado de São Paulo,* in its special supplement of April 13, 1960, published these figures taken in 1950:

Population of Rio

Whites 1,660,834

Blacks and mulattoes. 708,459
Population of Favelas
Whites. 55,436
Blacks and mulattoes. 113,218

(Nascimento 1968: 33)

This shows that for every three inhabitants of Rio, one is Black; for every white inhabitant of the *favelas,* two are Blacks. In other words, Blacks comprise a third of Rio's population, but their proportion in the *favelas* is 100% higher. Clearly, the colored population is subjected to a racist segregation of habitat.

For those who will protest that these Black people live in *favelas* simply because of "social" or "economic" discrimination that has nothing to do with race, or because they choose to, we pose the question: how is it that recent European immigrants who were also subject to "economic and social" discrimination when they arrived in the last few decades, have already risen to the higher and even highest levels of society, while Blacks have stayed for four centuries at the bottom of all social scales? In 1959, almost a decade after the passage of the Afonso Arinos law, racial prejudice was mentioned in the prominent newspaper *O Jornal,* in a report publishing the results of a research project conducted by the head of the Placement Section of the Federal Ministry of Labor: "It is color prejudice that is found to be in first place as a factor of unemployment." (Nascimento 1968: 29) the *London Times* also reported that "... racial discrimination really exists in Brazil, even though many Brazilians deny this fact." (Quoted in *Jornal do Brasil,* April 23, 1960. Nascimento 1968: 28-29) The *Times* went further. It answered the usual allegation that such discrimination was not racial in character, but simply a result of lower educational achievement on the part of Blacks, by citing the following result of its research: "But a black waiter is a rare thing in a hotel or restaurant of good quality, and the large stores never have them in service as sales people." (Nascimento 1968: 28-29) In other words, this disparity is not simply found in jobs of technical skill or educational requirement; it occurs in employment where a worker is visible and deals on a personal level with clients.

Employers do not want Black people serving their customers or waiting on shoppers -- this would be threatening to the store or business's image. This includes not only waitresses and salespeople, but also, according to the report in *O Jornal,* "porters, bartenders, hospital personnel, employees of foreign firms, or in any establishment that requires persons of 'good appearance'." (Nascimento 1968: 29)

Even in the field of sports -- apparently open to the protagonism of Blacks, and used heavily by the official spokesmen as an "example" of racial democracy -- discrimination is a fact as much today as yesterday. Mario Filho described in his book *O Negro no Futebol Brasileiro* (The Black in Brazilian Soccer) the struggles of the Afro-Brazilian to obtain a precarious place as soccer player. Precarious because even currently, an outstanding player such as Paulo César, considers himself condemned, a "damned player" by the fact of his epidermic color and his integrity as a Black man. In an interview given to Christina Lyro (1977) for the influential *Jornal do Brasil,* headlined "I am a Black man who didn't ask permission from the whites," Paulo César tells why he has irritated people so much:

- Because I am Black. A Black man who didn't ask for permission from whites, but demanded what I had a right to.

.- *Reporter:* You think, then, that you have been a victim of racial prejudice?

- *Paulo César:* Of course I do. In Brazil things are even worse than in the United States. There, prejudice is declared, and Blacks get together to free themselves from oppression. Here, no one admits that prejudice exists. Blacks themselves prefer to go through life trying to lighten their skins, instead of struggling for their rights. Prejudice is so great, that mulattoes don't like to be called Black.

- *Reporter:* But have you suffered any declared discrimination?

- *Paulo César:* When I was a kid, I was invited to a party here in Fluminense [famous athletic club] and they barred me at the door, they said Negroes couldn't enter the club.

Even after I was well known, I was barred from clubs in Porto Alegre and Santa Catarina. The truth is that whites don't allow a Black man into an elevated social position. We can only be porters, workers or truck drivers.

- *Reporter:* But, what about Pelé? He doesn't suffer this type of discrimination?

- *Paulo César:* Pelé is different. He's the "good boy", he never had the "audacity" to frequent nightclubs and restaurants in style, he never dressed extravagantly, he never tried to level himself with a white man. It's only been now, in the United States, that he's been seen dining in such and such a place, dancing I don't know where. I don't criticize anyone, but if I were him, I'd have been different. The truth is that Pelé has never contributed to help the Black race. That's what irritates me, the Black Brazilian cowers, he omits himself, he doesn't struggle for anything.

The report was provoked by the failure of the authorities to call this famous soccer player to participate in the Brazilian selective team which was to compete for the World Cup in 1978. My information as I write these lines (March 1978), is that Paulo César is now a member of the team, having paid a high price. He was coerced into making televised declarations which invalidated the statements in this interview.

The Afonso Arinos law has now been entered into the dictionary of the picturesque or folklore. To illustrate, let us look at one case among many: an event which took place in Bahia and was reported in the magazine *Manchete* of Rio de Janeiro, May 29, 1976. Irane Maria da Conceição attempted to enter the Maria Isabel Building to visit a friend. The porter of the building barred her from coming in the front door or using the main elevator -- "Black women only in the service facilities." When the incident was publicized by journalist Maria Carmelo Talento in the *Jornal da Bahia* and complaint registered, the administrator of the building, Teresa Falcão, fired the porter (who obviously had been following orders) protesting her innocence of any responsibility. Emanuel Araújo, interviewed about the situation, declared:

I think that's as far as it will go. I've never heard of a case in which the Afonso Arinos Law, which punishes those responsible for racial discrimination, has been applied...

We cannot leave this subject without mentioning Carolina Maria de Jesus. Almost illiterate, she wrote her testimony of life as a São Paulo slumdweller in her book *Quarto de Despejo* (literally, Room of Garbage). It is perhaps the most poignant document that anyone has ever written about the conditions of misery that Black people live in Brazil.

Education: Program of Discrimination

The fabric of social, economic and cultural control that we have been examining has pervaded Brazilian society on the political, social and educational levels throughout our history. Álvaro Bomilcar wrote:

> The organs and figures of public power in Brazil, the government, legislators, the system of criminal justice and law enforcement, intellectuals, the press, etc., in order to avoid violating their aesthetic values, wage a war against the black man without pity or compassion; a war never of direct confrontation, but of subtle, indirect, persistent but unhurried persecution of these victims of fatality, perverting or denying their civil rights, subverting their right to education, denying them public assistance or any type of official support for the cost of education or subsistence. (1916: 94)

The restrictions exercised over the Black population extend not only to social status and mobility, but also to the Black's and mulatto's patterns of thought, as Florestan Fernandes observes in *The Black in the White World:*

> To what point are the Black and the mulatto socialized not only to tolerate but to accept as a norm and actually endorse the existing structure, of racial inequality, with its dynamic components -- disguised racial prejudice and indirect racial discrimination? (1972: 10)

Black cultural heritage exists in a permanent confrontation with a system designed to negate African culture. Theoretical and practical obstacles were built by the Aryan elite to prevent the African descendant from establishing himself as an integral and valid element of Brazilian cultural life, and to protect the hegemony of Western European convention. Sílvio Romero noted the implications of a saying which expresses Brazil's perception of the Black person as a cultural entity: "We have Africa in our kitchens, America in our jungles, and Europe in our living rooms." (Rodrigues 1945: 15) I will further note that Africa entered the kitchen only by the service door.

The education system becomes a key instrument of control in this network of cultural discrimination. The material taught on all academic levels is simply the pomp and circumstance of Western Europe, and more recently of the United States. If consciousness is memory and future, where is African memory in the Brazilian consciousness? Where and when is African history or the development of African culture and civilization taught in Brazilian schools?

The treatment of Black history in school books has been deplorable, or absent. The facts and points of view presented are no more than testimonies to the alienation of Black identity; to the services we gave consciously or unconsciously for a cause or a culture that were not ours, and would never be allowed to be ours. In the university the only concepts, ideas, or forms of reasoning acceptable are Western European ones and their corollary and consequence; a difficult challenge for the few existing Afro-Brazilian students interested in their people's experience. When the chance for African studies apparently is created, it is illusory because the inevitably reactionary orientation defeats any possibility of meaningful, creative learning. An example is the African Studies Center at the University of São Paulo, under Fernando Mourão, a servile mouthpiece of the military dictatorship's delegation to Festac '77 in Lagos (see Nascimento 1977 for an account of his work).

There is in the University of Bahia a *Centro de Estudos Afro-orientais* (Center of Afro-Oriental Studies), aligned with those that advocate the disappearance of the African descendant under the aegis of miscegenation. In an article published in the official journal of the Center and signed by its then-director Waldir Freitas Oliveira, entitled "Considerations on Racial Prejudice in Brazil," we have an indisputable testimony of what the Center wants to combat: attempts at self affirmation by the Afro-Brazilian people at any level, be it social, aesthetic, political or other. Following the sinuosities of Oliveira's propositions, we find that after a traversal of history he comes to the conclusion that racial prejudice exists "with profound roots and difficult to be extirpated." One hopes that the Center or its director would articulate a suggestion or a measure to be taken against this evil. Vain hope. In fact it would be surprising, if it were not a commonplace among such "whites of Bahia," to note the untimely and aggressive attitude of Oliveira in attacking the few weak initiatives of Blacks themselves to combat the prejudice that he demonstrates is a concrete reality. Oliveira labels such initiatives

> ... disintegrationist tendencies which may evolve in the direction of the formation in Brazil of racial groups living together side by side, and not arriving at the point of definitively integrating themselves. Which may, in a long term future, lead us to a situation similar to that in which, today, the United States or South Africa find themselves. (1969: 17)

We should observe in the first place that it is regrettable that such a Center still lives in ignorance of the fact that the Black and the white in Brazil have been "living together side by side" for four hundred years. Never have they "integrated themselves" except for the insidious programs of acculturation, assimilation, miscegenation and syncretism of Black peoples and their cultures *into* the dominant white population and culture, processes that inherently involve their partial or complete destruction. Processes which are vertical, that is, coming from the top down, dictated by whites who have the entire social structure on their side as well as economic, military and political power. Blacks are forced to accept their dictates because of our relative lack of power. It is not necessary to wait for a "long term" future to diagnose in Brazil the same symptoms of race relations as the United States or South Africa. What differentiates Brazil from these racist societies is barely a difference in degree and appearance of the symptom. In essence, the identical racism can be verified in Brazil, with the subtle but uncompromising goal of liquidating the Black race through dissimulated methods and a sophisticated scheme of genocide. Ghanaian scholar Anani Dzidzienyo, in a comprehensive study of race relations in Brazil which was published in London by the Minority Rights Group, comes to this apt conclusion:

> The Black Brazilian's position in white-dominated Brazil differs from that of Blacks in similar societies elsewhere only to the extent that the official Brazilian ideology of non-discrimination, by not reflecting the reality and, indeed, by camouflaging it, achieves *without tension* the same results as do overtly racist societies. (1971: 14)

In his zeal to preserve the integrity of our "racial democracy," Oliveira does not spare ammunition for his attack on the

> ... small group of black intellectuals in Brazil who, agitating the banner of defense of the negro, still occupying in our society the lower posts and constituting the bulk of our proletariat, pass on to an ostensible position of combat against the white, even opposing miscegenation, according to them the most efficient arm the whites have to eliminate them and maintain their supposed superiority. Such an attitude, revealing a clearly racist content, cannot fail to constitute a motive for worry for all those who study and accompany the evolution of our society. (1969: 17-18)

The "our society" to which Waldir Oliveira addresses himself has nothing to do with the "our society" of Afro-Brazilians. For even in the state of Bahia where the Blacks are a large majority, Afro-Brazilian society is completely marginal to the entire structure of conventional (white) society. Blacks have no participation in political power, economic power, or the military; not even in religion, since Afro-Brazilian religions have suffered the persecution of the police and the pressures of the official Catholic church for four centuries (see analysis of this topic in detail in Chapter III).

It is strange that the director of a Center of African studies should state in one breath that Blacks even today "occupy in our society the lowest posts," and in the next breath deny them the right to defend themselves. We have configured here, in Oliveira's own findings, a situation identical to South Africa: a white minority monopolizing all power and dominating an Afro-Brazilian majority whose single-handed labor constructed the entire country.

The Center of Afro-Oriental Studies defines itself in such work less as a valid organ of study than as an instrument of domestication. As such it carries out studies of an immobilizing academic character with no value for the Afro-Brazilian community. Studies which lend themselves to the distraction of attention from emergent problems for Black people in the context of race relations. It is unpleasant to have to state the inescapable fact that the center assumes today the same function of apparently paternalistic character that was exercised by such Catholic exemplars as Antônio Vieira, in the strategy of domination, oppression and exploitation of the Afro-Brazilian people.

Conclusion

The political, economic, social and cultural repression experienced by the Black peoples of Brazil is deplorable. Its ultimate objective is the obliteration of the Black as a cultural, physical or ethnic entity. Florestan Fernandes points out:

> A situation like this one involves more than social inequality and insidious poverty. The individuals affected by it *are not included in the existing social structure, as if they were not human beings or normal citizens.* (my emphasis. 1972: 75)

In the face of the racist, genocidal character of the ideology of so-called "racial democracy," it would be irresponsible to fail to expose and roundly denounce the social structure supposedly básed on it. To be silent would be to give tacit approval to the exploitation and destruction of one race by another through dissimulated but systematic oppression and racial arrogance. It would be to condone genocide: a criminal act which perpetuates an unjust society totally iniquitous to Blacks and native Indians in Brazil.

BIBLIOGRAPHY

Azevedo, Thales de (1973) "Os grupos negro-africanos," in *História da Cultura Brasileira*. Rio de Janeiro: Ministério da Educação e Cultura.

Bomilcar, Álvaro (1916) *O Preconceito de Raça no Brasil*. Rio de Janeiro: Typografia Aurora.

Davis, David Brion (1968) *El Problema de la Esclavitud en la Cultura Occidental*. Buenos Aires: Editorial Paidos.

Degler, Carl (1971) *Neither Black nor White*. New York: Macmillan.

Diegues Jr., Manuel (1977) *A África na Vida e na Cultura do Brasil*. Published by official delegation of Brazilian Government to Festac '77.

Dzidzienyo, Anani (1971) *The Position of Blacks in Brazilian Society*. London: Minority Rights Group, Report no. 7 (mimeograph).

Fernandes, Florestan (1972) *O Negro no Mundo dos Brancos*. São Paulo: Difusão Européia do Livro.

Freyre, Gilberto (1976) "Aspectos da influência africana no Brasil", *Cultura*. Brasília: Ministério da Educação e Cultura, October - December (Vol. VI, no. 23), pp. 6-19.

Gilliam, Angela (1975) *Language Attitudes, Ethnicity and Class in São Paulo and Salvador da Bahia, Brazil*. Dissertation: Union Graduate School. (Unpublished)

Ianni, Octavio (1972) *Raças e Classes Sociais No Brasil*, 2nd edition. Rio de Janeiro: Civilização Brasileira.

Lyra, Christina (1977) "Sou um negro que não pediu licença aos brancos," *Jornal do Brasil*. Rio de Janeiro: January 29, p. 8. (Interview with Paulo César.)

Mortara, Giorgio (1970) "O desenvolvimento da população preta e parda no Brasil," in *Contribuições para o Estudo da Demografia no Brasil*, 2nd edition. Rio de Janeiro: Fundação IBGE. Cited in Mourão 1977.

Moura, Clovis (1972) *Rebeliões da Senzala - Quilombos, Insurreições, Guerrilhas.* Rio de Janeiro: Editora Conquista.

Mourão Fernando A.A. (1977) *The Cultural Presence of Africa and the Dynamics of the Socio-Cultural Process in Brazil.* Published by official delegation of Brazilian Government to Festac '77.

Nabuco, Joaquim (1949) *O Abolicionismo.* São Paulo: Instituto Progresso Editorial.

Nascimento, Abdias do (1968) *O Negro Revoltado.* Rio de Janeiro: Edições GRD.

——————— (1977) *"Racial Democracy" in Brazil: Myth or Reality?* Ibadan: Sketch Publishing Co., Ltd.

Oliveira, Waldir Freitas (1969) "Considerações sobre o preconceito racial do Brasil," *Afro-Asia.* Salvador: Centro de Estudos Afro-orientais, July - December.

Pierson, Donald (1942) *Negroes in Brazil.* Carbondale and Edwardsville: Southern Illinois University Press.

Reis, Rangel (1976) "Igreja junto aos indígenas," interview in *Jornal do Brasil* (Section I). Rio de Janeiro: December 28.

Rodrigues, José Honório (1961) Article in *O Jornal.* Rio de Janeiro: May 11.

Rodrigues, Nina (1945) *Os Africanos no Brasil,* 3rd edition. São Paulo: Companhia Editora Nacional.

Sena, Marina de Avellar (1977) *Compra e Venda de Escravos (em Minas Gerais).* Belo Horizonte: printed by Editora Littera Maciel Ltda.

Silva Mello, Antonio (1958) *Estudos sobre o Negro.* Rio de Janeiro: José Olympio Editora.

Skidmore, Thomas E. (1974) *Black into White.* New York: Oxford University Press.

——————— (1976) *Preto no Branco* (translated by Raul de Sá Barbosa). Rio de Janeiro: Editora Paz e Terra.

Verger, Pierre (1977) "African Religions and the Valorization of Brazilians of African Descent" (translated by W.F. Feuser). Faculty Seminar, Department of African Languages and Literatures, University of Ife, February 21. (Unpublished)

Viana Filho, Luiz (1946) *O Negro na Bahia.* Rio de Janeiro: José Olympio Editora.

Viana, Oliveira (1938) *Raça e Assimilação,* 3rd edition. São Paulo: Companhia Editora Nacional.

Vieira, Antonio (1940) *Sermões Pregados no Brasil.* Lisbon: Agencia Geral das Colonias. Cited in Oliveira 1969.

CHAPTER 3

RELIGION AND ART IN AFRO-BRAZILIAN CULTURAL EXPERIENCE

I. Antecedents

paper delivered to
Faculty Seminar
University of Ife, Department of
African Languages and Literatures
December 6, 1976
Ile-Ife
Nigeria

I believe that biological miscegenation, cultural miscegenation, elevated to the level of a political doctrine applied to a nation, is an error that can well lead to the most lamentable results. [...] And the fusion of the Brazilian ethnic elements will be done not on the anthropological, or the biological, but at the level of the heart, at the mental level, of sensibility.

Cheikh Anta Diop
(Interview with *Singular e Plural)*

It has been said that in the Afro-Brazilian context "... art fuses itself with worship; one cannot dissociate them, and when dissociation occurs it is because the faith has already begun to disappear." (Bastide 1973: 284) We have been assured by Professor Wande Abimbola's moving account of his visit with his Brazilian brothers in Bahia (1976) that we need harbor no fear of the faith's disappearance, so we can make full use of the observation. But if art cannot be dissociated from worship, neither can either of these be dissociated from the larger context in which they were born and evolved: the birth and evolution of Brazil itself. And in Brazil, it is slavery that defines the quality, the extensiveness, the intensity of physical and spiritual relationships between the children of three continents that met there, confronting each other in the epic of building a new country with its own characteristics, its specificity of spirit and people -- that is to say, a culture and civilization in its own right.

With the invasion of African soil, the rape, pillage, torture, murder of hundreds of millions of Africans, the plunder of the natural resources and artistic treasures of the continent, the negation of the African spirit, the debasement of African men and women to the condition of animals -- with these as the cornerstones of the building of Brazil, comes cultural domination, the denial of the history, culture, art, religion, philosophy, subtlety of the African peoples.

The brutality of slavery created severe difficulties for the survival of the art and religion of Africans in Brazil. Family and ancestral bonds were disintegrated by early death of parents, high infant mortality, breaking up of families for sale, and forced prostitution of African women. All of this disrupted the passing on of tradition. African religions were violently persecuted by secular authorities and the Catholic Church. These are just a few of the obstacles faced by slaves yearning to continue their practice and heritage. But even with tactics of degradation and distortion, the dominant Western culture was not able to suppress African cultures completely. Permanent victims of violence, some of their institutions disintegrated. African languages, the principal carriers of world-view, were

97

destroyed except for rare and isolated liturgical exceptions. But many institutions and traditions of the various African cultures did remain in all their brilliance and vitality. Some left indelible traces and influences in Brazilian culture. Others left whole theological systems and cosmologies intact. None of them passively or easily submitted to the white settlers' attempt to destroy them.

Interaction among various African Groups

According to a classification by Arthur Ramos, authoritative ethnologist, the main culture groups to arrive in Brazil were:

a) Sudanese cultures: represented primarily by the Yoruba peoples from Nigeria, the Fon or Ewe from Dahomey [now Benin], the Fanti and Ashanti from the Gold Coast [Ghana], and some less outstanding groups.

b) Guineo-Sudanese cultures: Islamized, originating mainly from the Peuhl, Mandingas, and Hausa groups from Northern Nigeria.

c) Bantu cultures, represented by the Angola-Congo tribal groups, and by those from the area called Contra-Costa [Mozambique, etc.].

(1946: 299)

Although most records and data about the slave trade were destroyed by order of Finance Minister Ruy Barbosa in 1891, and information on slave populations is therefore extremely precarious, it is evident that the relative predominance of the various cultural traits of ethnic groups is not related to the groups' numerical predominance in population. A subtle and complicated interplay between the various conditions of slavery and the characteristics of the cultures themselves led to diversity among them in terms of cultural development.

One key factor determining the circumstances of a group's cultural permanence was urban or rural placement of slaves. Urban slaves had greater opportunities for contact and communication among various households, more mobility and therefore more facility for transmission of cultural practice. The populations in the cities had more liberty of movement, houses were closepacked, and chances of getting out at night much better. City slaves known as *negros de ganho,* who worked in squads (of one ethnic group) carrying loads throughout the city, were natural carriers of cultural/ethnic communiques as well. Also, Catholic religious fraternities instituted among slaves were divided along ethnic lines. All of these elements contributed to the coherence of ethnic groups among city slaves.

The principal factor in this situation, however, was the formation of "nations," organizations based loosely on ethnic groupings, which functioned as social, cultural, religious and mutual aid societies. These played an essential role in cultural survivals. The "nations" were organized by the official authorities, which may seem ironic. To the white settlers, it was outrageous. Dr Melo Morais, of Bahia, for example, vigorously protested against the "... black men and women dressed in feathers, growling African chants and making barbarous noise with their rude instruments." (Rodrigues 1945: 283) The scene he is describing is a *Batuque,* one of the periodic celebrations and dances held by the nations at intervals, with the approval of authority. The reason for official consent is expressed clearly by Count dos Arcos, a colonial aristocrat and viceroy, in his reply to the complaints of the Melo Morais' of the day:

> The *batuques,* as seen through the eyes of government officials, are one thing; to private individuals they are quite another. The difference is profound. The latter regard *batuques* as simply a practice which runs counter to Sunday observance. [...] To the government, however, the *batuque* is an act which, once a week, forces all Negroes -- automatically, and without conscious realization -- to renew those feelings of mutual aversion that they have taken for granted since birth, but which tend gradually to vanish in the general atmosphere of degradation which is their common lot. Now, such sentiments of mutual hostility may be regarded as the most powerful guarantee the major cities of Brazil enjoy. Suppose that one day the various African nations forgot their tradition of inbred hatred for one another. Suppose Dahomeans and *Nagos* [Yoruba], *Geges* [Ewe] and Hausas, Tapas and Congos, in fact all the various ethnic groups, became friends and brethren: the result would be a fearful and ineluctible threat to Brazil, that would end up destroying our country entirely. (Bastide 1971: 91)

99

Catholic religious fraternities were organized among the slaves for the same purpose: to encourage religious disunity among groups and provide an effective instrument of social control.

Both the religious fraternities and the "nations" were used as buffers in carrying out disciplinary measures. To neutralize the anger and resentment of Black victims toward white rule, masters would send slaves before surrogate African "authorities" -- governors elected by these groups, or genuine ethnic kings from Africa -- to be flogged or otherwise tortured. These Black chieftains were given jurisdiction to settle disputes among slaves, maintaining order and maximizing efficiency in the work force, without any expense of time or energy by white masters or foremen.

Thus the nations and religious groups had a dual effect. On the one hand, they served as the vehicles and transmitters of African religious and cultural tradition, but on the other hand they were vital, effective tools of domination over Africans. Symptomatically, many revolts planned within these societies were betrayed by fellow slaves from some rival ethnic or religious group. This process resulted in the virtual disappearance of Muslim groups, who were notorious for their well-planned insurrections. After the first half of the nineteenth century, when Hausas attempted a series of uprisings, the leading exponents of Islam were killed in the violent repression or deported to Africa, and their followers were largely absorbed into other groups.

Among agricultural slaves in rural areas the situation was quite different, and the conditions they experienced had a marked effect on patterns of cultural survivals carried by them. Unlike city slaves, they were kept in populations of mixed ethnic composition, creating language and cultural barriers to communication. Nations were not organized. Plantation slaves were very closely surveilled by masters and foremen who did their best not to allow the formation of groups of any kind among slaves. Religious organization and practice was virtually impossible to sustain under these circumstances.

Despite the barriers in communication, which hindered the organization of planned insurrection, agricultural slaves, who were largely Bantu in origin, used many other methods of escape and revolt. Those individuals who did escape often managed to form communities, called *quilombos*. These were usually well-organized societies, functioning as self-sustaining farm collectives which used traditional African production methods and conserved African forms of social and economic organization. The most outstanding of these was the Republic of Palmares, a union of several *quilombos,* which resisted armed siege by both the Dutch and the Portuguese for 64 years. The sovereign African state of Palmares, with its last king Zumbi, immortal hero of Pan-African struggle, represents the seeds of Pan-Africanism sown in the 1600's in the forests of Brazil.

Because of the lack of ethnic coherence in the communities of agricultural slaves, the cultural traits that did get passed on were of a different nature and origin. On Sundays and festival days the plantation slaves were allowed time off -- not out of any generosity of the master, as most Brazilians would have it, but because the extremely high death rate made it imperative. On these days, they would entertain themselves with music, dance, chants, anecdotes or tales. But because of the problems of communication and diverse origin, the cultural survivals in this context had to be more haphazard, more subject to mixture and confusion, amalgamation and variation.

These considerations account, at least in great part, for the apparent prevalence of certain African cultural forms. Because Yoruba, Fon and Ewe peoples were mostly urban slaves, their religions were able to survive nearly intact with the structural support and protection of the nations and fraternities. Bantu slaves, on the other hand, were used in their great majority as field hands on plantations, and their cultural traits are preserved mainly in music and folklore. To this day, the Yoruba culture seems more prevalent because of its visibility in organized religion. But the folklore of the Bantu civilization, in the phrase of Roger Bastide, "... has been preserved from one end of the American continent to the other, from Louisiana to Rio de la Plata." (1971: 106)

Naturally, the characteristics of the cultures themselves contributed to their respective preservation in certain aspects.

Another reason for the apparent disappearance of Bantu religion, perhaps, is that it was heavily based on ancestor worship, which was devastated by the destruction of family and inheritance groups. Also, its deities were often localized and identified with specific places in Africa.

Despite its visibility and preponderance, Yoruba religion in Brazilian African worship is not monolithic, and Bantu and other influences were never absent from Afro-Brazilian religion. In Rio de Janeiro there existed until very recently no fewer than three independent religions: that of the Orisha, that of the Alufa (descendants of the Muslims) and the Cabula (descendants of Bantus). At present in Bahia, at least five groups are represented: Bantu, Ketu, Ijesha, Yoruba, and Ewe. The Afro-Brazilian worship prevalent in São Paulo and Rio de Janeiro is called *macumba*. Although it is progressively assimilating indigenous Brazilian, Yoruba, spiritist and Catholic elements, the Bantu influence in this cult is dominant. This is evident from the deities it emphasizes, including Ganga Zumba, Zambiapongo, Calunga, Zumbi, Calandu. (Bastide 1971: 108) Another outgrowth of the *macumba* strain has been *Umbanda,* an eclectic variation with spiritist, Catholic, Yoruba, Brazilian native Indian, and even some Hindu and Buddhist elements. *Umbanda* has recently expanded greatly and enjoys tremendous popularity both inside and outside of Brazil. There are some subtle and serious implications in this phenomenon which we shall examine presently.

Other African ethno-cultural groups preserved their own deities within a predominantly Yoruba religious structure in Brazil, by establishing a system of correspondence between the deities. There are *Candomblés* of Angolan or Congolese origin in Bahia which borrow their ceremonial and priestly organization from Yoruba religion. And often, the Yoruba orisha are identified with Bantu, Angola or Congo gods in a system of reciprocal transfer in which Xangô for example, becomes for Angolan worshippers Kibuko or Kibuko Kiassubanga: and for Congolese, Kanbaranquanje. Oxunmarê is the Angolan Angorô and Exu the Congolese Bombonjira. (Bastide 1971: 109) Roger Bastide in his studies has elaborated a table of corresponding deities among eight groups in African worship in Brazil. (1973: 216)

The liturgical music of Afro-Brazilian religion reflects this rich and vivid syncretization among African religions themselves, as can be observed in the following *ponto* (ritual invocation music or song) for Exu:

Ê pomba-gira ê -- Vamos saravá
Exu Tranca Rua ê -- Vamos saravá
Exu Tiriri ê -- Vamos saravá
Exu Barobo ê -- Vamos saravá

Ê Kolobo ê
Abre caminho ê
Na fe de Zambe ê
Esse Quimbanda ê

Ê pomba gira ê -- Vamos saravá
Eu quero pemba ê -- Vamos saravá
Pra risca ponto ê -- Vamos saravá
Na minha terreiro ê -- Vamos saravá

(Nascimento 1961: 185)

Another example can be seen in the *"Ponto de Oxunmarê,"* by the same composer, Abigail Moura, founder and conductor of the Afro-Brazilian Orchestra:

Oxunmarê tem as sete cores
As sete cores tembem tem neste pegi
Oxunmarê ê meu orixa
Oxunmare é um amigo leal

Oxunmarê é um grande general
E'mandão da agua doce
Em Angola é Angorô
Oxunmarê vem que vou te coroá
E na fé de Zambe-Ampungo
A demanda vou ganhá.

(Nascimento 1961: 194)

(Oxunmare has the seven colors
The seven colors have we also in this shrine
Oxunmare, eh, my orisha
Oxunmare is a loyal friend

103

Oxunmare is a great general
Commander of the sweet waters
In Angola he is Angoro
Oxunmare come, for I will crown you
And in the faith of Zambe-Ampungo
The vindication I will win.)

These examples are only a few suggestions of the syncretic nature of the interaction among African (and also native Brazilian Indian) religious practices, which was determined not only by the religious needs of the worshippers but also by their diverse circumstances in servitude, as discussed earlier. Although the Yoruba religion is clearly ascendant among Afro-Brazilian forms of worship, it has incorporated and been incorporated into many other African religious practices. The most important aspect of this interaction among religions has been pointed out by Wande Abimbola:

> African traditional religion does not regard itself, unlike Christianity, as the only way leading to salvation. African traditionalists respect the faith of others as equally authentic and as an experience which they themselves can take part in. (1976: 49)

Catholicism and African Religions

Although they are often referred to in "scientific" circles by the same name, this process of syncretization among African religions was of an entirely different nature from the interaction between the official state religion, Catholicism, and African worship. It is misleading to suggest that syncretism occurred between Catholicism and African religions, because the implication is that the exchange would have occurred on a level of equality and spontaneity. Olabiyi Babalola Yai of the University of Ife has made a serious and authoritative study of Yoruba religion in Brazil, in which he comments:

> The Nigerian religions in Brazil cannot adequately be qualified as syncretic if by syncretism is understood an intimate amalgam of what Santayana called "marked dissyncracy" and "special message" of two religions. (1976: 99)

104

In reality, African religion was subjected in Brazil to a violent imposition of forced "syncretism" with Catholicism. African religions were outlawed by a colonial regime which knew that in order to maintain complete control over Blacks they must enslave not only their bodies but also their spirits. Slaves were baptized compulsorily either in their ports of embarcation (Ouidah, Lagos, Bissau, Dakar, Luanda, etc.), or upon arrival in the New World. The Catholic Church proselytized with the armed support of the state. It also maintained through its religious brotherhoods and orders many profitable rural estates where it exploited African slaves with the "Christian charity" characteristic of sadism and tyranny.

What scholars have called "syncretism" between Catholicism and African religion was really a cover under which Africans continued clandestinely to practice their own religious worship. It is a tribute to the ingenuity of the Black people in preserving their own cultural heritage in the face of Aryan cultural repression: not, as Brazilian official history would have it, a symptom of liberalism and generosity of the colonial white aristocracy. The true reaction of whites to Afro-Brazilian worship was expressed in the action of the Bishop of Espirito Santo, who upon witnessing a Bantu religious ceremony called Cabula in that state, promptly pronounced a sentence of anathema against it. (Bastide 1971: 107-108) Another significant sample of Catholic "tolerance" is the famous "syncretic" ceremony of the cleaning of the Church in the festivals of the *Senhor do Bonfim* in Bahia. This ceremony, evoking mythical celebrations of Obatala in Yoruba religion, transforms Catholic mass into a veritably African event. Far from being encouraged, it was in fact prohibited for years by Catholic and governmental authorities, who would not allow savage and pagan rituals to defile their churches.

This attitude, to the contrary of popular opinion, has not substantially changed over the centuries. Recently in the city of São Paulo, there was an attempt to initiate a Day of Ogum and a Day of Oxosse as religious festival holidays. The Catholic Archbishop denounced their celebration, as a defilement of the religious purity of São Paulo. A strange "syncretism," in which one element is so intensely despised by the other...

There is a tendency among "scientists" to sanctify the taboos of the Catholic attitude by labelling *Candomblé* and other African religious faiths as "black magic," superstition, animism, or other pejorative euphemisms. A typical manifestation of this attitude among white academics is illustrated in the following statement by Donald Pierson, social scientist from the U.S.: "The Catholic Church at Bahia, by exercising almost infinite patience and tact, has now incorporated into its organization all members of the Bahian fetish cults." (1942: 305) Predictably, Pierson uses the racist terminology of Eurocentrism by designating Afro-Brazilian religion as "fetish cults." What exactly are the implications contained in this expression? It may seem fairly innocuous on first glance, but a look at the definitions of "fetish" and "fetishism" from *Webster's Seventh New Collegiate Dictionary* will soon reveal its inherently derogatory content. For "fetish" we have:

> ... any material object regarded with superstitious or extravagant trust or reverence *b*: an object of irrational reverence or obsessive devotion *c*: an object or a body part that rouses libido often to the exclusion of genital impulses. (1971: 309)

Here we detect the two elements which characterize the biased treatment given to African religions. First, non-recognition of a spiritual or genuinely religious content in them, replacing these concepts with phrases like "superstition" and "extravagant trust." Second, the banal representation of sensuality expressed in spiritual devotion in the reference to "libido." Since European religion creates shame and guilt complexes around human sexuality, in an unnatural rejection of our most sacred responsibility, procreation, European "scientists" cannot conceive of a religion in which sexuality is seen as an integral part of divine and spiritual being. They therefore render religious expressions of sensuality as insipid, petty eroticism (we shall see an example of this in literature when we examine the work of Jorge Amado). Thus we find in the dictionary definition of "fetishism," not only the element of "extravagant irrational devotion," but another meaning "the pathological displacement of erotic interest and satisfaction to a fetish" (1971: 309). And here we encounter another facet of Eurocentric arrogance: the assumption, explicit or implicit, that African religions are demented psychotic phenomena.

Pierson was incapable of perceiving that the real situation is exactly the opposite of what he postulates. It is the Afro-Brazilian religions that have, in spite of being belittled by such loaded concepts as "fetishism" and being persecuted and repressed by Catholicism, exercised centuries of tolerance, patience and generosity by respecting the arrogant Christian faith and assimilating elements of it.

In the scheme of conventional scholarship, the metaphysical conceptions of Africa, her philosophical order, the fabric of her religious ritual and liturgy, never receive their deserved respect or consideration as values constituting the identity of a national spirit. They were made the *material,* the *objects* of curiosity and commerce by the Aryan society, which used them to its own benefit and high profits. Nina Rodrigues, the man who is considered the pioneer of Afro-Brazilian studies, typifies this attitude. A psychiatrist, he wrote a book called *Os Africanos no Brazil* (The Africans in Brazil) in which he makes use of European theories to characterize the African as a "savage." From a psychological vantage point, Rodrigues contends, the African "... showed an obscure consciousness; from a social perspective, he preserved totemic conceptions." (1945: 279) The phrase "totemic conceptions" is only one among a myriad of contemptuous expressions prevailing, all of which demonstrate the utterly ludicrous character of the phrase "syncretism" as applied to Catholic and African religions.

The real indication of the status of *Candomblé* and other African religions in Brazilian society is the fact that they are the only religious entities whose places of worship are compulsorily registered with the police. Only in Bahia has this exigency been revoked, by decree of the governor. Much has been made of this, and claims that African religions are enjoying a new "status" because of it are common. But the fact remains that Bahia is only one state, and it is the state with the largest majority of Blacks. In all the rest of Brazil, the exigency still stands. And the revocation of it in Bahia in 1976 merely accentuates the fact that for more than four centuries African religions in this state with its African majority, have been harassed and surveilled by the police. (For a more in-depth discussion of this event, see Nascimento 1977: 96-98)

Constituting the source of African cultural resistance and the cradle of Afro-Brazilian art, the *Candomblés* have had to seek refuge from police violence in hidden places of difficult access. The temples, or *terreiros,* in the heart of the jungle or on the slopes of remote hills, were and are often attacked and ransacked by the police, who confiscate ritual sculptures, icons and other objects used in worship, and liturgical vestments - not to mention priests, priestesses and believers themselves. Anonymous Black popular poetry informs us how the priests of African religions are treated by official Brazil:

> Dá licença Pai Antonio
> Eu não vim te visitá
> Eu estou muito doente
> O que quero é me curá.
> Se a doença fôr feitiço
> Me cura no seu Congá;
> Se a doença fôr de Deus. . .
> Pai Antonio vai curá!
> Coitado de Pai Antonio
> Preto velho rezadô
> Foi parar numa prisão
> Ah! por não ter um defensorô.
> Pai Antonio na Quimbanda. . .
> E'curadô
> E'pai de mesa, é rezadô
> E' pai de mesa, é rezadô
> Pai Antonio da Quimbanda
> E'curadô!

(Seljan 1967: 70)

> (Let me come in, Father Antonio
> I'm not here to visit,
> I am very sick

108

What I want is that you cure me.
If the sickness is of witchcraft
Cure me in your Congá;
If the sickness is of God. . .
Father Antonio has the cure!
Poor Father Antonio,
Old Black man of prayer,
Ended up in jail
Ah! For not having a defender.
Father Antonio in his Quimbanda. . .
Is a healer
He's head of the table, he's a man of prayer,
He's head of the table, he's a man of prayer,
Father Antonio of the Quimbanda
He's a healer!)

One result of police persecution of the *Candomblés* has been the creation of a new order in the hierarchy of the religion: the *ogan*. These patrons of *terreiros*, usually prominent members of the community, well-to-do and therefore usually white, have the singular and revealing function of protecting the *terreiros* and their faithful in the event of police or legal action, arranging for attorneys or bail, etc. Whatever the good intentions of these patrons, their origin and existence as a social phenomenon speaks to the real historical situation of Afro-Brazilian religion: marginalized and harassed.

Another effect of police harassment has been disruption of the continuity and permanence of religious communities due to the dislocation of priests and priestesses, as Roger Bastide testifies:

> With the persecution of the police many *pais-de-santo* [priests] and *mães-de-santo* [priestesses] wander to more hospitable regions: I met in Bahia many Pernambucans who preferred to emigrate than to abandon their faith; Dona P. went to Alagoas. In earlier years, the opposite happened: people fled from Alagoas, where persecution reached a peak, to Recife, where at that time the *terreiros* had a nominal protection. (1973: 165)

This process has also contributed to the continued contact and mutual influence of different forms of worship on each other.

Macumbas, of mainly Bantu derivation, share and swap elements of religious practice with chiefly Yoruba faith through dislocated victims. Unlike Catholics, however, the adherents of these faiths do not see this sharing as a "foreign" or "defiling" corruption. They are seen as identical spiritual entities in different languages. In interviews with people in Recife, when Bastide asked how a Catholic saint could be an African deity at the same time: "All the members of the old *Xangôs* [temples] which had been closed by the police . . . repeated obstinately: 'But it's the Portuguese name for Orisha!'" (1973: 181)

Another circumstance that has been observed in Brazil is the rigidly preserved character of the *Candomblé* ceremony in Bahia. This situation has socio-historical implications which arise from the severe repression suffered by Afro-Brazilian religion. Why, throughout four centuries of life in a totally new and different environment, have many *Candomblés* preserved so markedly without change the cultural tradition brought from home? So much so that some practices ". . . can be observed in Bahia as [they were] probably being observed two hundred years ago in Africa." (Abimbola 1976: 4) Clearly one factor is the strength and tenacity, the very metaphysical viability of Yoruba religion. But during these centuries the same religion changed considerably in Africa itself. Other forces must have contributed to the extreme conservation of these cults in Bahia.

One explanation is that cultural conservation was a reaction against the threats and infringements of the dominant culture, so forcefully imposed by the ruling Aryan groups. As an act of immobilization, a turning-in from this imposition, the African culture refused to move in any direction, in case such moves proved fatal. Cultural stasis becomes a defense mechanism developed by an entity threatened, endangered by a hostile outside world. Perhaps Muniz Sodré, a contemporary Brazilian writer, offers the most apt response to these considerations when he remarks:

> ... Black culture in Brazil maintains itself, in great part, due to its possibility to mask and to silence itself. We mean by this that Black culture was able to survive, to escape extermination (the same extermination of which the Muslims of the first half of the nineteenth century were victims), be-

cause it hid itself in the seclusion of the religious communities (the *terreiros*), disguising itself when it wanted to, silencing itself when it had to. The history of Afro-Brazilian culture is principally the history of its silence, of the circumstances of its repression. (Santos 1974: 5)

Observing the phenomenon of conservation in Brazil, Roger Bastide compares it with the situation of Haiti, which won its independence and the elimination of white domination in the beginning of the nineteenth century. Haitian Voodoo has developed into a specifically and originally Haitian form of worship, characterized by innovation and dynamic variation:

... the Negroes no longer had to fight against the Europeans' desire to assimilate them. They were not obliged to erect that double barrier of social resistance (such as we find in other Antilles or on the mainland) against racial prejudice on the one hand, and the imposition of Western values on the other. [...] The Haitian Negroes had no longer anything of the sort to struggle against, and their religion could thus more easily adapt itself to changing conditions -- which, inevitably, soon took place in the infrastructures of the peasant communities. (1971: 131)

Aryan Cultural Chauvinism

The imposition of Western European culture was not unique to the era of slavery, nor has it disappeared with the coming of the present century. The attitudes of the Aryan-aspiring society toward Black cultural expression remain virtually unchanged. We mentioned the case of the Days of Ogum and Oxosse which were vigorously opposed by the Church of São Paulo only a couple of years ago. This reaction is almost identical to an editorial which appeared in the powerful newspaper *Jornal de Notícias* on February 12, 1901. The editorial asked for police intervention to stop the *batuques* -- African music and dance celebrations -- which it said were spreading through the streets "... singing the traditional *samba,* for all of this is incompatible with the state of our civilization." (Rodrigues 1945: 255) And in February of 1977, to complete the cycle, we have the prohibition by the highest authority of the Catholic Church in the

111

metropolitan area of São Paulo, the *Cúria Metropolitana,* of a mass which was to be celebrated in the traditionally Black church of the Rosary (dating back from the African religious fraternities of colonial times). The mass, in commemoration of the inauguration of the largest *Candomblé* temple in Brazil, would have been an authentic celebration of syncretism between Catholic and African religions, so often flaunted by Brazil as a symbol of its "racial democracy." But not only did the Church forbid such a desecration of its sanctity. The police authorities prohibited Black priests and priestesses of the *terreiro* Ache Ile Oba from singing religious songs in the street procession which they held in lieu of the mass. (*Folha de São Paulo,* February 13, 1977, cited in Nascimento 1977: 105-106)

That the "state of our civilization" is exclusively Aryan according to the dominant strata, is evident one more time in 1955 with the attempt to encourage the elaboration of a Black aesthetic in the artistic portrayal of a historical figure who was undoubtedly Black: Jesus Christ. In that year the *Teatro Experimental do Negro* (Black Experimental Theater) sponsored a contest in plastic arts around the theme Black Christ. Predictably, the major organs of the press came out vehemently against the very idea of such a contest. The eminent *Jornal do Brazil* published its indignant response in an editorial of June 26, 1955:

> Through her example of abnegation, of renunciation, of goodness, the Black Mother, who rocked us to sleep, who gave us milk, was the great formulator of our heart. [...]
> This exhibition which is being announced should be prohibited as being highly subversive. Such an event, realized on the eve of the Eucharistic Congress, was prepared intentionally to serve as a stone of scandal and a motive of repulsion. Our moral lack of control, our great lack of respect toward good taste, cannot be given as spectacles to those who visit us. We register here our shout of alarm. The ecclesiastical authorities must, as soon as possible, take measures to prevent the realization of this attack on Religion and the Arts. The Brazilian people themselves will fall down, shocked by the affront committed. (Nascimento 1968: 18)

The role of Black people, according to this mouthpiece of the

112

ruling classes of Brazil, is abnegation, renunciation, suffering quietly without complaint. For us to assert our own artistic creativity is a crime of subversion. More specifically, the suggestion of a Black Christ becomes not only a degrading insult, but an "attack on Religion and the Arts!" If this is the situation of a Black *Christ,* we can be certain that the situation of African deities is not one of status in this Catholic society...

Since this represents the typical attitude of conventional society toward works of art which reaffirm the Black aesthetic, it is not surprising that the most concerted of efforts has been made to eradicate Afro-Brazilian creativity from the mainstream of Brazil's artistic production. The "scientific proofs" of African savageness and inferiority gave birth to the eulogy of mixed breeding with the objective of producing a lighter population. Corollary to this process was the operation of transculturation, with the stated purpose of incorporating Blacks and mulattoes into a culture and a population that would soon be white.

Thus "acculturation" and "assimilation" became the passwords of Aryan domination, representing the absorption and co-optation of Black culture. This was the cultural basis of "racial democracy" in Brazil: a strange democracy indeed, which only allowed the Black people the right to become white, inside and outside, culturally and aesthetically as well as epidermically.

Cultural domination of the majority of Brazilians by a Europe- or U.S.-identified Aryan minority elite is so vassalizing that even those who seek to defend the Brazilian image of "acceptance of Africanity" cannot help but betray it, often explicitly upholding its tenets. They cannot avoid belying the innate contradictions of their position as proponents of a transparently hypocritical mythology.

Among the ideologues we have in mind, two stand out for the prestige they enjoy as scholars and for the influence they exert among those who study Afro-Brazilian culture: Gilberto Freyre and Pierre Verger. Freyre's Eurocentrism is explicit in all his work, but let us look at the way it emerges when he claims to be defending himself from certain protests against his praise of the cultural contributions "... of Negroes from Africa, as very valuable to Brazilian development:"

> Curious it is that some of these objections have come from intellectuals, later eminent public figures; and, as such, enthusiasts of the cause -- for it is today a cause -- of the approach of Brazil to the Black cultures -- for they are now seen without tension as cultures -- of Africa, without this signifying a repudiation of the predominance of European cultural values in Brazilian development. For what Brazil intends is to be, not anti-European, but the contrary, sub-European, with the non-European presence in her population and in her culture, valorized as they deserve. (1976: 7)

This passage summarizes a great part of the ideology that attempts to hide the realities of African experience in Brazil. Meanwhile Freyre reveals that: 1) Conventional Brazilian society has never considered African culture as true culture. 2) The management of this conventional Brazil has always been opposed to African cultures, so that in order for an "approach" to occur, it is necessary that it be made a "cause." That is, Africans and African cultures represent something strange, something alien, an ideal to be reached at and not a daily reality and integral part of the entire process of Brazilian history. 3) The most progressive exponents of liberal generosity, upon "recognizing" the African cultural contribution to Brazil, still emphasize the predominance of European cultural values *over* those of the majority of the population which is of African origin.

With almost the same words, Pierre Verger, a Frenchman who for almost thirty years has been carrying out research on African cultures in the Americas and in Africa, observes: "... there is a hybrid Brazilian civilization open to all influences, among them, clearly in the ascendant, that of African religions, but not involving an alienation from Western values." (1977: 19) Whether or not African cultures are really the "ascendant" values depends upon where we look. If we are speaking of schools, theater, museums, festivals of plastic arts, the Academy of Letters, or the universities of Brazil, anyone can observe that Verger is just wrong. If referring to the tourist industry whose

profits go to Aryans, or to clowning e
Carnaval Schools of Samba, which have
to the organized profits of whites, then he
even Verger cannot deny that Western value.
the society at large.

The encouragement of acculturation was an integral part of
colonial policy from the beginning of slavery in Brazil.
Compulsory baptism was the first step in the process, outlawing
from the beginning the spiritual life of African men and women.
As a European traveller to the colony, Henry Koster, testified in
his account published in 1816:

> No one asks the slaves if they want to be baptized or not;
> their entrance into the community of the Catholic Church
> is considered a question of duty [on the part of the slave-
> owner to impose it]. Really they are seen less as men than
> as ferocious animals until they enjoy the privilege of going
> to mass and receiving the sacraments. (Freyre 1966: 493)

Slaves soon learned that they were able to improve their status
and living conditions only if they took on the white man's
religion and ways of life.

Guerreiro Ramos, the Black sociologist and writer who best
expounds the Black aesthetic, comments upon the continuation
of this situation today: "This acculturation is so insidious that
even the most generous are affected, domesticated,
indoctrinated into whiteness, and are convinced that the
opposite is true." (1966A: 131) Thus, a man like Raimundo
Sousa Dantas, the only Black man ever to be appointed by Brazil
as an ambassador to any country (Ghana), declares himself
outrightly to be culturally Aryan, a Western man. (1975: 14)
Much more than an integrationist preoccupation, this attitude
advocates the unqualified disappearance of Black people as a
spiritual entity, the first justification for their ultimate
eradication physically.

This line of reasoning is currently being developed into a
strategy of cultural infiltration, in the form of a movement
toward what is already being referred to as *Umbandomblé,* the
latest novelty of religious syncretism. *Candomblé,* having
maintained itself for centuries as the bastion and shelter of

rican culture, is today undergoing a process of interaction and involvement with other religious forms of African origin. I want to emphasize *Umbanda* in particular, because it symbolizes the front line that conventional society is using surreptitiously to bastardize the integrity and independence of the religion of the Orixas. *Umbanda* is the popular religion which is growing most rapidly in Brazil, precisely because it finds stimulus and support in the ideology of "racial democracy." Originally compressed in the structures of *Candomblé, Umbanda* found itself increasingly infiltrated by enormous contingents of the "white" elements of the middle and upper-middle classes. Concurrently and quite rapidly, the command and management of its *terreiros* are passing from the hands of Blacks into those of whites. With the perspective of past experience, one can easily foresee that within a short time *Umbanda* will share the fate of the *escolas de samba* -- schools of samba. From being meaningful cultural organizations of Black community music and dance, they were transformed into business enterprises controlled by white people and commercialized to their profit. *Umbanda,* analagously, if the current trend continues, will soon absorb *Candomblé* to create a new entity, *Umbandomblé*. This institution would encompass Blacks, mulattoes and whites, in the rosy embrace of racial democracy -- with whites, of course, in positions of power as *Babalaôs* or *Babalorixás*. It would not be at all surprising if this entity were brought to birth by the midwife commercial tourist market, wielding the forceps of governmental tourist agencies, to suck at the same breasts of folkloric fanfare and Carnivalistic commercial ridicularization that nourish the new "schools of samba." It will not be exceptional either, to find among the new priests many *Babalaôs* who, outside the *terreiro,* put on the uniform of the Army, display the stripes of officialdom or even the stars of Generals, Admirals and Brigadiers.

The military dictatorship which seized Brazil in 1964, through its organs of information, control and repression, is alert to the expansion of Afro-Brazilian religions. Its agents do not let any opportunity slip by to infiltrate themselves among the devotees and make their way into positions of control, especially in

Umbanda. To illustrate, we have the name of General Mauro Porto, who is Secretary General of the Spirit Confederation of Umbanda and the Afro-Brazilian Cults, located at Rua Isidro de Figueiredo (Maracanã) in Rio de Janeiro.

Suffering every class of pressures, direct or subtle, Afro-Brazilian religions are obliged to defend themselves as much from declared enemies, such as the Catholic Church (even after the Ecumenical Council of Pope John XXIII), as from those theoreticians, priests, writers, researchers, and others who ostensibly belong to the community of *Candomb'é* or *Umbanda.* This warning emerges, for example, from the journal *ADJA - Afro-Brazilian Cultural Organ* (1978), in its editorial entitled "President Ernesto Geisel in Afro-Brazilian Culture:"

> We are discerning today an Afro-Brazilian expansion never observed in our history. This expansion has propitiated a considerable gamut of information, making possible for us a more objective vision of the ethical and philosophical concepts of Afro-Black religious culture. [...] We register with joy that this expansion owes itself to the "responsible pragmatism" of the President of the Republic, General Ernesto Geisel; a fact that shall fix his name in our history, constituting, still more, a motive for eternal gratitude of Blacks, mulattoes, of the Brazilians who are active in the area of the samba, of Black literature or of the religious societies: *Candomblé* or *Umbanda.* (1)

And so the white establishment obtains through coercion, direct or indirect, its inglorious gratifications...

Black Brazilian Literature

Cultural bias and assimilation have had their effects on Black arts in Brazil. In the first two centuries after the so-called "discovery" and colonization, participation of Blacks in the literary life of the colony in a formal sense was nil. Literary creation by Blacks was possible only in the anonymous form of folklore, as narrators, recalling the *arokin* or *akpalo* of Nigeria or the *griots* of other parts of Africa. It was a contribution within the parameters of oral tradition: tales, divination, verses, sayings, word-puzzles, and satires, but principally the history of the Black race, of its heroes and its religious myths.

A permanent and vital influence of Africans in the literary arts has been the transformation of the Portuguese language, by alterations, additions and transformations made in it by Africans. Morphology, syntax, and phonetics were all affected. Nigerian scholar Ebun Omowunmi Ogunsanya in her excellent study concludes that "... more in-depth scientific research needs to be undertaken to show the influence of Yoruba language on the Brazilian language." (1971: 66)

From the beginning, in order to enter the literary world or gain access to higher levels of the educational and social hierarchy, Black and mulatto writers were subjected to a process of cultural whitening. Examples are numerous: Domingos Caldas Barbosa (1739-1800); Manoel Inácio da Silva Alvarenga (1730-1800); José Basílio da Gama (1741-1795), epic poet; Gonçalves Dias, one of the foremost poets of our literature, a Romantic. The most consecrated name in Brazilian literature is Machado de Assis (1857-1913). Assis portrayed in his work principally the middle classes, which were white. His acculturation to the norms and standards of European language is clear. His novels deal with themes and problems of the Aryan strata of society. The problems or aesthetics of the Blacks of his time do not enter into his literature. Africans sometimes appear as slave figures, evanescent and tangential, but never as central or developed characters. His language is singularly the language of the Portuguese Academy in Europe, cementing his cultural affiliation with the metropolis.

Similarly to Machado de Assis in literature, there are also various examples in politics of mulattoes ashamed of their racial origin: the Baron of Cotegipe (Empire period), Nilo Peçanha, Rodrigues Alves (former Presidents of the Republic), Otávio Mangabeira (former governor of the state of Bahia), senators Mello Viana and Afonso Arinos, and others.

A unique personality, unrivalled in Brazilian literature, was the Black poet João da Cruz e Sousa (1809-1861). Born in Florianopolis a slave, and subsequently adopted by a white family, he later lived in Rio de Janeiro a life of searing pain. Despite shame and persecution, he left immortal poetic works in

118

the symbolist tradition; now he is held by critics on a plane with Baudelaire and Mallarmé. Among his works are *Faróis* (Lighthouses), *Evocações* (Evocations), and *Ultimos Sonetos* (Last Sonnets). In prose, he wrote a moving testimony to his existential adventures called *O Emparedado* (The Walled-In Man). His profound suffering in everyday life and the content of his literary work are symbolic of the condition of all Black people in Brazil -- imprisoned in the aesthetic walls of whiteness:

Ó formas alvas, brancas, formas claras
De luares, de neves, de neblinas! ...

(Bastide 1973: 65)

(O forms of light, white, clear forms
Of moonrise, of snow, of mist!)

The recurrent images of Northern or Nordic and white themes are significant. From *Missal* we have *"Estesia Eslava"* (Slavic Ecstacy):

... então claramente, vejo e sinto, desiludido das Coisas, dos Homens e do Mundo, que o que eu supunha, embriagamento, arrebatamento de amor nas tuas asas, ó loira Águia Germânica! -- nada mais foi que o sonambulismo de um sonho à beira dos rios marginados de resinosos alcentros em flor, na dolência da lua nebulosa e fria ...

(Bastide 1973: 67)

(... so clearly, I see and I feel, disillusioned of Things, of Men and of the World, that what I supposed, inebriation, rapture of love in your wings, O blond Germanic Eagle! -- no more was it than the somnambulism of a dream on the banks of the rivers lined with resinous trees in blossom, in the melancholy of a cold, clouded moon ...)

In spite of his profound acculturation, Cruz e Sousa combatted the slavery of the Black people. He emerges as a great Black poet with a deeply African heritage underlying in his work, perceptible primarily in his use of rhythm.

Lima Barreto (1881-1922) was a novelist who wrote tales of the people of the suburbs of Rio de Janeiro, home of the poor Blacks. Afro-Brazilian people enter into his novels, although he does not actually deal with Black culture. His language is a colloquial Brazilian Portuguese, a style closer to the people and problems of Brazil.

Castro Alves (1847-1871), who is considered white but was of evident African origin, was called the Condor of Bahia. He raised in flight the defense of the slaves in his poem *Vozes da África* (Voices of Africa), and also *Navio Negreiro* (Slave Ship), and *Poema dos Escravos* (Poem of the Slaves) -- all of them pieces of tragic beauty describing the horrors of the slave trade and of slavery. His poetry is a sharp contrast to the satire of a Gregório de Matos (1633-1696), who, although he was of direct African descent, went so far in his acculturation as to satirize mulatto men who had Black or *mestiço* lovers.

One implacable voice was that of Luis Gama, who was also a slave himself. Born in Bahia in 1830, his father a Portuguese aristocrat and his mother a Black woman who was a great struggler and historical figure in her own right, Luisa Mahin, Gama was sold by his father to pay off a gambling debt. He was sent to São Paulo, and there he became a free man. With hard work he achieved a position as a journalist, attorney and orator, dedicating himself totally to the cause of the liberation of his race. In his evocation of his mother, he does not flee, as did many Afro-Brazilian writers, from his African heritage:

> Era a mais linda pretinha
> Da adusta Líbia rainha
> E no Brasil pobre escrava.

(Bastide 1973: 34)

> (She was the prettiest little Black woman,
> Of sunburnt Lybia queen
> And in Brazil poor slave.)

Attacking the anomaly that at one time Guerreiro Ramos characterized as the "social pathology of the 'white' Brazilian" (1957: 138) -- that is, the morbid anxiety to become white, Luis Gama wrote a biting satire called *"Bodarrada,"* an excerpt of which follows:

> Se os nobres desta terra empanturrados,
> Em Guiné têm parentes enterrados;
> E cedendo à prosápia, ou duros vícios,
> Esquecem os negrinhos, seus patrícios;
> Se mulatos de cor esbranquiçada,
> Já se julgam de origem refinada,
> E curvos à mania que os domina,

120

Desprezam a vovó que é negra-mina;
Não te espantes, leitor, da novidade,
Pois que tudo no Brasil é novidade!

(Bastide 1973: 34)

(If the nobles of this land so gorged and haughty,
In Guinea have relations buried;
And succombing to bragging pride or heavy vices,
Forget the Blacks, their countrymen;
If mulattoes of lightened color,
Now judge themselves of refined origin,
And curved under the mania that dominates them,
Despise the grandma who is Mina Black;
Don't be surprised, reader, by the novelty,
For everything in Brazil is novelty!)

As it happens, some Blacks did reveal themselves to be both aggressive and competent in the improvisation of poetic *desafios* (challenges): an oral tradition of literary contest. The Northeast of the country has conserved for history the names of some of the talented *repentistas* (improvisors) who were of African descent: Inácio da Catingueira, Azulão, Manuel Preto, Theodoro Pereira, Chica Barbosa and others. An example of the oral satire that has been recorded in this form:

Cantor branco

Moleque de venta chata
de boca de cururu,
antes de treze de maio
eu não sei o que eras tu
O branco é da cor da prata
O negro é da cor do urubu.

Cantor negro

Quando as casas de negócio
fazem sua transação,
O papel branco é lustroso,
Mas não vale um tostão;
Escreve-se em tinta preta,
Fica valendo um milhão.

(White singer:
Flat nosed little black kid,
with *cururu* toad mouth,
Before the 13th of May
I don't know what you were;

121

White is the color of silver,
Black is the color of vultures.

Black singer:
When the houses of business
engage in their transactions,
The white paper is lustrous,
But it ain't worth a penny;
Write on it with ink of black,
Then it's worth a million.)

More recently, other Black and mulatto voices have emerged in poetry: Lino Guedes, from São Paulo; Omar Barbosa, from Espirito Santo; Solano Trindade, from Pernambuco; Osvaldo Camargo of São Paulo; Aladir Custódio of Rio de Janeiro; Jorge de Lima from Sergipe; Fernando Góes, critic from São Paulo. Romeu Crusoé, of the Northeast, wrote *A Maldição de Canaan* (The Damnation of Canaan), a novel which deals with the racial situation in his home region, as well as the play *O Castigo de Oxalá,* based on the Yoruba mythology of *Candomblé.* (Nascimento 1961: 73-125) Eduardo de Oliveira, of Sao Paulo, wrote the volume of poetry *Gestas Líricas da Negritude* (Lyrical Gestations of Negritude). Ironides Rodrigues is a dramatic author from Minas Gerais. His *Estética da Negritude* (Aesthetic of Negritude) unfortunately still awaits publication.

The man responsible for the most serious conservation and divulgation of African tales with the dignity and integrity of African religion, is Deoscoredes Maximiliano dos Santos (Didi). *Pai-de-Santo* (priest) of the *terreiro* Axé Opô Afonjá in Salvador, Bahia, and also High Priest -- *Alapini* -- of Egungun at Itaparica, Didi is also the author of several books. He has collected with devotion, fidelity and patience the *Contos Negros da Bahia* (1961) (Black Tales of Bahia), *Contos Nagô* (1963) (Yoruba Tales), and *Contos Crioulos da Bahia* (1974) (Native Black Tales of Bahia) among other publications.

Antonio Olinto, a "white" Brazilian writer, paints a vast portrait of the life and mores of the descendants of slaves who returned from Brazil to Nigeria and Dahomey in his novel *Casa d'Agua* (House of Water). It follows three generations of Africans and their descendants on both sides of the Atlantic.

Among other contemporary Black writers are ethnologist Nunes Pereira, cultural anthropologist Edison Nunes da Silva, J. Romão da Silva, historians Beatriz Nascimento and Marina Avellar Sena, and Africanists Lélia Gonzales and S. Rodrigues Alves.

Despite the efforts of certain writers and artists who deal with Black problems and themes with dignity and respect, the norm in the treatment of the Black character in Brazilian literature is the stereotype. We noted previously, for example, the Black Mother or Black Mammy stereotype, the all-suffering, abnegating, humble and tragic figure of maternal goodness. Roger Bastide makes an extensive study of this tendency in poetry, prose and folklore (1973: 113-128). One is surprised at the viciousness unleashed against blackness by the writers he examines, among them Bernardo Guimarães, Gregório de Matos, Mello Morais Filho, Joaquim Manuel de Macedo, Manoel Antonio de Almeida, Machado de Assis, Julio Ribeiro, Adolfo Ferreira Caminha and others. Some of the stereotypes registered:

the good nigger: stereotype of submission and servility;

the bad nigger: innate cruelty, unharnessed sexuality, filthiness, laziness, and immorality;

the African: physical ugliness, crude brutality, witchcraft and superstition;

the creole: slyness, cunning and deceiving savageness;

the free mulatto: pretentious and ridiculous vanity;

the mulatto or creole woman: voluptuousness and seduction.

The last stereotype, Black female sensuousness, is resultant from the overall sexual objectification of Black women.

Doris Turner, in her "Symbols in two Afro-Brazilian Literary Works: *Jubiabá* and *Sortilégio*" (1975) studies the work of Jorge Amado, an author who has capitalized immensely on his supposedly "sympathetic" treatment of Afro-Brazilians and their culture. Religious trance and dance of Black people are portrayed by Amado in terms of buttocks, thighs, breasts and "foaming sex." The protagonist Antonio Balduino is described in this manner: "Era puro como um animal e tinha por única lei os instintos" (He was pure as an animal and had as his only law his instincts). To cite one passage from *Jubiabá,* typical of Amado's attitude toward Black religion, we have the following:

Ela rebola as ancas. [...] Desapareceu tôda, só tem ancas. As suas nádegas enchem o circo, do teto até a arena. Rosenda Roseda dança. Dança mística de macumba, sensual como dança religiosa, feroz como dança da floresta virgem. [...] A dança é rápida demais, é religiosa demais e eles são dominados pela dança. Não os brancos, que continuam nas coxas, nas nádegas, no sexo de Rosenda Roseda. Mas os negros sim... dança religiosa dos negros, macumba, deuses da caça e da bexiga, a sáia voando, os seios saltando. (in Turner 1975: 13)

(She wiggles her hips... She has disappeared completely, she has only hips. Her buttocks fill the circus, from ceiling to sand. Rosenda Roseda dances. She dances the mystic dance of *macumba,* sensual like religious dance, ferocious like the dance of the virgin forest. ... The dance is too rapid, it's too religious and they are overcome by the dance. Not the whites, who are still absorbed in the thighs, the buttocks, the sex of Rosenda Roseda. But the blacks, yes, ... religious dance of the blacks, *macumba,* gods of the hunt and of smallpox, skirts flying, breasts jumping...)

Here Afro-Brazilian religion is equated with circus events through symbolic setting, revealing not only the typically folkloric approach but also the commercial aspects of the conventional "sympathy" of Brazil toward Black worship. The offspring of the literary and symbolic prostitution of Black women, then, becomes the bastardization of Afro-Brazilian religious worship. As Turner, a Black American scholar, incisively concludes in her study,

The aggregate of images used to create the vision of *Jubiabá's* Candomblé manifests implicitly a denial of the Afro-Brazilian religion as a religion, rendering it a wild emotional manifestation of primitive sensuality and eroticism. (1975: 15)

The stereotype of sexual abandon is one of the most pernicious and pervasive in the literature, since the sexual appeal of the mulatto woman to the white man is held up as one of the "proofs" of Brazilian racial democracy. Such appeal, however, is, in reality, at best the reflection of an unadmitted, perhaps unconscious process of contemptuous belittling of the Black woman as a human being, and at worst a demented and violent act of aggression against her. We have another example of its use in literary creation with *"Essa Negra Fulô"* (That Black Girl Fulô) by Jorge de Lima; probably the most famous Brazilian modern poem. An excerpt will give the reader a sense of the poem's treatment of slave life:

O Sinhô foi ver a negra
Levar couro do feitor.
A negra tirou a roupa,
O Sinhô disse: Fulô!
A vista se escureceu
que nem a negra Fulô.

O Sinhô foi açoitar
Sòzinho a negra Fulô.
A negra tirou a sáia
e tirou o cabeção,
De dentro dele pulou
Nuinha a negra Fulô.

(Vizo 1972: 126)

(Master went to see the black girl,
Took the overseer's whip.
The darkie took off her clothes,
The Master said: Fulô!
His vision blacked right out,
Blacker than nigger Fulô.

Master went to whip
All alone the darkie Fulô.
The nigger jumped out of her skirt
And then out of her camisole,
Out from inside it she jumped
All naked the darkie Fulô.)

And so, with all reason, Guerreiro Ramos concludes that "... what is important to point out is that among us was formed a literature, principally of poetic character, that exploits black motifs in reactionary terms, even if the authors are of the best intentions." (1966B: 142)

Blacks in Brazilian Theater Before 1944

Katherine Dunham touched upon the tragedy of Black

Brazilians in the arts when she singled out as the most rarefied form of deprivation and usurpation the one that brings on spiritual starvation as a result of cutting off the roots of origin and tradition. (1950: 6) The history of Brazilian theater is another aspect of the tragic suppression suffered by African culture at the hands of dominant white society.

The first attempts at theater in Brazil, like so many other aspects of our culture, were part of the systematic proseletyzing of the Catholic Church. They were made by Father José de Anchieta, one of the many Jesuit missionaries who came to convert the "pagans" and contribute to the success of slavery. Anchieta was the author of European religious plays which were called *autos sacramentais,* roughly similar to mystery plays, and were used as platforms of preaching and conversion rites. The first play in Brazil, in 1570, was called *Auto da Pregação Universal* (Auto of Universal Preaching).

Within this Catholic tradition, slaves were allowed to present folkloric entertainment during the season between Christmas and Epiphany: the *Congada* or *Congo,* the *Quicumbre,* the *Quilombos. Bumba-meu-boi* is a dramatic dance considered widely to be the most original creation of Brazilian folklore. It is generally considered to be of European origin, but it presents Black African magical characteristics and influences in the theatrical part *(auto)* as well as the action itself. Obvious adaptations by slaves are found in the inclusion of characters such as "Mateus" and "Bastião," the little pet niggers, foretelling the picturesque Black pickanninies that are one of the few stereotype roles in which Black actors have been tolerated, up until very recently, on Brazilian stages.

Several of these dramas and dramatic dances in Brazil act out the tale of death and resurrection of the protagonist. To me, these are projections of ancient African beliefs, the Egyptian myth of Osiris brought through a long physical and spiritual journey in time and space, and incorporated into Yoruba cultural foundations which came to Brazil in bondage.

Perhaps one of the most tragic figures in the colonial epoch was the mulatto. He was kept in a constant state of oscillation between his maternal African family and his Portuguese father,

126

who most often rejected him wholly. His status was ambivalent: as child of a slave woman he was legally a slave, but as child of the white master he had certain privileges within his functions as slave. The mulatto was set against his Black ancestors and family to the greatest extent possible; he was used as hunter of runaway slaves and as overseer. He was kept in servitude, but with the vain hope of entering his father's "society" always frustratingly dangled before him.

Another assignment given the mulatto was that of actor. It must be remembered that at that time the stage and theater were considered, along with music, most worthless activities of the day: lower than the most infamous of occupations. Why not open it to those restless mulattoes, as long as they cover their faces with a coat of red and white paint?

A typical example of the conditions under which Black people were able to enter theater otherwise is Chica da Silva. In the eighteenth century she became the bold and brazen mistress of a tax collector -- who was white, of course -- in Palha, a suburb of Diamantina in Minas Gerais. Her illicit but public relationship with this man gave her the means of operating a private theater where the classical repertory of the day was presented. Later, when theater became more prestigious as "culture" or "art," whites began taking over positions in theater.

The profession having been made respectable, the stages of Brazilian theater as well as the auditoriums, were now exclusively reserved for whites. Blacks entered only after the spectacle was over, to clean the stage and washrooms. The plays presented reflected the life, customs, aesthetics, ideas, problems -- in sum, the entire social and cultural milieu -- of a dominant society which was white: as if more than half the country's population, of African origin, did not exist. When an actor or actress of African origin had the opportunity to appear, it was invariably to play an exotic, grotesque or subaltern role, one of the Black stereotypes destitute of humanity, such as the pretty and easily accessible smiling maid, the grinning pickaninny with his limited repertoire of antics and clowning, the weeping or guffawing Aunt Jemima, the Black Mammy, or the domesticated and servile Uncle Tom.

When the role of a Black character demanded any dramatic quality of the actor -- that is, when the Black man's role on stage was something more than clowning or local color -- the "artistic norm" was to paint up a white actor in blackface. A caricature of the Black as nigger: this was Brazilian theater before 1944.

Dramatic literature ignored the tremendous potential, cultivated through centuries of suffering and creative labor, of Black people. Centuries also of insurrection and revolt in search of liberty, which inscribed in the territorial vastness of the country an indelible cartography of heroism and legend; with leaders of the stature of King Zumbi of Palmares. Of Chico-Rei, African king who toiled in slavery to buy the liberty of his enslaved tribe, which then founded a thriving mining community in Minas Gerais. Of Luiza Mahin of Bahia and her son Luis Gama who worked in São Paulo. Of Karocango in the state of Rio de Janeiro. Of João Cândido, the sailor who led the *Revolta da Chibata* (Revolt of the Whip) in the Navy in 1910. All of these African heroes and many others still await the dramatists who will recount their sagas for the stage, thereby elevating the consciousness of Blacks and Africans of the world.

Conventional dramatic literature included the Black in roles which can be inferred from their titles: *Demônio Familiar* (Family Demon) (1857) and *Mãe* (Mother) (1859), both by José de Alencar; *Os Cancros Sociais* (The Social Cancres) (1865) by Maria Ribeiro; *O Escravo Fiel* (The Faithful Slave) (1858) by Carlos Antonio Cardoso; *O Escravocrata* (The Slaver) (1884) and *O Dote* (The Dowry) (1907) by Arthur Azevedo; the comedies of Martins Pena (1815-1848).

Music and Dance

The most recognized and inescapable influence of Afro-Brazilian arts has been in music and dance. The Brazilian samba, famous throughout the world, is a Black creation. Despite the objections of the white communities of the day, *batuques* in colonial times had their profound effect on the musical world of Brazil. The Angolan wedding dance *Quizomba* and the Angolan-Congo *batuques* contributed such forms as the

Umbigada or *semba,* literally the "meeting of navels," which is widely taken to be the origin of the name Samba. From Angola also came the *capoeira,* orginally a form of martial arts, which was banned as such and subsequently developed into a dance done to the African musical instrument called the *berimbau.* It has become a beautiful and exquisite expression of African heritage in Brazilian dance.

Africans brought several other musical instruments, some of which persisted and are in use among us today, especially the *atabaques,* drums of various styles and sizes, the *ganzá,* the *adjá, agogô, urucungo, gongué.* These percussion instruments generated an aura and creation which seduced even composers of classical music of the Western European tradition.

The most successful and famous of early Black musicians, however, did not get their inspiration from these sources. Father José Maurício (1767-1830) had a musical formation which was strictly European. He sang, played the harpsichord and viola, and wrote Catholic religious music. He was Master of the Royal Chapel under Dom João VI (1808-1821). More recently we can name the mulatto conductor and composer Francisco Braga, and Paulo Silva, teacher of fugue and counterpoint at the National School of Music. Some of the most recent musicians of current times, though, are not subject to such pretentions. Black and Afro-Brazilian musical tones are clearly evident in such creators as Donga, Ismael Silva, Ataulfo Alves, Luis Soberano, Zé Keti, Sinval Silva. Many will recognize the names of Milton Nascimento, Caetano Veloso, Candeia and Gilberto Gil.

Brazilian music is the richest and most creative of our artistic tradition, and it would be impossible to present a full list here. But it would be unpardonable to omit the great female vocalist Clementina de Jesus, whose hauntingly African interpretive singing represents one of the high points of Black musical creativity. Carmen Costa is a more recent singer of African origin, and Gal Costa and Maria Bethania also use African musical motifs in their contemporary singing.

Two names deserve special place, Mercedes Batista, a choreographer and dancer of superb talent who made tireless and dedicated efforts towards the development and valorization of Black values in Brazilian dance, maintaining high artistic standards and preserving the genuine African roots of our musical and dance heritage. Along with her, Abigail Moura, recently deceased, conductor and composer in the same tradition, as well as creator and founder of the Afro-Brazilian Orchestra.

Of central importance is the profound effect Afro-Brazilian religion has had upon Brazilian popular music as a whole. We find the deities of the Yoruba *Candomblé* in our folk songs everywhere. *Pontos*, ritual songs and rhythms, have deserved many recordings in themselves and have exerted great weight among the writers of popular music. One of these, Bahian songwriter Dorival Caymmi, has written a tribute to the celebrated *Mãe-de-Santo*, Menininha do Gantois. A short transcription from memory:

> Coro: Ai, minha Mãe,
> Minha Mãe Menininha,
> Ai, minha Mãe,
> Menininha do Gantois. (Bis)
>
> E o sol mais brilhante, heim?
> Tá no Gantois.
> E a estrela mais pura, heim?
> Tá no Gantois.
> E o consolo da gente, heim?
> Tá no Gantois.
> E a Oxum mais bonita, heim?
> Tá no Gantois.
>
> Olorum que mandou, essa filha, de Oxum,
> Tomá conta, da gente, e de tudo cuidar.
> Olorum que mandou, ei-ô!
> Ora-yei-yei-ô.
> Ora-yei-yei-ô.
> Ora-yei-yei-ô.
>
> (Coro)
>
> Chorus: (Ai, my Mother
> My Mãe Menininha,
> Ay, my Mother,
> Menininha do Gantois.
>
> (repeat)

130

And the most brilliant sun, eh?
It's in the Gantois.
And the purest star, eh?
It's in the Gantois.
And the comfort of our people, eh?
It's in the Gantois.
And the most beautiful Oshun, eh?
In the Gantois.

Olorun who has sent
This daughter of Oshun,
Take care of us all and of everything.
Olorun who has sent, eh-oh.
Ora-yei-yei-o.
Ora-yei-yei-o.
Ora-yei-yei-o.

(Chorus)

Ornamental, Visual and Plastic Arts

African elements blended in the development of the clothing and ornamentation so famous worldwide, of Black women in Bahia. Making clothes and jewelry is a tradition of handcraft which has persisted since colonial times. It has also turned out to be the basis of a profitable tourist trade run by white business and governmental commercial interests. African masks left their mark on Brazilian handicrafts. Shawls, bracelets, earrings from Nigeria are still elaborated and innovated with. Turbans and *rodilhas* of Muslim origin, probably Hausa, are still used. And beads and *balangandãs,* jewels and bangles, from Angola or Congo origins, also contribute to the typical Bahian attire.

The development of plastic arts of Afro-Brazilian creation has been subject to limitations and impediments ever since colonial times. Because of official prohibitions such as the decree of October 20, 1621, which banned Africans from working in goldcrafting, and other limitations inherent to slave life, Africans were forced to produce their artistic works in hiding. The only visible outlets for their talents were the few Catholic churches that allowed Blacks to create. Of course, paintings and sculptures in this medium had to be reduced to Catholic orientation. In order to reach the "artistic level" of Aryan

131

"sacred art," Blacks had to empty their creations of any African character, using prevailing European norms and techniques. Thus Francisco Chagas of Bahia realized important achievements within these criteria in the eighteenth century at the Church of Carmo. In Rio de Janeiro, a slave called Sebastião revealed qualities worthy of respect in the several churches he decorated with oil paintings. Also Valentim de Fonseca e Silva (1750-1813) of Minas Gerais elaborated a prolific and diversified body of work in Rio de Janeiro, sculpting in wood, cast iron and gold. Black painter Oseas dos Santos was born in Bahia in 1865.

The most remarkable artist of the colonial period was Antonio Francisco Lisboa, who was born of African descent in Sabará, Minas Gerais, in 1730. At forty years of age he was stricken with leprosy, which devoured his hands and fingers; hence his nickname *Aleijadinho* (Little Cripple). A church architect, he was the powerful sculptor of twelve prophets of soapstone in Congonhas do Campo. Despite his disease and the crippling of his hands, he managed to paint saints and angels on the ceilings and walls of churches throughout Minas Gerais, and he represented the genial explosion of the Baroque in Brazil. But, underlying the European forms in his woodcuts, figures and images, a definite African ferment reveals itself. He created forms of communicative magic, fiery and powerful force.

Estevão Silva, a Black painter who died in Rio de Janeiro in 1801, became famous through his painting about slavery called "Charity." Pedro Americo, a mulatto native of Paraiba, painted historical scenes in grandiose dimensions.

Afro-Brazilian religion, though, remained the cradle and the inspiration of the art that Africans and their descendants created in the occult in the *terreiros* and *pegis* (shrines) of their worship. *Candomblé,* sacred locus of the cult, point of social convergence and cultural citadel, provided the Afro-Brazilian artist with a means for resisting. A means for keeping in his heart, in the light of Xangô's fire and "safe from the deluge and the ice," in the words of Gerardo Mello Mourão (1957: 26), that physical and spiritual force with which Mother Africa branded him: her indelible stamps of love and identity.

The objects used in worship have never lost their character as genuine works of art. However, the demeaning status of Afro-Brazilian religions within the larger European-oriented society had a marked effect on their development, acceptance and encouragement as art. Sculptures, icons and vestments were continuously confiscated in police raids. They were collected and displayed as ethnographic exhibits by psychiatrists and mental institutions like the Nina Rodrigues Institute of Bahia. Or they bore testimony to the "innate criminality" of Black Brazilians in police exhibits such as the Police Museum in Rio de Janeiro. Clarival do Prado Valladares, referring in his document submitted to the Second World Festival of Black and African Arts and Culture, to the collection of "totem elements and masks" apprehended by police agents and now the property of the Institute of History and Geography in Alagoas, remarks:

> This collection gains additional significance when it is realized that the seizure in Maceió in 1910 had no connection with those of the ensuing period, in the second decade, which took place in Bahia, Recife, Rio de Janeiro and elsewhere, aimed at the overthrowing of the African cults in Brazil. It was on that account that these objects were zealously safeguarded and not done away with, so that they now open up the way to further study. (1977: 7)

This is the way the white Catholic dominant classes deal with religions of African origin. They are cases for the police, raw material for "scientific" studies.

Nina Rodrigues, "pioneer of Afro-Brazilian studies," epitomizes such trends in his analysis of a Xangô sculpture. He uses theories of European racists to expose the representation of the *demon* or *devil* in African art forms. From there, he sets the trend concluding that Black people have innate criminal tendencies. This criminological approach to African art is important to point out, as it repeats itself in the early works of Fernando Ortiz of Cuba, and other prominent "scientists."

Nina Rodrigues goes on to say that the sculptor of the Xangô piece has no technical capability, mostly because he did not use the "proper proportions" between the legs and arms. A piece so deplorably deformed, in the eyes of this self-righteous Aryanoid, could not satisfy the fundamental requisites of artistic work. Rodrigues died in 1906, and did not see the paintings of a Modigliani or a Picasso. If he had seen these works unsigned, they would have been for him merely another monstrosity of African barbarism, evincing the artistic incompetence of African creation. Seeing them signed with the names of Europeans, however, his colonized compulsion to bless anything Aryan would have altered his judgment considerably.

Nina Rodrigues is not unique. He is only one example of a trend which has not disappeared. When Africans create works of art in their own cultural context, they are considered, at best, ethnographic curiosities and at worst, proofs of African inferiority. When white artists begin to use their motifs, suddenly African art is "discovered," as if it had never before existed. Aryan artists are accredited with great innovation — on the basis of plagiarism. The Black artist, throughout this entire process, remains in the same position as before: marginalized and ignored.

A timely example of the continuity of the attitudes expounded by Nina Rodrigues comes from the pen of the present General Coordinator of the Brazilian official representation at the Second World Festival of Black and African Arts and Culture, Clarival do Prado Valladares, white critic and aristocrat from Bahia. In 1974, he wrote an article published by Brazil's Ministry of Education and Culture, with the interesting title "On the Archaic Comportment of Brazil in Popular Arts." "Archaic" comportment, according to Valladares, is "... the opposite of rational logic, which is the inevitable premise of Classic comportment." (1974: 63) Naturally, "archaicism" is characteristic of Afro-Brazilian arts, in which Valladares encounters a "syncretic imaginary" of African worship in liturgical objects, votive offerings sculpted in wood, pieces in clay, etc. It need hardly be mentioned that "rational logic" (the enlightened superior of "archaicism") is characteristic of white European convention.

Valladares is the very personification of "white" Brazilian behavior toward fellow citizens of African descent. He was Brazilian representative and member of the Jury of the First Festival of Black Arts in Dakar in 1966. When he returned to

Brazil after this activity, he wrote an article with another interesting title: "The African Out-of-Phase State or Chronicle of the First Festival of Black Arts." In this document he makes the following comments: "The whites did not hunt blacks in Africa, but rather they peacefully bought them from the black tyrants." He continues,

> It is no surprise that a better understanding and analysis of Africa is not to be found among Africans themselves, [since] concerning the historical dimension there seems to exist a certain feeling of inferiority that is African. Thus it is not possible to present a historical text running parallel to that of Western countries. (1966: 4)

Here we have the case of the victim who, aside from being robbed, is accused by the very robber of having committed the crime! Valladares assumes the negation of African history is a natural fact, resultant from a supposed historical inadequacy on the part of Africans; and not the fruit of a systematic ideology of Aryan imperialism, devised to justify Europe's merciless aggression against the people of Africa. From the denial of African history and civilization, nothing prevents such mythmakers from going on to elevate, as a superior and absolute value, the virtues of whiteness and European supremacy. From this sacred pedestal of arrogant self-righteousness the Aryan disciples of Euro-ascendancy in Brazil were able to construe the "feeling of inferiority innate to Africa" in the first place.

This history of the Brazilian "intelligentsia" summarizes, in a frightening dossier, the racist framework of Brazilian society. I use the example of Valladares as one more focal beam which helps to illuminate the paths that lead to true liberation -- economic, political, cultural, social. His kind of paternalistic "sympathy" with Afro-Brazilians must be exposed for what it is: subtle, disguised social control. This is the most pernicious form of oppression suffered by Black Brazilians. Hidden under the sugar-coating of generosity and magnanimous sponsorship of aspiring young Black people, the true ideas of this class of paternalists emerge only rarely in publicized statements. Meanwhile, the Black Brazilians they take under their wing are

135

expected to remain grateful, humble, obliging and quietly agreeable to the dictates and superiority of their patrons.

The example of Valladares only represents the same thing that has occurred systematically in Africa, Australia, and all of the Americas: the attempt to negate, and if this does not work, to co-opt and absorb, Black being on all levels. The denial of our history is the means used to hide from Black people the more profound causes of the secular oppression of which we are victims; in the direct form of physical genocide and exploitation of our labor, or in the contempt and eradication of our culture. From this historical experience, from the depths of our cultural heritage, emerges the lesson: the Black people will never be liberated by falling into the trap of "racial integration" in the form of miscegenation, so conveniently praised by the apostles of "racial democracy." It is easy to perceive the falsity of the argument these apostles generally present, that in the process of ethnic integration white disappears as much as Black. For the values, references, definitions, ideas and orientations that control the direction of such "integration" are Euro-Aryan. They are the pointers indicating the true objective of "integration" : *whitening,* if not in blood and color of skin, at least in culture and personality. A Black country with a white soul -- that is the dream of Brazilian racism!

But Africans in Brazil have their heritage in Zumbi, in the democratic collective, egalitarian African community of Palmares. They have their legacy in Luis Gama, in João Cândido. Afro-Brazilians know that our liberation is inextricably linked to the liberation of our African brothers in the rest of the Diaspora, and that is why we accept the teachings of Marcus Garvey, W.E.B. DuBois, George Padmore and Malcolm X. Afro-Brazilians also understand that our fate is connected to the fate of Black Africans in the continent of origin, and the examples of Nkrumah, Lumumba and Nyerere are our inspiration. They are our authentic heroes and theoreticians, who knew how to hurdle the walls that white supremacy built around the Black world. They fought, they clamored, they revindicated, and they left us an inheritance of struggle for the liberty and dignity of the Black race.

RELIGION AND ART IN AFRO-BRAZILIAN CULTURAL EXPERIENCE

II. Reflections on the contemporary scene

paper delivered to
Faculty Seminar
University of Ife, Department of
African Languages and Literatures
December 9, 1976
Ile-Ife
Nigeria

... we black Africans have been blandly invited to submit ourselves to a second epoch of colonisation - this time by a universal-humanoid abstraction defined and conducted by individuals whose theories and prescriptions are derived from the apprehension of *their* world and *their* history, *their* social neuroses and *their* value systems.

Wole Soyinka
Myth, Literature and the African World

I t is not superfluous to repeat the truism that "Being an act of love, Art implicitly signifies an act of human and cultural integration. An act carried out in the direction of a continually re-evaluated civilization created for and shared by all of humanity." (Nascimento 1976: 54) But love does not exhaust itself in the simple gesture of sympathy. It implies and demands something more decisive: the active engagement of he who loves. For this reason love, rather than being static or simply contemplative, affirms itself as a dynamic value, indeed often aggressively dynamic. In consequence of the quality and character of his sensitivity, the artist lives under compulsory obligations of love, feeling, interpreting, and expressing his concrete relationship with the life and culture of his people. A relationship that is complex and subtle, woven into the act of receiving and the act of giving; into the act of re-creating the culture of his people in all its levels, forms, meanings, implications and connotations. There is, in this context, no room for the vaccuum of "art for art's sake," that is, the exercise of nothing, the gymnastics of pure abstraction.

It is obvious that art is a phenomenon that involves an entire mechanism of meaning and a process of visual perception, of intercommunication between the artist and his environment. The integrity of this relationship is basic, and when it suffers arbitrary influences, that is when it becomes the victim of aggression, that flux and re-flux which sustains the healthy equilibrium of the interplay is broken.

What has been the significance of Afro-Brazilian art? What has been the process of Black art in Brazil? A creativity that has been continuously, from the beginning, besieged by the aggression of forms, symbols, themes, ideals and ideas of white European culture. We are not dealing here with a normal reciprocal influence between two different cultural milieus. More correct would be to characterize it as an act of white cultural-aesthetic exclusivism, which excludes from the plane of the eminent and the honorable all that escapes the determinations of its artistic code. In this code beauty is unswervingly white, as also are goodness, nobility, and value. At the other extreme we find what the color black signifies: the ugly, the evil, the inferior. Thus the definition of the word *negro* (black) from the *New Appleton Dictionary of the English and Portuguese Languages:*

> *negro, -gra* ('negru, -gra). I. a. black (also fig.); dark; (anthropol.) Negro; somber, gloomy, funereal; shadowy, tenebrous; sinister, threatening; ominous, portentous; cloudy, obscure, stormy; horrible, frightening; adverse, hostile; wretched, odious, detestable. (1967: 417)

Webster's Collegiate Thesaurus gives us the following synonyms for "black":

> 2 *syn* DIRTY 1, filthy, foul, grubby, impure, nasty, soily, squalid, unclean, uncleanly. 3 *syn* GLOOMY 3, bleak, depressing, depressive, dismal, dispiriting, dreary, funereal, oppressive, somber. (1976: 89)

In such circumstances the Black person finds himself imprisoned in a net of aesthetic alienation so powerful that one begins to detest one's own color, to hate one's own race. There are many public manifestations of this sentiment of self-contempt, such as that of a Black Commissioner of Police, Dr. Lirio Coelho, who once declared his race to be a race of ugly persons. The cases are not isolated ones, of Black girls who have committed suicide because they could not tolerate the "ugliness" of their skin, or fathers who have killed their daughters rather than see them marry a Black man.

This aesthetic race bias is expressed in the often cited and discussed painting by Modesto Brocos, *The Redemption of Ham,* which has a venerated place in the Museum of Fine Arts in Rio de Janeiro. It portrays, in the words of Antonio Olinto, "... an old Negro woman, a grandmother, who has at her side her mulatto daughter and white grandson, while her son-in-law, a happy and smiling Portuguese, stands nearby." (1967: 5) This is only one of the renditions in plastic arts of the dream of whitening the Brazilian family through the generations, which is encouraged and propagated in Brazil for the "betterment of the race." It reflects the pathological desire, aesthetic and social, of the Brazilian people to become white, imposed by the racist ideology of the dominant elite.

In 1955, this abnormal situation provoked the *Teatro Experimental do Negro* - TEN - (Black Experimental Theater) to hold the Black Christ contest in plastic arts, as well as a series of beauty contests, entitled Queen of the Mulattoes and Tar Doll, with the collaboration of Arthur Ramos, prominent anthropologist, and leading sociologist Guerreiro Ramos. The objective was to correct this aesthetic and social pathology. It was as much a technique of educating popular aesthetic taste as it was an attempt to purge collective emotional tensions born of these questions of the concept of beauty and aesthetic preference. Thus the necessity of statements such as this one by Guerreiro Ramos: "Black beauty is not simply a cerebral creation of those whom circumstance has given a black skin, a mode of rationalization or self-justification; but an eternal intrinsic value, worthy even if it is never discovered." (1966: 130)

In colonial times in Brazil and in all parts of the Americas where Europeans practiced enslavement of Africans, Aryan colonial powers attempted with all tactics and tools available to dehumanize the African people. The aim was to smash totally the possibility of creation or continuance of cultural traditions specific to the Black people. In Africa itself, this was carried out with the sacking and destruction or stealing of artistic and religious treasures. The destiny of these stolen legacies? The year 1842 heralds the launching of P.F. von Siebald's idea of founding ethnographic museums in the European countries, among other reasons because it was a "lucrative trade." (Goldwater 1967: 4) From then on these institutions flourished, the outstanding models being the museums of Berlin, Rome, London, Paris, Leipzig -- all agencies of African "studies" at the service of the oppressor. These joined with scholars, scientists, theoreticians and researchers in conjuring up elaborate theories of African exoticism, inferiority, picturesqueness and savageness.

In this respect, we should not lose sight of a curious continuity in Afro-Brazilian studies, ever since their inception with Nina Rodrigues. In general, studies of African *culture and religion* are done by *psychiatrists*. We mentioned last week the psycho-criminological approach to the "scientific" analysis of a Xangô sculpture, taken by Nina Rodrigues, a psychiatrist, author of the unequivocal statement that the natural inferiority of the Black people accounted for their failure to "establish themselves as a civilized people." (1945: 24) Much time and energy is spent apologizing and rationalizing the inescapable racism of his work, which is less subtle than current scientists would prefer. It has merited the conclusion of Brazil's most authoritative and innovative sociologist, Guerreiro Ramos, that "Nina Rodrigues, in the plane of social science, is a nullity, *even considering the period in which he lived.* [...] His work, in this particular, is a monument of assininity." (emphasis added. 1957: 144) Nevertheless, Nina Rodrigues headed an entire school of anthropology and ethnology known as the School of Bahia (including such names as Arthur Ramos, Edison Carneiro, Luis Vianna Filho, and others) which continues his living tradition to this day.

Following Rodrigues in time and tradition are fellow psychiatrists Arthur Ramos, and currently René Ribeiro and George Alakija. What are the implications of the fact that one of the qualifications for studying Black culture is a degree in psychiatry? The underlying implication is that Afro-Brazilian culture, especially religion, is considered indicative of mental disequilibrium, and its practitioners pathological beings in a society of healthy Christians.

George Alakija, another Bahian psychiatrist, was sent by the Brazilian Government to Lagos for Festac '77. His mission: report the astounding conclusion from his study of fifteen religious mediums from *Candomblé* and Kardecist spiritism: that they were *not* pathological! The good doctor, a Black man himself, was quick to add that "... this does not preclude the possibility that in one or other group there may be individuals who present overt psycho-pathological anomalies." (1977: 10) On the next page, he proceeds to classify all of the subjects' levels of intelligence as "low," and general knowledge as "poor." (1977: 11) Alakija, while diverging from the sanctified conclusion of Nina Rodrigues that spiritual ecstacy among Afro-Brazilians was hysteria, a form of pathology, is careful not to exaggerate. In the name of objectivity, perhaps, he insists upon continuing the use of long-outmoded pejorative labels coined by Euro-centric "scholars" to describe African religion: "primitive cults," "animistic religion," or "magic-primitive guise." (1977: 8, 9) In the last analysis, Alakija prefers the easy way out: he classifies spiritual trance as a "sophronic state" that "cannot be classified as either ordinary or pathological." (1977: 4)

The very existence of Alakija's "radical" and "astonishing" finding that African religion is *not* a psycho-pathological disorder indicates the ingrained, deep-rooted notion of Aryan-aspiring intellectual circles that Black religion was and is an abnormal, psychopathic departure from the healthy norm of Christian society. I belive it will be useful to evoke an idea of the development of this normal, wholesome community of upright white citizens.

What were the character and moral fiber, the preoccupations and activities of the noble Aryan masters? Gilberto Freyre writes extensively of those first centuries when the Brazilian "family" was formed: "In the white master the body almost became exclusively the *sex organ*. Hands of a woman; feet of a little boy; only the penis was arrogantly virile." (1966: 599) They lived their days stretched out in hammocks, lazy, immersed in the only worry that consumed them: sex. As for their wives, the white mistresses, their principal task, in a life of complete idleness, consisted of screaming orders at slave girls. They were easily exasperated, since they had been born, raised and lived surrounded by slaves, which enabled them to conceive "... an exalted opinion of their superiority over other human creatures and never to imagine that they could be in error." (Koster, cited in Freyre 1966: 469) From the cultivation of laziness and indolence, the white mistresses went on to jealousy and sexual rancor:

> There are not two or three, but many cases of cruelty of the *senhoras de engenho* [mistresses] against defenseless slave girls. Young missies who would have the eyes of pretty maids torn out and brought to the husband at dessert time, in the compote of sweets and floating in the still-fresh blood. Baronesses of middle age, who out of jealousy or spite would have little mulatto girls sold at the

age of fifteen to old libertine men. Others would shatter slave girls' teeth with the high heels of shoes or have their breasts cut off; yank out their nails, burn their faces or ears. (Freyre 1966: 470)

Targets of the vindictiveness of the white "ladies," and permanent victims of the sexual violence of Aryan "men" from the tenderest age, little Black girls confronted a veritable sexual calvary.

It is sad and revolting, to find white "scholars" of today registering such facts as positive achievements in Brazilian race relations. Pierre Verger croons, for example, that the sons of white masters

... would undergo their sexual initiation with the coloured girls working in the big house or in the fields, thus infusing elements of sensual attraction and comprehension into their relations with what one has chosen to call persons of different races. (1977: 10)

If Verger has "chosen" to call them persons of different races, the Black women who were tortured and raped had no such privilege. They did not "choose" to be Black, but it was because of their Blackness that they were brutalized and oppressed, along with their Black men who were subjected to the humiliation and castration of this nefarious creation the Aryans called "society."

Where are the elements of "comprehension" in this ritual of rape, practiced with religious fervor by white aristocrats against African women? There are answers that speak to the pursuance by white men and women of the lucrative business of pimping:

At times little Black girls of ten, twelve years were already in the street offering themselves to enormous sailors, blond Jack-tars that disembarked from the English and French sailing ships with a mad hunger for women. And all of this superexcitation of the gigantic, fair-haired, bestial men, was discharged on little pickanninny girls; and, beyond superexcitation, syphilis; the diseases of the world -- of the four corners of the world; the international putrescences of blood. (Freyre 1966: 628)

If this kind of "sensual comprehension" were to be visited by African men upon French and English women, the attitude of Aryan "scholars" would be quite different.

144

These are crimes that shall never be erased from the Afro-Brazilian memory. To extinguish the memory of Black people has been the constant preoccupation of those who rule the country. But Black Brazilians, if they want to have a future, will have to build it from the debris left over from the misfortune that befell them in slavery, never by appealing to the facile escapism of pardoning the tormentors who martyrized the African race, principally in the flesh of Black women. We shall not forget that thousands of their bodies were pitilessly sacrificed not only to the sexual appetite of the Aryan male, or the jealousy of white "ladies," nor even just to the profit interests of the pimping profession:

> It was the bodies of Black girls -- sometimes children of ten years of age -- that constituted, in the moral achitecture of Brazilian patriarchy, the magnificent block which defended the virtue of white mistresses from the attacks and the audacities of the Don Juans. (Freyre 1966: 628-629)

Meaning that the debasement and degradation of the Black woman was the bastion of honor of the "ladies" of white Brazilian society. This situation has not been significantly altered to this day.

It is curious to note that the man who divulged and studied these historic acts of crime, Gilberto Freyre, sees them as positive and idyllic scenes of cultural progress, deserving of the adjective "magnificent" *(formidável)*. "Magnificent" is the block of Black girls sacrificed on the altar of white virtue; "magnificent" also the contribution by licentious priests of their "better stock" to the pool of Brazilian genetic selectivity:

> The sexual intercourse of white males of the best stocks -- including clerics, without doubt some of the elements most select and eugenic in the Brazilian makeup -- with black and mulatto slaves was magnificent. From it resulted a great multitude of illegitimate children -- little mulattoes brought up many times together with legitimate offspring, in the liberal patriarchalism of the mansions; others in the

145

shadow of the mills of priests; or in the "wheels"* and orphanages. (1966: 618)

Freyre caps his insensitivity and colonial mentality by calling "selective and eugenic elements" those common criminals, bandits and nefarious renegades, the outcasts of Europe, who enslaved and ravished African women in Brazil.

White researchers, with Freyre at the forefront, have indeed developed a viable profession of turning Afro-Brazilian people into a *question, ethnographic material*: the Black as a museum piece, stuffed and displayed. Our *exotic* (ex-optic) configuration aroused the curiosity of scholars, who explored the oddities of our cooking, our lovemaking, the shape of our skulls, the recesses of our "demented" minds, our ways of dancing and of drumming, of worshipping our god. Juana Elbein dos Santos, in her important work *Os Nagô e a Morte,* remarks that

> It is necessary to admit that the majority of work done on Afro-Brazilian culture is resented either because of its superficiality, or the lack of a consequential methodology, and generally, because of its ethnocentric focus. (1977: 22)

And Olabiyi Babalola Yai corroborates this conclusion when he writes from the African perspective:

> The subject of African religions, and notably of religions of Nigerian origin, is the most discussed in what there is a habit of calling "Afro-Brazilian studies." It is perhaps equally the most badly treated. [...] for a long time anthropologists avoided analyzing these religions from inside, preoccupied as they were with the superficial and "folkloric" aspects. [...] It is not rare for them to begin with theoretical presumptions in vogue, attempting to lead into constructions which justify them; not to speak of prejudices of ideological order, which have not failed to influence the conduct and results of their research. [...] [From them] the African religions emerge uncomprehended and impoverished. (1976: 99)

Rodas (wheels) were revolving platforms upon which mothers who did not wish to be identified would put their unwanted babies, who then would ride into the orphanage on the wheel. (Translator's note)

146

The outcome of this tendency? We have witnessed one "expert" whose literature presents spiritual ecstacy in religious worship as nothing more than erotic stimulation and sexual primitivism: Jorge Amado. There are many other examples of the kind of racist logic that still labels us "folkloric," "picturesque," psychiatric "curiosities," "exotic phenomena." Not to mention the great white benefactors who come to our festivals of art and culture to "archaicize" and dehistoricize us!

It is revealing to focalize, if only briefly, upon the newest challenge that the *Candomblé* must confront in order to continue existing: commercialization and profiteering by white moneyed interests. Pierre Verger affirms that:

> The Yoruba Oriṣa are recognised as a living reality and highly appreciated in the daily life of Bahia and of Brazil in general.
> The recognition and status accorded the Yoruba Oriṣa is in fact such that numerous buildings in Bahia, even among the most modern and luxurious ones in residential areas, bear their names.
> Quite recently a real-estate agency successfully staked on the popularity and the confidence the names of the Oriṣa will inspire among the upper class of citizens, the only people able to afford to live in luxurious apartments. This agency has already constructed 23 buildings with up to 30 storeys which are placed under the patronage of Yoruba gods and goddesses. (1977: 13)

According to such ideologues of "racial democracy," the sale of the Orixás constitutes a positive fact. It follows the business tradition of Aryans who bought and sold African people, profited from the compulsory prostitution of Black women and children, transacted with the blood of Africans in the wars of slavers, trafficked the sweat of the Black man and the milk of the Black woman. Now has come their time to corrupt and market the very divinities of Africa on the counter of real estate enterprise. In a state like Bahia, with a population seventy percent of African descent, Black people build a high rise where they themselves cannot even live. Because of racism? "No," respond the proprietors of Bahian life, "Never racism! It's just that Blacks don't have the economic means."

What these "whites" of Bahia, white supremacists of all

Brazil, carefully do not mention is the fact that Afro-Brazilians lack financial means because they are Black. And economic, political, cultural and social power "naturally" remain a monopoly of the chosen ones of European origin, i.e., the minority Aryanoid classes of society. Even the advertisements of the apartment buildings in question betray this objective. We have, from the ads for the "Oşaguian Building:"

> Oşala is the greatest Orişa.
> The Oşaguian Building is one of the highest on 7th avenue.
> Oşaguian is dressed in white and marble is his symbol.
> The Oşaguian Building is made of marble.
> *By virtue of his colour* and his symbol, Oşaguian is the Afro-Brazilian god of peace and love.
> The Oşaguian Building features calm and luxury.
> (emphasis added. 1977: 14)

Underneath this apparently calm and peaceful land speculation, how much unscrupulous activity, how much aggression against the legitimate interests of Afro-Brazilian religion and culture goes on! The fact is that such real estate deals have practiced and continue to practice various types of encroachments threatening to the survival of the *Candomblé terreiros*. The magazine *Veja* of São Paulo, in its December 10, 1975 issue, registers a news item from Salvador, Bahia entitled "Support for the Orixás:"

> Since their remote appearance in Salvador, almost two centuries ago, the *Candomblé terreiros* have always been harassed by severe police restrictions. And, at least in the last twenty years, the blockade erected by the police has been noticeably strengthened by a powerful ally -- real estate expansion, which has extended itself to the areas distant from the center of town, where the drums resounded. Further, never has the Mayor outlined legal barricades to protect these strongholds of Afro-Brazilian culture -- although Bahian capital has collected fat dividends from the exploitation of tourism fomented by the magic of the Orixás. [...] The mayor's office itself, in fact, is frequently accused of trampling with viaducts and avenues certain sites which, though belonging officially to the public, for more than 100 years have sheltered venerated temples of the *Candomblé*. And never has the application of sanctions been heard of, against unscrupulous proprietors of land neighboring to the houses of worship, who seize with impunity the land of the terreiros. (1975: 52)

I transcribe this text at length to compare its terms with the statements of Verger. Contrary to the euphoria of the French researcher, the article denounces the contemptuous treatment of Afro-Brazilian religion not only by businessmen with real property interests, but also by governmental powers who, after condoning the exploitation of *Candomblé* as tourist merchandise, usurp the terrain of its temples. Where is that "high appreciation of the Orişas" preached by Verger? Maybe exclusively in his own interest as an ideologue at the service of the status quo, disguised as disinterested investigator...

Considering the samples, representative and typical, that we have examined here, of the tone and tenor of "scientific" research in Afro-Brazilian studies, I propose that we organize and execute an *International Congress for the Study of White Europeans and Aryanoid Euro-Surrogates in Brazil*. We would scrutinize the mental and psychiatric phenomena which motivated Aryans to enslave their fellow human beings with a sadistic brutality unprecedented in the history of man. We would delve into the physio-neurological and psycho-criminological origins of their emotional need to attempt to justify their acts of murder, torture and robbery with facetious fantasies of "white man's burden," "manifest destiny," "bringing civilization to the native savages," "philanthropy" and "economic necessity." We would record the measurements of the white man's mind, which motivate them to steal artistic treasures from other peoples, and arrogantly and obstinately refuse to return them for the celebration of those peoples' cultural and artistic heritage, as the British government is currently doing on the occasion of Festac '77.

From a psychiatric point of view, we would analyse the formalistic, unemotional, mechanical attitudes that Europeans and their imitators display in religious worship. These betray, from an anthropological and psychological perspective, a profound lack of identity and attachment with their gods, as well as a strange absence of spiritual contact. We would also study from a sociological and ethnological standpoint the singularly dehumanized, mechanistic nature of white European and North American society, whose ultimate achievement in the rigid, distant coldness of its "objectivity" has been the invention of weapons of destruction capable of obliterating the human race. We would investigate the origins of the pathological avariciousness which drives Aryans to poison their own food supplies and those of the rest of the world with chemicals and dyes, in the pathetic search for profit, which also moves them to senselessly destroy millions of tons of foodstuffs, and slaughter, for no other reason than waste, millions of heads of cattle per year. For it is not the people of Africa or the Black people of the Americas who commit such absurdities. They would feed their children with those products if they could.

It is imperative to understand that the historical experience of Africans and their Diaspora has been and is one of essentially *racist* content, which transcends and surpasses the simplistic formulas by which many consider slavery and the subsequent oppression of Black people to be merely a branch of capitalist production, a result only of an economic system. Such facile constructions speak of systems as if they were some lofty, intangible abstractions not made up of human beings and their motivations, attitudes and cultural aspirations. In the human configuration of Western society, it is racism and its derivatives -- cultural chauvinism, race and color prejudice, and discrimination -- that are the operative elements in the existential dilemma of Black people. Ignorance, belittling, or underestimation of the impact of racism makes it difficult or impossible to obtain a realistic vision of the conditions suffered by Blacks in Brazilian society and in the Americas generally.

Black Artists in Brazil

Despite the precepts of the white scholars, slaves in Brazil proved the racist concepts of their incapability and primitiveness to be false, from the very beginning. Africans from the Gulf of Guinea proved themselves highly developed with the famous bronzes of Benin, Dahomeans in their works of copper, Ashantis in their textiles. From the Ivory Coast, Dahomey (now Benin) and Nigeria, came specialists in wood sculpture and metal working, while from Mozambique came artesans of iron and from Angola the *Capoeira*.

150

In the course of the early centuries of the colony we witness the transmission of painting of African origin in ritual symbols of the *terreiros,* ornamentation of shrines, and decoration of residential walls. This was an occult production, almost secret. With the abolition of slavery in 1888, and subsequent arrival of European immigrants, the situation did not change substantially. Theoretically free, but without work opportunities since the white immigrant was preferred, the Black remained slave of unemployment, underemployment, crime, prostitution and hunger -- all forms of personal and family disintegration -- while the white immigrant rose rapidly in the socio-economic world and in the levels of power.

Is it surprising in the social, economic, cultural and racial context we have described here, that from the point of view of plastic arts Blacks almost do not exist in Brazil? We represent more than fifty percent of the Brazilian population of more than 120 million inhabitants; at least seventy million Afro-Brazilians. Black artists who are meaningful from the Afro-Brazilian cultural perspective are rare. Nevertheless, Roger Bastide bears witness to the emergence of an Afro-Brazilian aesthetic: "Afro-Brazilian art is a living art, quite unstereotyped. But in its evolution, up to the latest of its transformations, it has preserved the structures, mental and purely aesthetic, of Africa." (1968: 404)

Working with symbolic forms of African origin, recreating ritual symbols, manipulating graphic signs and signifying traits of our liturgy, attempting to capture the plastic values of Yoruba mythology or Bantu legend, art has functioned as a spiritual force which sustains, to whatever extent possible, the identity and visibility of the African in Brazil, unalienated from his existential self and his original culture. The Black artist, through the crystallization of his plastic language, re-establishes and re-creates his bond with the history and culture of his people, retains and enriches a system of concepts and values which signify the vestments and substance, lively, dynamic, which the existential parable of Africans in the Diaspora has written for history.

We had the opportunity, in the previous seminar, to refer to the popular plays, the *autos,* dramatic dances, ritual music and popular music of African origin in the creative production of African art in Brazil. These represent the expression of ancient tradition from the Black Continent, which have been examined by many authors. The continuity of African themes, motifs and techniques in wood sculpture and painting, has been studied by Arthur Ramos, Roger Bastide and others. Traditional African techniques in sculpture transcended the socio-geographic boundaries of the Black artist's and artesan's world. Their influence projects far into the Northeast of the country, in the production of *ex-votos.* These are sculptures, generally small in size, which the faithful of Catholicism make in payment of promises to their saints. Painter Antonio Maia re-elaborates these anonymous popular sculptures in his creative and beautiful pictorial work. Another manifestation of the widespread African continuity exercising its influence in the Northeast is the tradition of oral literature in the form of the *desafio* (challenge) which we referred to last week. Its literary form and style are reminiscent of the oral literature of traditional Africa, particularly songs and chants to Ogun, in Yoruba culture.

Black artists who focalize traditional African themes in their Brazilian dimension are often labelled by conventional critics as primitive, archaic, naive, and other classifications of pejorative connotation, laced with paternalistic condescension. My response to these pompous passers of judgement is this:

What you manipulators fail to see is that by concretizing our myths and legends rather than submitting our art to the dictates of Western critics and cultures, we are historicizing ancient mythical origins, turning age-old foundations into current and timely forces of social transformation. For Black art is the practice of Black liberation -- reflection and action, action and reflection -- in all levels of existence: material and spiritual; social and religious; cultural/aesthetic; economic and political. By keeping our specific logic and our artistic integrity unalienated, Black art becomes the exorcism of the whiteness resulting from centuries of denying, perverting and deforming our formal and essential values through social, cultural and police pressure. The art of the Black people in the Diaspora objectifies the world around us and furnishes a critical image of that world. It fulfills a need of utmost relevance: critically historicizing the structures of domination, violence and oppression which characterize the Western capitalist civilization created and controlled by Aryans. As Paulo Freire has said: "... this is the great humanist and historic task of the oppressed -- to liberate themselves and the oppressors." (1975: 41)

It is not sufficient for Black art to be the "living art preserving the ancient structures of Africa" which Bastide describes. It must have the courage and capacity to incorporate into the expression of traditional Africa new forms, new spaces and volumes, new cultural values, all of which are valid only after critical selection, demonstration of their adequacy to our creative integrity.

The Black and African people are experiencing the living plenitude of a sociological and cultural historical phenomenon radically opposed to the context of white European society. From this experience springs a specific aesthetic whose implications for the artistic heritage common to all cultures do not invalidate its inalienable identity. Black art in the Diaspora, peripheral relative to the art sanctified by local dominant societies, carries implications dictated by history, by environment, by the cultures of various enslaving groups. But it never ceases to conserve in its themes, forms, and content, and revolutionary function as an instrument of conscientization, its character as an integral part of the vital system of African creativity.

In this light we can begin to understand the work of a painter as sensitive as Sebastião Januário, born in Dores de Guanhães in the state of Minas Gerais. He began his work constrained by Catholic motifs and models. Experience and intuition united to liberate and guide him to the evolvement of mature, truly Afro-Brazilian paintings. Then there is the sculptor of wood, José Heitor, whose strength and self-taught technique explode in a work marked with profound Africanity. And what can be said of an artist like Iara Rosa, painter and tapestry-weaver of such rich and beautiful recourse? Or Cleoo, whom Guerreiro Ramos once called the "rose of the winds," open to all voices of creative imagination? Raquel Trindade elaborates the poetic heritage of her father, Solano Trindade, in colors, forms, and visual themes. Yeda Maria transfers to her canvasses the human and geographic landscape of African Bahia. Agenor realizes in wood all of the "miracles" of forms and proportions in Afro-Brazilian character. Celestino actively develops his own creative and artistic work, and also promotes Black artists, their identity and creativity, through critical action and reflection around Afro-Brazilian art. Deoscoredes Maximiliano dos Santos, also called Didi, recently installed as Alapini of Bahia, high priest of Egungun, realizes in various kinds of material the forms and themes of ritual objects, works of great artistic merit and significance in their own right.

In the selection of Brazilian representation in Festac '77, would these artists and others of like merit in the affirmation of Afro-Brazilian culture receive any gesture of respect from the Ministry of Foreign Relations, a body of notoriously racist character which has no Black diplomatic representatives in any country? Its Commission is in charge of the selection process for the Festival, with a few members from the Ministry of Education and Culture, which is also all-white. Yet Black artists themselves, those who produce and promote Black culture in Brazil, should *be* the selectors and organizers of their delegation to Lagos.

In this vein it is appropriate to remember the example of the United States, which the dominant strata in Brazil proclaim as land of racism, contrasting it to the "racial democracy" of Brazil. Undoubtedly the U.S. is a bastion of racism. But the North American Black community, minority in its country, is solely and exclusively responsible for its own representation in the Second Festival of Black Arts, despite being partially funded by the government. Is it necessary to ask which of these racisms commits, in this case, the most radical discrimination against Blacks? The veil of so-called "racial democracy" cannot continue to hide indefinitely and with impunity this condemnable reality of an ethnic majority secularly oppressed and controlled, even in its artistic participation in its own international community, by a minority of white European origin.

For me, ontological mystery and the vicissitudes of the Black race in Brazil come together, merged and fused, in the religion of the Orixás -- *Candomblé*. Experience and science, revelation and prophecy, communion of men and divinities, dialogue between the living and the dead, *Candomblé* marks the point where the existential continuity of African life has been recaptured. Where Black people can look at themselves without seeing reflected the face of the physical and spiritual rapist of our race. In *Candomblé* the paragons of white power and culture, which for four centuries have enriched themselves on the product of African sweat and blood, have no place and no validity.

This is why the Orixás are the foundations of my painting. For me their image and significance surpass visual-aesthetic perception. They are the basis of a process of struggle for liberation, because their love is commitment. The Orixás are far from a purported "archaicism" and far from "remissive images of a harmonious past" compensating "an arid factual reality." (Coelho 1974: 55) Wọle Ṣoyinka's definition carries more truth: the Orixás are our "sources of strength," the reality of our own being; they are "the Gods who make the energies of the Black Continent." (1975: 48)

What does it matter, then, to be labelled "painter of instinct," *artist insitu, neoprimitive,* or any of the many codifications of conventional criticism, when I paint Ogum, god of iron, of war, of vengeance, companion in arms of his brothers in the fight for liberty and dignity? Or Yemanjá, mother of all the waters of the world and of all the Orixás, keeping faithful vigil over Black fertility, alert against the contained aggression of the white man's birth control and forced sterilization? And Xangô -- storm, fire and lightning -- practicing justice, militant of all movements for the fundamental rights of human beings? When I paint Ossaim, the leaf-divinity, I am evoking the reign of Nature, of raw materials; she is the enemy of pollution and she cultivates the plants and herbs of the traditional medicine and pharmacology of Africa.

Ifa reveals the past, examines the present, and discloses the future: he gives us knowledge and enables us to make plans and projections. Oxunmarê condenses the colored vital joy of our race and its playful content. Oxalá, in his masculine-feminine duality, structures the primal egg of the procreation of the species. Oxum, patroness of the arts and bestower of love in all moments of life. Exu, whom the Catholics wrongly identify with the devil, commands the roads and crossings of the universe. Messenger, interpreter of human and divine languages, Exu embodies the principle of contradiction, dialecticizes human existence, ritualizes the perpetual motion of the cosmos and of the history of men and women.

The Afro-Brazilian in Cinema

In its intrinsic unity, art manifests itself in various and multiple forms, the film being one of the most recent expressions of human creativity. This artistic expression of our century does not yet exist as an Afro-Brazilian product; cinematic production is an exlusive monopoly of directors and producers of white origin. It happens that cinema is, simultaneously, a manifestation of art and also a techno-industry of high economic and financial development. This fact constitutes an effective impediment to the entrance of the Black, who is synonymous with pariah, dispossessed and at the lowest levels of the social and economic hierarchy. He enters only as subject, or more frequently, object, of cinematographic activity controlled by whites.

As a mere object the Black actor marks his presence in film, interpreting, as a rule, roles insignificant from the artistic point of view. Within this negative general context we can distinguish attempts of certain white writers and directors in films portraying the life and customs of Blacks. Examples: the late Alinor Azevedo wrote *Tambem somos irmãos* (We are also Brothers) in 1947, which was directed by José Carlos Burle, with two of the most important actors of Brazilian theater and cinema: the late Aguinaldo Camargo and Grande Otelo. *Amei um Bicheiro* (I Loved a Numbers Runner), in 1951, directed by

Jorge Ileli, offered another good opportunity to Grande Otelo. Director Nelson Pereira dos Santos initiated a cycle of what has been denominated *Cinema Novo* (New Cinema), with *Rio 40 Graus* (Rio 40 Degrees) and *Rio Zona Norte* (Rio North Zone) in 1957. Tom Payne directed *Sinhá Moça* (Young Missy) in 1953, in which Ruth de Sousa played an impressive role.

A French director, Marcel Camus, made the well-known *Black Orpheus* in 1958, which won the Grand Prix in Cannes. Lea Garcia interprets with great intelligence and sensitivity one of the leading roles. This film effectively illustrates the commercial exploitation to which Blacks, in their marginal position in economy and society, are constantly subjected. The film is a transposition of the Greek myth of Orpheus to a *favela* in Rio de Janeiro, portraying in picturesque and rosy hues the Black people's preparations for Carnaval. Music, dance, rhythm, colors, happiness and love, everything contributes to the product destined for the international markets, avid consumers of the exotic and folkloric. And when Euridice disappears from the *carnaval* parades, ultimately to be murdered, Orpheus looks everywhere for her. When he doesn't find her, decides to descend into Hell to look for her. And where is Hell? A temple of Afro-Brazilian religion!

Meanwhile, in *Assalto ao Trem Pagador* (Assault on the Payment Train), 1962, director Roberto Farias, unlike Camus with his rosy portrayal of blissfully innocent *favela* dwellers, presents on the screen the desperate misery and poverty of *favelados* who, not out of choice but forced by circumstance, assault and rob in order to survive, turning to the recourse of outlaw life.

When we do not have a visual degradation of Afro-Brazilian religions as in *Black Orpheus,* the cause becomes exposure of the religious intolerance of the Catholic Church. Based on a play by Dias Gomes, *O Pagador de Promessa* (The Payer of a Promise) by Anselmo Duarte is the story of a certain humble man from the interior of the state of Bahia who in his ingenuousness makes a vow in a *terreiro* of Iansan (the Afro-Brazilian version of Yoruba goddess Oya) to carry a huge cross to the Church of Santa Barbara (who is syncretized with Iansan) in Bahia. The vow is related to his donkey, as is his name, Zé do Burro. After laboriously carrying the heavy cross on his back through a long journey, Zé do Burro and his cross stand on the steps of the church, which is still closed at this early hour of the morning. Here commences the drama and tragedy of the hero: the great doors of the church open for Mass, and the priest forbids the entrance of this blasphemous cross -- the object of a promise made in a *Candomblé,* a pagan temple of Black infidels! This film portrays faithfully the tone and the mode of the religious syncretism so highly praised as a value of the Catholic culture of Brazil.

The Black artists most active in Brazilian film are: Grande Otelo, whose life is identified with the very history of Brazilian film through his forty years of activity. Lea Garcia and Ruth de Sousa are two of the most prominent Black actresses of quality in Brazilian film as well as television. Zózimo Bulbul is a Black actor who has attempted to make his own films and pursues cultural activity in other fields also. Milton Gonçalves, also active as actor and director in television, and Antonio Pitanga, Jorge Coutinho, Zeni Pereira, Luiza Maranhão, figure among the other Black actors and actresses in Brazilian cinema.

From the perspective of culturally valid film, it is worth mentioning the experiments of Glauber Rocha, continuing the movement of *Cinema Novo* founded by Nelson Pereira dos Santos. Glauber has obtained international fame with his many creative ventures, one of the most famous being *Antonio das Mortes.* His first film, *Barravento* (1961), merits consideration in our discussion of Black participation on the cultural level in Brazilian film. It is a work which uses strong and beautiful images of the life and customs of a village of Black fishermen in the interior of Bahia. The nerve center of the film is the contrast between tradition and the conquests of modern technological life. In this case it is represented in the contrast or conflict between the beliefs of Afro-Brazilian religion and the dynamics of class struggle. The artistic quality of the film does not stop with the defense of a theory, and various paths of resolution remain open to contemplation and interpretation.

One of the most promising attempts in Afro-Brazilian film is *Ganga Zumba* (1968) by Carlos Diegues. A retrospective look at African history in Brazil, focalizing on Zumbi, the last king of Palmares, when he is still a young slave. We accompany on the screen the future hero's escape from captivity and struggle against his pursuers, opening the path to the Black Troy, where he will soon assume command of the struggle for liberation of the race.

Let us return to the work of Nelson Pereira dos Santos, who in *Vidas Secas* (Barren Lives, 1963) based on the book of the same title by Graciliano Ramos, represents another turning point in the development of Brazilian film. A fleeting but powerful statement of race relations comes when the protagonist, a poor peasant, hungry and miserable victim of the drought which periodically devastates the Northeast of Brazil, attempts to confront the contemptuous and unjust treatment meted out to him by the all-powerful landowner and cattle rancher boss. He bursts out, in a flare of repressed anger, in words to the effect of "Do you think I'm a nigger?" This phrase, in the mouth of such a hero, accurately rebuts the frequent allegation that in the lower classes suffering from poverty there is no racial prejudice. The same can be said of another moment in his later film *Amuleto de Ogum* (1974), where the leader of a group of marginal outlaws asks about a young bandit aspiring to be admitted to the gang, "But at least he's not a nigger, is he?", or words to that effect.

Amuleto de Ogum offers a glimpse of the definition of Afro-Brazilian culture that Nelson Pereira dos Santos will later develop more profoundly: a magic culture, with positive, constructive values, its own intrinsic power and validity, and a persuasive spiritual force that transcends the limitations of conventional faith and wisdom, as well as the boundaries of the Black community, to embrace enormous sectors of the "white," traditionally Aryan-aspiring population.

The culminating work of this creator thus far, however, is in the incomparable film *Tenda dos Milagres* (Tent of Miracles), made in 1977 and executed with a socio-historical insight and cinematographic subtlety that have no percedent in Brazilian film. Its unmasking of the racial hypocrisy of the Bahian dominant society (white or Aryanoid) is taken to its ultimate consequences. The socio-ethnic analysis that the filmmaker evolves is valid for the entire country. One of the most beautiful and useful films that Brazil has produced, *Tenda dos Milagres* can be criticized only for its implicit and explicit endorsement of the ideology of mulattization or miscegenation as it has been practiced for centuries in Brazil. For the film's critique of the racist orientation of Brazilian scientific convention stops with the exposure of explicit theories of white supremacy, disappointingly and rather artificially avoiding delving into the more subtly racist content of scientific advocacy of mixture of races. The truth is that we are dealing with a colonialist-reactionary theory preached by Jorge Amado, author of the book on which the film is based. "Mulattization" is the ethno-genetic counterpart of the policy of "cultural assimilation" made famous by certain European colonial powers in Africa and used in Black communities in Western multiethnic societies. It means Aryanization through the absorption of African ethno-cultural identity. Along with Amilcar Cabral, we consider it dangerous and unacceptable,

> ... not only from the theoretical point of view but even more so in practice. It is founded on the racist idea of the "incapability and lack of dignity" of Africans and it implies that African cultures and civilizations have no value. (1975: 77)

The ideology of miscegenation or "mulattization" defended in *Tenda dos Milagres* is a *modification* of Victorian white supremacy, not its opposite. (see Skidmore 1974, Nascimento 1977 and the essay by Joan R. Dassin "Inside the Tent of Miracles," unpublished as yet, written for the cinema magazine *Jump Cut,* special issue dedicated to Brazilian film). The film, so effective in its exposure of the racist fundaments of Brazilian science, fails its own insight when it neglects to deal with the implications of miscegenation ideology.

Despite this shortcoming, *Tenda dos Milagres* remains the most courageous and definitive statement yet made by a Brazilian filmmaker on the history of race relations in my

160

country. Certainly any criticism of Brazilian cinema must be made with due consideration of the limitations imposed by government censorship, arbitrary and implacable. Nelson Pereira dos Santos has overcome both the formidable obstacle of censorship and the more subtle coercion of entrenched racial ideology, to make a lucid and creative statement, of artistic and intellectual integrity, in *Tenda dos Milagres*.

One very promising development in the perspective of a meaningful Brazilian-African cinema is appearing with the collaboration of Brazilian and African actors, producers, and directors. The first step has been taken with the making of *Deusa Negra* (Black Goddess), directed by the talented Nigerian cinematographer Ola Balogun, which has not been released at the time of this writing. It was filmed in Brazil.

Whatever the merits of these developments, however, a valid Afro-Brazilian film will not be achieved until Black Brazilians themselves are able to overcome the obstacles to their creative activity and penetrate into the fields of directing, producing and writing films. Such work, of course, cannot be considered truly Afro-Brazilian unless it makes creative attempts to deal seriously with Black experience, socio-economic, religious, aesthetic and cultural, and political, in Brazil. Purely commercial, folkloric, picturesque or sexual exploitation of Blacks by Blacks in film will simply represent a continuation of the current situation with sad implications of betrayal the only added elements.

Afro-Brazilian Theater: TEN

With its great power to penetrate and illuminate the most profound regions of the human soul; with its capacity to reveal hidden aspects of the history of men and the societies they create, dramatic theater exercises a role more than relevant in the function of art as a liberating force. It should be clear that I do not refer to the presentation of picturesque dances or of folklore. I am speaking of dramatic theater in its real artistic sense: using the verbal and visual, the poetic and plastic resources of drama to articulate problems, ideas, beliefs, experiences; proposing paths of change, pointing the way to the assumption of the Black and African Revolution in its most radical engagement.

In this field of creative endeavor Black Brazilians have sustained a tenacious and arduous struggle. Anyone who is familiar with the evolution of Brazilian theater will remember the role of divider of waters played by the *Teatro Experimental do Negro - TEN* (Black Experimental Theater), founded in Rio de Janeiro in 1944 by myself and the late Aguinaldo Camargo, the finest actor Brazil has yet produced, Black or white, and many other persons of courage, vitality and excellence. We were not a group that simply wished to present a few plays on the stages of Brazilian theaters within the dominant norms including stereotype, white actors in blackface, plays reflecting the white culture's aesthetics, problems and situations. Attempting to counteract the forces of cultural Aryanization through dynamic work and constant research, TEN trained a body of Black dramatic actors and actresses, the first that had existed outside the stereotypes mentioned earlier. At the same time it stimulated the creation of dramatic texts in which Black experience was reflected, where the Black artist could search and explore, with respect and dignity, his own human and humanistic personality and values.

Our objective in the TEN was the liberation of Black people by means of education, culture, and art. The work was urgent on two fronts: to denounce the errors and alienation purveyed by the prevalent studies of the Afro-Brazilian, done by white conventional scholars; and to see that the Black himself became aware of the objective situation in which he found himself culturally, socially and aesthetically.

The first task of TEN was therefore to make literate the first participants, who were recruited from among workers, maids, slum-dwellers without any definite occupation, humble civil servants and the unemployed, and offer them new alternatives in attitude, a criterion and concept of their own value, a new vision of the position they occupied as Afro-Brazilians in the national context. We organized courses in reading and writing, the history of Africa and Africans in Brazil, the history of theater and art, dramatic literature of Africans in the Diaspora, and more. Indeed, a veritable university for consciousness raising among eager and knowledge-hungry Black Brazilians.

The next step was to find a play consonant with the artistic and social level of the movement. What repertory existed was terribly weak -- the few inferior plays in which the Black appeared ephemerally as comic element or local color. The most viable solution was *The Emperor Jones* by Eugene O'Neill, a play which sums up the experience of the Black man in the white world, where after having enslaved him, they "free" him, cast him into the lowest levels of society, and teach him that the only way to survive is by fraud, tricks, robbery. Having degraded and humiliated him, they ultimately send him to confront the fact of his own perdition. We requested the author's permission to produce the play without royalty payments, and received the following answer from O'Neill in his sickbed in San Francisco:

> You have my permission to produce *The Emperor Jones* without any payment to me, and I want to wish you all the success you hope for with your Teatro Experimental do Negro. I know very well the conditions you describe in the Brazilian theatre. We had exactly the same conditions here in our theatre before *The Emperor Jones* was produced in New York in 1920: parts of any consequence were always played by blacked-up white actors. After *The Emperor Jones,* played originally by Charles Gilpin and later by Paul Robeson, made a great success, the way was open for the Black to play serious drama in our theatre. What hampers most now is the lack of plays, but I think before long there will be Black dramatists of real merit to overcome this lack. (Nascimento 1967: 41-42)

The reaction in Brazil to the formation of TEN and the announcement of our first production was not so enthusiastic. The atmosphere of pessimism and disbelief that a group of "ignorant negroes" could dare to undertake such a project is expressed in the words of critic Ascendino Leite:

> Our surprise was all the greater because of the doubts we had relative to the choice of repertory, which started no less than with the inclusion of an author of the strength of expression of O'Neill. We predicted that the Experimental Black Theater would be a resounding failure. And we had privately already thought about the criticisms we would make of the audacity of this group of actors, almost all

unknowns, who dared to come before a public that was already beginning to see in the theater more than entertainment and instead a more direct form of penetrating the heart of life and human nature. Aguinaldo Camargo in *The Emperor Jones* was therefore a revelation. (Nascimento 1967: 42-43)

The Black Experimental Theater had won its first victory; the Black actor's clownish phase on the Brazilian stage was over. *The Emperor Jones,* directed by myself and played by Aguinaldo Camargo, had struck the first blow at white monopoly of the stages of dramatic theater in Brazil. Grande Otelo would still exhibit his comic ability, which is tremendous. But now it was known that other paths were open. Only the blindness or ill-will of producers would prevent the public from coming to experience what Grande Otelo and his fellow Afro-Brazilian actors and dramatists, directors and producers, were capable of. In the Municipal Theater of Rio de Janeiro, where never before had any Black person set foot, on the stage or in the audience, except to clean, the Black Experimental Theater had, on May 8, 1945, presented an Afro-Brazilian production. R. Magalhães Junior of the Brazilian Academy of Letters and a playwright himself, exemplifies the critical reception of *The Emperor Jones:*

> The opening production of the Teatro Experimental do Negro merits repetition because it was a notable production. Notable for several reasons. For its assured and firm direction. For the splendid and artistic sets by Enrico Bianco. And for the masterful interpretation by Aguinaldo de Oliveira Camargo of the role of Jones. (Nascimento 1967: 43)

This first victory opened the road for the second phase, that Eugene O'Neill had emphasized in his letter: the creation of Afro-Brazilian plays for the Afro-Brazilian actors and their stages. In 1947 Lúcio Cardoso's *O Filho Pródigo* (The Prodigal Son) was written, and it was the first of a group of Afro-Brazilian plays produced and inspired by the work of the TEN. Using the deities and religious context of Black culture in Brazil, Joaquim Ribeiro's *Aruanda,* produced by TEN immediately after *O Filho Pródigo,* studies the effects of cultural assimilation and juxtaposes it with the real circumstances brought to the fore by African religious possession.

There is one author who divides Brazilian theater into two phases, modern and pre-modern. Nelson Rodrigues ushered in the age of modern theater with his unprecedented creative drama. In 1946 he wrote *Anjo Negro* (Black Angel), a penetrating study of race relations with an entirely new level of tragic language. The play presents a study of a Black/white marriage, in which the circumstances of color breed a morbid hypersensitivity that turns the protagonists, Virginia and Ismael, into two hermetic, implacable islands incapable of communication. They are monsters bred by racism, which in this play has its most beautiful and terrible condemnation. In the words of Roger Bastide, this play is "... the one that penetrates most deeply into the revelation of the ideology of whitening that we have criticized because it is nothing but a hypocritical form of genocide." (1972: 4) Unfortunately, its production in 1948 by the Maria della Costa Company did not measure up to the creative authenticity of Nelson Rodrigues' creation. The director, Ziembinski, overplayed the aesthetic elements of the play to the detriment of the racial content. Worse, he conformed to the usual "artistic norm" of blacking up a white actor to play the part of Ismael. Indeed, Maria della Costa herself repeated this artistic calamity once more when she put on *Gimba,* by Camargo Guarnieri, in which she wore blackface to play the leading role of the mulatto woman from the hillside slums.

This situation was repeated with *Pedro Mico* by Antonio Callado in 1957. Callado's play, a work of major importance, was sacrificed in its production by the National Comedy Theater, an institution of the Ministry of Education and Culture, by the presentation of a caricaturesque figure of Pedro Mico by a white actor in stove-black. The racist excuse of the director, Paulo Francis, was to allege that there was a lack of Black actors. The usual pretext...

These two works illustrate the reaction and reception of Brazilian authorities to the new genre of Afro-Brazilian plays, through another common circumstance, one which they share with *Sortilégio (Mistério Negro)*, my own play, written in 1951. This circumstance is their repression by censorship. *Anjo Negro,* after having several difficulties with the censors, was selected to be part of the repertory of the official season of the Municipal Theater of Rio de Janeiro. The authorities imposed one absolute condition: that the main role be played by a white actor in blackface. It seems that they were afraid that after the performance, the actor playing Ismael, if he were Black, would join up with other hungry niggers and go out on the streets to find a white woman to rape. It may sound like a joke, but there was no humor in the situation. The play was not put on. The blackface performance of *Pedro Mico* by a white actor was mandated for similar reasons: the press loudly expressed the great apprehension of certain classes that the play might incite the Black *favela* population to some direct action. They were afraid that the *favelados* would come down from their hills and create havoc and destruction, aroused by the example of Pedro Mico, who tries to repeat the deeds of Zumbi, leader of Palmares and legendary hero of the Black people. A Black actor playing Pedro Mico constituted a threat to private property and persons -- it being quite clear exactly which "persons" those were.

Sortilégio was banned by the censors for six years, on the grounds of "immorality" of language, despite the author's intense efforts to free it from suppression. It was forbidden from Brazilian stages from 1951 to 1957, when at last it was produced at the Municipal Theater in Rio de Janeiro and in São Paulo. The prohibitions by official censorship have marked for history the attitude of Brazil's dominant classes to the Black's assumption of his historical protagonism. It shows the threat felt by these strata when the Black people make any move toward altering the real nature of the "racial democracy" of Brazil, as expressed in this widely known popular saying: "In Brazil there is no racism. The negro knows his place."

Afro-Brazilian dramatic texts are collected in an anthology which I compiled, entitled *Dramas para Negros e Prólogo para Brancos* (Nascimento (ed.) 1961). It includes the following plays: *Auto da Noiva* (Rite of the Betrothed) by Rosário Fusco;

O Castigo de Oxalá by Romeu Crusoé; *Além do Rio* (Beyond the River) by Agostinho Olavo; *Filhos de Santo* (Children of God) by José de Morais Pinho; *O Emparedado* by Tasso da Silveira; and the four we have already mentioned: *Anjo Negro, O Filho Pródigo, Sortilégio* and *Aruanda*. An English language version of the anthology has been prepared, including six of these plays as well as *A História de Oxala* (The Story of Oxala) by Zora Seljan. This translation awaits a publisher. In his Introduction to the English edition, Roger Bastide gives brief impressions of some of the plays. A sample of his reactions:

> *Auto da Noiva* (Rite of the Betrothed) retakes the whitening ideology but, through a wise humorous strategy, turns it against the whites who created it for their own profit after the suppression of the Black to servile work. It is the most beautiful inversion of whitening that I have come across... Rosário Fusco makes, out of a systematic policy of the white man, a boomerang that turns against its maker to bless his death.

> *Aruanda* is a Bantu-Caboclo myth that creates men of today, ruled by African gods, the masters of their destinies.

> *A História de Oxalá* (The Story of Oxala) by Zora Seljan, is a Yoruba myth that was kept in Brazil in the interior of the *Candomblés*.

> *Sortilégio* by Abdias do Nascimento occupies in Brazilian literature, exactly the same place that *Native Son* occupies in Afro-American literature of the United States. Certain phrases answer back, from one hemisphere to the other, from Richard Wright to Abdias do Nascimento, demonstrating the *fundamental* unity of the Black Americas, beyond the diversification of ideologies, the political situations and the various strategies of the white man... A rotating blade born of fear, that establishes crime as an expression of revolt, of liberation.

(1972: 4)

The Black Experimental Theater in Brazil did not stop at producing plays and dramatic literature. It was also an active organizer of Blacks in the process of conscientization and social revindication. The TEN organized the Afro-Brazilian Democratic Committee in 1945. Under TEN's patronage, two sessions were held of the National Black Convention, in São

Paulo in 1945 and in Rio de Janeiro in 1946. It organized the National Black Conference in 1949, the forerunner of the First Congress of Brazilian Blacks in 1950 in Rio de Janeiro, also under the aegis of the Black Experimental Theater. In 1955 we held the Week of the Black People, a series of cultural events including debates, panel discussions, speeches and conferences. The documents, speeches and debate of the First Congress are compiled in a book called *O Negro Revoltado* (The Black in Revolt) (Nascimento 1968). TEN also published the newspaper *Quilombo,* a journal of cultural and current events of the Afro-Brazilian community in 1949 and 1950.

The birth of the Black Experimental Theater also inspired the organization of other Black groups in different areas. Blacks in São Paulo formed a Black Experimental Theater which produced among many other works, Langston Hughes' play *The Mulatto.* Langston Hughes also exempted us from royalty payments. In Rio de Janeiro the Brazilian Popular Theater was founded by the Black poet Solano Trindade, inspired by the production of *Aruanda* by TEN, with the objective of bringing to the stage Brazilian folklore in its purity and integrity. Milton Gonçalves organized the short-lived Action Group in Rio de Janeiro.

To look retrospectively at the facts of our existential vicissitudes does not mean that we are advocating the immobilization of our future with an emphasis on the past. I am not suicidal or nostalgicist. But I believe I have demonstrated, throughout these pages, what has been the function of art in the development of Afro-Brazilian culture in all its phases: a) to maintain and enrich the values of African cultural origin in their eminent universal significance and not simply as "curiosity," "picturesque events," "folklore," "primitivity," or "ethnographic material." b) To sustain the humanity of the African people and their Afro-Brazilian descendants in their specific ethno-spiritual identity, transforming them from *object* to *subject-protagonist* of their own history. c) Utilizing all forms of artistic manifestation (song and dance, sculpture and painting, literature, metalwork in iron, silver, gold, ceramics, dress and cuisine, film and theater) to conquer the maximum

168

liberty as much on an individual and interior level as on the collective social, economic, political and cultural levels of Black existence. d) To critically expose the Aryan structures of domination over Black people, in Brazil and also in other parts of the world. e) To enrich and elevate Afro-Brazilian culture to the level of an original civilization, through the creation of artistically significant work elaborated from an intrinsic aesthetic and world-view immune to the cultural domestication of Aryanoid and European-aspiring ruling classes.

The survival and persistence of the Black people in Brazil owes a fundamental debt to the action and influence of art in an environment where everything negates and works against our continued existence. It is my profound conviction that Afro-Brazilian art, with the stimulation and support of independent Africa, the inspiration and guidance of Afro-Brazilian religion, and the support and example of the strengths, struggles and consciousness of our brothers in Africa and her Diaspora in all parts of the world, is revitalizing itself, growing more aggressive in its liberating protagonism. Without abdicating its intrinsic qualities of artistically elaborated creation; with the loving care of Oxum, the heat and light of the fires of Xangô, Afro-Brazilian art will wield the arms forged by Ogum and assume the responsibility that befits it in this Black-African dawn against colonialism and white supremacy. The dawn of the struggle which Exu is articulating and unleashing from the four cardinal points as the irresistible phenomenon of our century.

-O', Yemanjá, our mother and mother of all the Orixás
        sovereign of the waters of eternity:
                Odomi! Odoceiaba!

- I proclaim the omni-science of Ifa,
        master of the mysteries of existence
        and of human history:
                Saravá!

- I invoke the healing power of Omolu,
        doctor of the poor and the dispossessed:
                Saravá!

\- Hail Oxunmarê,
    rainbow of alliance between deities and mortals:
              Saravá!

\- I salute the purifying winds of Oya-Yansan,
    source of lightning and storms
    of liberation:
              Eparrei!

\- Honor and Glory to Obatala,
    founder of our human race
    founder of our sacred primal city of Ile-Ife
    founder of the world:
              Saravá!

                              Saravá!

BIBLIOGRAPHY

Abimbola, Wande (1976) "The Yoruba Traditional Religion in Brazil: Problems and Prospects." Faculty Seminar, Department of African Languages and Literatures, University of Ife, October 18. (Unpublished)

ADJA - Orgão Cultural Afro-Brasileiro (1978) Editorial "Presidente Ernesto Geisel na cultura Afro-Brasileira." Rio de Janeiro, January/February (Ano I, no. 1), p. 1.

Alakija, George (1977) *The Trance State in the "Candomblé."* Published by Official Delegation of the Brazilian Government to Festac '77, Lagos. Designated "Colloquium: Black Civilization and Science and Technology."

Anonymous (1975) "Apoio aos Orixás," *Veja.* São Paulo: December 10, pp. 52-53.

Bastide, Roger (1971) *African Civilizations in the New World* (translated by Peter Green). New York: Harper and Row Publishers.

- (1972) "Introduction" to *Afro-Brazilian Drama: An Anthology of Seven Plays,* (English Edition of Nascimento, ed., 1961) translated by Erica Fritz and Elisa Larkin Nascimento . (Unpublished)

- (1973) *Estudos Afro-Brasileiros.* São Paulo: Editora Perspectiva.

Bastide, Roger et. al. (1968) *Colloque Sur l'Art Negre.* Paris: Présence Africaine.

Cabral, Amilcar (1975) *L'Arme de la Theorie.* Paris: Francoise Maspero.

Coelho, Lélia Frota (1974) "Criação individual e coletividade," in catalogue *7 Brasileiros e seu Universo.* Brasília: Ministério da Educação e Cultura.

Dantas, Raimundo Sousa et. al. (1975) "Abdias e a questão racial." Public debate transcribed in *Crítica* (edited by Gerardo Mello Mourão). Rio de Janeiro: June 16-22 (Ano I, no. 25).

171

Dunham, Katherine (1950) "O estado dos cultos entre os povos deserdados." Lecture transcribed in *Quilombo*. Rio de Janeiro: June-July (Ano II, no. 10), pp. 6-7, 10.

Freire, Paulo (1975) *Pedagogia do Oprimido*. Porto: Afrontamento.

Freyre, Gilberto (1966) *Casa Grande e Senzala,* 14th edition, 2 vols. Rio de Janeiro: José Olympio Editora.

- (1976) "Aspectos da influencia africana no Brasil," *Cultura*. Brasília: Ministério da Educação e Cultura, October-December (Ano VI, no. 23), pp. 6-19.

Goldwater, Robert (1967) *Primitivism in Modern Art*. New York: Vintage Books.

Mourão, Gerardo Mello (1957) *"Sortilégio,"* program of Municipal Theater production of Nascimento 1960. Rio de Janeiro: Teatro Experimental do Negro.

Nascimento, Abdias do (1960) *Sortilégio (Mistério Negro)*. Rio de Janeiro: Teatro Experimental do Negro.

-(1967) "The Negro Theater in Brazil" (translated by Gregory Rabassa), *African Forum*. New York: The American Society of African Culture, Spring (Vol. II, no. 4), pp. 35-53.)

- (1976) "Afro-Brazilian Art: a Liberating Spirit" (translated by Elisa Larkin Nascimento), in *Black Art: an International Quarterly*. New York: Black Art, Ltd., Fall (Vol. I, no. 1), pp. 54-62.

- (1977) *"Racial Democracy" in Brazil: Myth or Reality?* (translated by Elisa Larkin Nascimento). Ibadan: Sketch Publishing Co.

Nascimento, Abdias do (ed.) (1961) *Dramas para Negros e Prólogo para Brancos*. Rio de Janeiro: Teatro Experimental do Negro.

- (1966) *Teatro Experimental do Negro - Testemunhos*. Rio de Janeiro: Edições GRD.

New Appleton Dictionary of the English and Portuguese Languages (1967) eds. Antonio Houaiss and Catherine B. Avery. New York: Appleton-Century-Crofts.

Ogunsanya, Ebun Omowunmi (1971) "Residual Yoruba-Portuguese Bilingualism." B.A. Thesis, Harvard University, Cambridge Mass. (Unpublished)

Olinto, Antonio (1967) "The Negro Writer and the Negro Influence in Brazilian Literature" (translated by Gregory Rabassa), *African Forum*. New York: The American Society of African Culture, Spring (Vol. II, no. 4), pp. 5-19.

Pierson, Donald (1942) *Negroes in Brazil*. Carbondale and Edwardsville: Southern Illinois University Press.

Ramos, Arthur (1946) *As Culturas Negras no Novo Mundo*. São Paulo: Companhia Editora Nacional.

Ramos, Guerreiro (1957) *Introdução Crítica à Sociologia Brasileira*. São Paulo: Editorial Andes.

- (1966A) "O negro desde dentro," in Nascimento (ed.) 1966.

- (1966B) "Semana do Negro de 1955," in Nascimento (ed.) 1966, p. 142.

Rodrigues, Nina (1945) *Os Africanos no Brasil*, 3rd edition. São Paulo: Companhia Editora Nacional.

Santos, Deoscoredes Maximiliano dos (Mestre Didi) (1961) *Contos Negros da Bahia*. Rio de Janeiro: Edições GRD.

- (1963) *Contos Nagô*. Rio de Janeiro: Edições GRD.

- (1976) *Contos Crioulos da Bahia*. Petrópolis: Editora Vozes. (Preface by Muniz Sodré)

Santos, Juana Elbein dos (1977) *Os Nagô e a Morte*, 2nd edition. Petrópolis: Editora Vozes.

Seljan, Zora (1967) "Negro Popular Poetry in Brazil," (translated by Gregory Rabassa), *African Forum*. New York: The American Society of African Culture, Spring (Vol. II, no. 4), pp. 54-77.

Skidmore, Thomas E. (1974) *Black into White*. New York: Oxford University Press.

Şoyinka, Wọle (1975) "An Interview with Louis S. Gates," *Black World.* Chicago: August (Vol. XXIV, no. 10), pp. 30-48.

Turner, Doris J. (1975) "Symbols in Two Afro-Brazilian Literary Works: *Jubiabá* and *Sortilégio.*" Commissioned by the Latin American Studies Association and Consortium of Latin American Studies Programs. Delivered at National Seminar on the Teaching of Latin American Studies, University of New Mexico, Albuquerque. (Unpublished)

Valladares, Clarival do Prado (1966) "A defasagem africana ou Cronica do Io Festival de Artes Negras," in *Cadernos Brasileiros.* Rio de Janeiro: July-August (Ano VIII, no. 36).

- (1974) "Sobre o comportamento arcaico brasileiro nas artes populares," in catalogue *7 Brasileiros e seu Universo.* Brasília: Ministério da Educação e Cultura.

- (1977) *On the Ascendancy of Africa in the Brazilian Arts.* Published by the Official Delegation of the Brazilian Government to Festac '77, Lagos. Designated "Colloquium: Black Civilization and the Arts."'

Verger, Pierre (1977) "African Religions and the Valorization of of Brazilians of African Descent" (translated by W.F. Feuser). Faculty Seminar, Department of African Languages and Literatures, University of Ife, February 21. (Unpublished)

Viana, Oliveira (1938) *Raça e Assimilação,* 3rd edition. São Paulo: Companhia Editora Nacional.

Vizo, Hortensia Ruiz del (ed.) (1972) *Black Poetry of the Americas (A Bilingual Anthology).* Miami: Ediciones Universal.

Webster's Collegiate Thesaurus (1976) Ed. Mairé Weir Kay. Springfield: G&C Merriam Co.

Webster's Seventh New Collegiate Dictionary (1971) Ed. Philip B. Gove. Springfield: G&C Merriam Co.

Yai, Ọlabiyi Babalọla (1976) "Alguns aspectos da influencia das culturas nigerianas no Brasil em literatura, folclore e linguagem," *Cultura*. Brasília: Ministério da Educação e Cultura, October-December (Ano VI, no. 23), pp. 94-100.

CHAPTER 4

AFRO-BRAZILIAN ETHNICITY
AND
INTERNATIONAL POLICY

these ideas were originally developed
in my speech to the National Black
Leadership Symposium on the War in
Southern Africa in African Liberation
Day Celebration sponsored by the
All-African People's Revolutionary Party
May 21-23, 1976
Washington, D.C.
U.S.A.

and

were discussed at the Scandi-
navian Symposium "Brazil at
the Doorstep of the Decade of
the 80's"
December 1-4, 1978
Stockholm, Sweden

paper presented to
First Congress on Black
Culture in the Americas
August 24-28, 1977
Cali, Colombia

I, for one, would like to impress, especially upon those who call themselves leaders, the importance of realizing the direct connection between the struggle of the Afro-American in this country and the struggle of our people all over the world. As long as we think - as one of my good brothers mentioned out of the side of his mouth here a couple of Sundays ago - that we should get Mississippi straightened out before we worry about the Congo, you'll never get Mississippi straightened out. Not until you start realizing your connection with the Congo.

Malcolm X Speaks

Here in this historic assembly, the First Congress of Black Culture in the Americas, where for the first time in four centuries the African descendants of the Americas have an opportunity to meet together, I am highly honored and happy to represent, as an Afro-Brazilian, the Project on African Cultures in the Diaspora, of the University of Ife in Ile-Ife, Nigeria. The University is located in the neighborhood of the very city where Obatala, sent by Olorum his father, descended over the inchoate waters of Olokun to create the earth and human beings. Ile-Ife signifies for the black African world not only the cradle of our existence, but also the place where the modes of black artistic creation reached their highest peaks in technique and symbolic significance. It was as if I were practicing a ritual return to my origins, when I stayed there for one year as Visiting Professor in the Department of African Languages and Literatures. During that stay I was able to witness firsthand what is being realized in that beautiful institution of advanced learning, in the sense of attending to the exigencies of the reconstruction of an Africa that for centuries suffered colonialist destruction. And in this movement to recover the physical and spiritual riches of Africa, the University of Ife, of which I consider myself spiritually a permanent member, in its wisdom included among its preoccupations the Africans of the Diaspora: we here reunited and all those whom the circumstances of history scattered to the four corners of the universe. But the diaspora in this epoch of human history has an inverse sense of dispersion: we are the diaspora that turns itself in a concentric rhythm toward the pristine center of historic and spiritual origin of our ancestors. We salute the hour of Africa! We hail the inaugural hour of the ascent of Black people of the Americas, and our collective effort to organize the future according to our own definition and determination.

In the terms and space of this informal communication there is not room for a detailed analysis, or an exhaustive one, of the experience of Africans and their descendants in Brazil, who constitute an Afro-Brazilian ethnicity of almost 80 millions of Blacks and mulattoes, in a country of 115 million inhabitants. Be it emphasized from the start that this is an ethnic group

179

fenced in by a system of pressures that range from prejudice and discrimination, veiled and dissimulated, to psychological and cultural aggressions, and the open violence of police. This fabric of subtle or explicit violence has transformed Brazilian Blacks into victims of an internal colonization of unparalleled cruelty in history. Since the times of slavery, the African and his descendant, the Brazilian Black people, have been subjected to a consummate technique of elimination which is characterized by the form of implacable genocide. Thus the Afro-Brazilian -- be he *negro* (Black), mulatto, *moreno* (brunette), *pardo* (brown), *escuro* (dark), *crioulo* (Black Brazilian), or any of those euphemisms of African descent in various gradations of epidermic color and ethnic classification -- forms a human group condemned to disappearance. For such is the rhythm, the logic of the racial policies of Brazil.

The aggressions of which blacks are victims can be found on the physical/biological level, in the *ideology of whiteness,* which dictates that they must turn progressively lighter in color, through miscegenation, in order to obtain better living conditions, employment opportunities, social relations and respect, in short, to fully exercise their very human condition and citizenship. On the order of economic aggression operates perhaps the most intensely negative factor, throwing Blacks into unemployment and underemployment, subverting their domestic organization and personality, leaving them without resources to attend to their minimal necessities of housing, education, health, etc. The collusion of these factors of criminal and inhuman racism is described and documented in detail in a recent work of the present author (1977), entitled *"Racial Democracy" in Brazil: Myth or Reality?.* Here I can only reiterate some of the already divulged notions, which are crystallized in various stereotypes that for centuries have constituted the identity of the African and the image of Black people still dominant in Brazilian society. The situation is quite complex, and it looms as an obstacle, almost insuperable, impeding, denying to the African-Brazilian his basic right to a peaceful and creative existence based on self-respect and security.

One of the reasons for the long duration of slavery, which legally lasted in Brazil from 1500 to May 13, 1888 -- and thus my country was the last in the Americas to abolish this atrocious economic system -- was emphasized by historian Nelson Werneck Sodré in his book *Formação Economica do Brasil* (Economic Development of Brazil): "... the African slave is marked by his color, which is like a label." (1970: 248) The obvious implication is that ever since the beginnings of colonization there existed an identification -- race/color -- marking the presence of the African. It is important to underline this fact because of the great role it shall play when we analyse the factors that produce racism. Various ideologues of racism, whether through mistaken notions, ingenuousness, or maliciousness, make a habit of appealing to conceptual metaphors like "the exclusive relation of *master* and *slave*" which would be possible only on a purely subjective plane. Not by any means can it be said that by coincidence or quirk of fate Black Africans are the only people of all times to have been subjected to the chattel slavery of Europeans. It is only futile and facile escapism to deny the fact that the slaves' bondage was inextricably bound up with their *race;* a fact easily confirmed by the enslavement of the white masters' own sons and daughters of mixed blood. Yet many of our own best minds fall into such a fallacy.

What is curious in this treatment of the matter is that the occurrence conjoins researchers, scientists, writers and ideologues of all tendencies, including those of the so-called left. In Brazil they pontificate theories and behave pragmatically, when it comes to the anti-racist struggles of the black people, by directly following the models and definitions of the ruling strata, exclusively white or white-aspiring: a society which for centuries has been immersed in a culture that is intrinsically prejudiced and prejudicial to the Black. We see reactionaries sustaining the liberal-paternalist myth of "racial democracy," a formula of domestication that is extremely efficient in perpetuating, transfigured, the concepts of inferior race predominant in the past, today out of mode. But let there be no mistake: in essence nothing has changed. For the dominant classes, exploitation, disdain toward the Afro-Brazilian and his aspirations remain inalterable. The Brazilian left, with its endorsement of "racial democracy" or with its systematic refusal to see social facts objectively, implicitly supports the most retrograde positions regarding the possibilities of a society truly multiracial and multicultural. The attempt to mask racism, or better, the custom of substituting its identity by labelling racism as a simple accident in the dialectics of class, in practice becomes a valuable service to the anti-national forces that threaten the legitimate interests of the Brazilian people, of whom African descendants are more than half. As such, we constitute a majority to whom is denied not only our inalienable original identity, but also our right to reclaim it.

Those who act in this way reinforce the manipulations of the reactionary right, collaborate with the elites of Aryan origin, in the propagation outside the country of a false image. According to it, Blacks, after the abolition of slavery in 1888, in the words of Marxist historian Caio Prado, Jr., would have been integrated and absorbed "... by the new social order and economic structure in which they came to participate, and which conditioned them entirely in their culture and personality." (1966: 222) Following this line, assuming such postulates, Brazil goes on to become a rich exporter of models. The model of cruel military dictatorship fancied as democratic revolution. The model of giving away the country's resources to the multi-nationals, with the blessings of the "economic miracle." The model of ethnic oppression and genocide under the label "racial democracy."

We mentioned previously the constant pressures and threats to which Afro-Brazilians are subjected inside the borders of our country. The opportunity arises to point out that external threats are also configured in this scheme, as of now looming not only before Black Brazilians, but also before Africans and their descendants in every part of the world. I refer to an old project, which presently is being once more dynamized by virtue of the contingencies in the dispute for influence and power among the world giants: the Alliance or Treaty of the South Atlantic.

182

Let us look rapidly at the behavior and attitudes of Brazil in questions and decisions on her international policy. In this area, obviously, Blacks have never participated nor had a voice. In fact, as a group or community, Afro-Brazilians have never participated, on any level, in power: be it economic, political or administrative; be it judicial, executive or legislative. Never have they belonged to the circles of decision-making, even in matters that affect them immediately, much less in the international policy of the country. For example, Blacks have never been heard when in the United Nations the decolonization of the African continent is discussed or voted on. During the entire process of decolonization Brazil voted with Portugal -- that is, against independence for the colonies of Guinea Bissau, Angola and Mozambique. At times Brazil opted for the recourse of abstention, which in practice is the same as the voting against.

Portugal inaugurated the historical epoch of imperialist aggression in Africa when, in 1482, Diogo Cão "discovered" the Congo. From this point on, until about 1945, the end of the second world war, European colonizers -- large and small -- took upon themselves the mission of "civilizing" slices of African territory, which they sacked, terrorized and enslaved in the name of Christ. Portugal, having been the first to enter, was the last to leave Africa -- following, it would seem, a sort of family tradition in which Brazil participated by being the last in the Americas to abolish slavery...

The foreign policy of Brazil is based upon, and indeed subordinate to, colonialist interests of all species and forms. Our own President, Juscelino Kubitchek, declared that Brazil's foreign policy was the same as Portugal's, going to the extreme of stating that our independence had been a "gift" from Portugal. (Rodrigues 1964: 395) Brazil signed a Treaty of Friendship and Consultation with Portugal on November 16, 1953, in the time of Getúlio Vargas' presidency. The treaty favored exclusively the international manipulations of Salazarist colonialism, in radical detriment to Africa. Around this time Portuguese writer Almerindo Lessa stated: "Brazil is and will increasingly be a cornerstone of our Atlantic policy, and specifically in our African action." (Rodrigues 1964: 356) A

183

statement of predictive truth, as we shall see below.

To this line of activity in the United Nations and the wider context of international politics is aligned a tendency of Brazilian thought which has in Gilberto Freyre one of its most conspicuous representatives. Freyre took on a role of veritable justifying ideologue of Portuguese colonialism. He began the praise and valorization of the Portuguese in Brazil with his book *Casa Grande e Senzala* (Mansions and Shanties), following with a celebration of Lusian superiority in colonizing the tropics in another work entitled *O Mundo que o Português Criou* (The World that the Portuguese Created).

Under such ideological direction Brazil voted in the U.N. in favor of Portugal when, in 1957, the euphemism of Portuguese colonialism designating her colonies in Africa as "provinces" was discussed. (Rodrigues 1964: 366) The Ministers of Foreign Relations of Brazil -- be they formally entrenched in the most illustrious reactionarism as a Raul Fernandes, or socialist-laborite as a Hermes Lima, or of liberal-reactionary tendency as Negrão de Lima or Afonso Arinos de Melo Franco -- all of them facilitated, with their particular gestures, the expansion or permanence of Portuguese colonialism. One of them, Minister João Neves da Fontoura, with an amazing lack of decency, modesty or shame, declared in 1957: "Our policy with Portugal is not even a policy. It is family business." (Rodrigues 1964: 357)

In 1969, a Special Committee of the United Nations was created to investigate the implementation of the General Assembly's Declaration on the Granting of Independence to Colonial Countries and Peoples of December 14, 1960. This committee documented and reported on the continuing horrors of the colonial situation in all of Southern Africa (Rhodesia, Namibia and the Territories under Portuguese Administration). The Committee reported on the bloodletting and atrocities committed by Portugal in Africa, *condemning*

> ... the persistent refusal of the Government of Portugal to implement General Assembly resolution 1514 (XV) and all other relevant resolutions of the General Assembly, the Security Council and the Special Committee, as well as the

colonial war being waged by the Government against the peoples of the Territories under its domination, which constitutes a crime against humanity and a grave threat to international peace and security. (Report 1974: 115)

At the same time, the Committee declared itself

Deeply disturbed by the intensified activities of the foreign economic, financial and other interests which impede the realization of the legitimate aspirations of the African peoples in those Territories to self-determination and independence,

Noting further with profound concern that Portugal continues to receive aid in the form of military training, equipment, weapons and logistic and other assistance from certain States, and in particular from its military allies, which enables it to pursue its military operations against the population of those Territories. (114)

In a section entitled "International Relations of Portugal Affecting the Territories under its Administration," the Report devotes a whole subsection to "Luso-Brazilian relations:"

101. As reported previously (A/6700/Rev. 1, chap. V, paras. 91-93), in September 1966 Portugal and Brazil signed agreements on trade, technical and cultural cooperation and a joint declaration on economic cooperation. Instruments of ratification in these respects were exchanged between the two Governments only in March 1968, although both countries appear to have considered the provisions of the agreements to have taken earlier effect and the Economic Committee established under the provisions of the new trade agreement, had already met several times before that date.

102. In July 1968 Mr. Franco Nogueira noted that within the United Nations, the Governments of Portugal and Brazil took the same positions on the problem of international control of atomic energy, and that as a result, Portugal furnished Brazil with uranium completely free of any conditions. Later, in October, the Minister for Foreign Affairs of Brazil, Mr. Magalhães Pinto, said at a press conference in New York that the links of sentiment and friendship between Portugal and Brazil were very sincere and that in the General Assembly Brazil would vote against any measures hostile to Portugal; it would abstain

on sanctions against Portugal and vote against any proposal of a boycott.

103. For the first time in their history, in August 1968, Portugal and Brazil held joint naval manoeuvres in Brazilian waters. Participating Portuguese naval craft included the newly delivered frigates, the Admiral Pereira da Silva and the Admiral Gago Coutinho. (Report 1974: 149)

These actions and attitudes on the part of Brazil, of course, were in direct violation and persistent non-compliance with the many United Nations General Assembly resolutions condemning Portugal's colonial wars of aggression. Resolution 2395 (XXIII) of November 29, 1968,

5. *Appeals* to all States to grant the peoples of the Territories under Portuguese domination the moral and material assistance necessary for the restoration of their inalienable rights;

6. *Reiterates* its appeal to all States, and in particular to members of the North Atlantic Treaty Organization, to withhold from Portugal any assistance which enables it to prosecute the colonial war in the Territories under its domination;

9. *Urgently appeals* to all States to take all measures to prevent the recruitment or training in their territories of any persons as mercenaries for the colonial war being waged in the Territories under Portuguese domination and for violations of the territorial integrity and sovereignty of the independent African states;

11. *Deplores also* the activities of the financial interests operating in the Territories under Portuguese domination, which obstruct the struggle of the peoples for self-determination, freedom and independence and which strengthen the military efforts of Portugal. (Report 1974: 122)

Brazil ignored this and continued her collaboration with Salazarism.

In return for this collusion, this familiarity with that colonial impotency which imagined itself a potency, according to a denunciation made by Mr. Dadet of the Republic of the Congo

186

(Brazzaville) to the United Nations, Portugal offered Brazil a participation in its colonies as compensation for her help in maintaining the Portuguese Empire. (Rodrigues 1964: 4) José Honório Rodrigues sketches the perfect portrait of these events:

> We voted always with the colonial powers in the United Nations, we gave in to all the Portuguese pressure, that of the oligarchical government of Salazar or that which emanated from the colony, and from time to time we would mask our colonial alignment with abstentions. We had not one word of sympathy for African liberty.
>
> (1964:372)

To illustrate this fact we will list a few of the innumerable resolutions discussed and approved by the General Assembly of the United Nations, underlining the vote of Brazil. Of eleven resolutions supporting the independence of the Portuguese colonies in Africa, there were three votes by Brazil against, six abstentions (these can be counted as votes against), and two votes in favor, one of which, in 1974, took place on the eve of the winning of independence by the Africans, at a time when it was no longer possible to try to impede it.

In its single meaningful vote for independence, Brazil voted in favor of Resolution 2288 (XXII), adopted by the General Assembly on December 7, 1967 (Round-up, Session XXII, Part VI: 13-16). The resolution approves the report of the Special Committee on the Situation with regard to the Implementation of the Declaration on the Granting of Independence to Colonial Countries and Peoples in Southern Rhodesia, South West Africa and Territories under Portuguese domination and reiterates its call to all member states to support resolution 1514 (XV) and other relevant resolutions calling for decolonization.

A year later, however, when Resolution 2425 (XXIII) was voted on December 18, 1968, repeating essentially the same principles, Brazil abstained: Portugal and South Africa being the only countries to vote against. The United States took the same recourse of abstention along with the United Kingdom. This resolution contains the following clause:

> *Requests* all States to take practical measures to ensure that the activities of their nationals involved in economic, financial and other concerns in dependent Territories do

not run counter to the rights and interests of the colonial peoples in conformity with the objectives of resolution 1514 (XV) and other relevant resolutions (Round-up, Session XXIII, Part VI: 18-20)

This clause was the major difference from the 1967 resolution.

On November 21, 1969, the General Assembly adopted Resolution 2507 (XXIV), the first of these to deal specifically with the Portuguese government itself. A few of its clauses will be instructive here:

Condemns the persistent refusal of the Government of Portugal to implement resolution 1514 (XV) and all other relevant resolutions of the General Assembly and the Security Council; [...]
Deploring the aid which the Government of Portugal continues to receive. [...] *Urges* all States, and particularly the States of the North Atlantic Treaty Organization, to withhold or desist from giving further military and other assistance to Portugal which enables it to pursue the colonial war in the Territories under its domination.
(Resolutions, Session XXIV, VI: 3-5)

The resolution also

Reaffirms the inalienable right of the peoples of Angola, Mozambique and Guinea (Bissau) and of other territories under Portuguese domination to self-determination and independence in accordance with General Assembly resolution 1514 (XV);
Reaffirms the legitimacy of the struggle by the peoples of those Territories for their independence and freedom; [...]
Condemns the collaboration between Portugal, South Africa and the illegal racist minority regime in Southern Rhodesia, which is designed to perpetuate colonialism and oppression in Southern Africa;
Deplores the activities of the financial interests which obstruct the struggle of the peoples under Portuguese domination for self-determination, freedom and independence and which strengthen the military efforts of Portugal. (Resolutions, XXIV, VI: 4)

Brazil abstained on this resolution also. (6)

Resolution 2795 (XXVI) -- adopted on December 10, 1971 -- eloquently evokes the deteriorating situation of the Portuguese colonies and the progressively more intense violence and horror of Portuguese attacks on innocent Africans. In it the General

188

Assembly

> *Condemns* the indiscriminate bombing of civilians and the
> ruthless and wholesale destruction of villages and property
> being carried out by the Portuguese military forces in
> Angola, Mozambique and Guinea (Bissau); [...]
> *Calls upon* the Government of Portugal to refrain from
> the use of chemical substances in its colonial wars against
> the peoples of Angola, Mozambique and Guinea (Bissau),
> as such practice is contrary to the generally recognized
> rules of international law embodied in the Protocol for the
> Prohibition of the Use in War of Asphixiating, Poisonous
> or Other Gases, and of Bacteriological Methods of War-
> fare, signed at Geneva on 17 June 1925, and to General
> Assembly resolution 2707 (XXV) of 14 December 1970;
> *Calls upon* the Government of Portugal to treat the free-
> dom fighters of Angola, Mozambique and Guinea (Bissau)
> captured during the struggle for freedom as prisoners of
> war in accordance with the principles of the Geneva Con-
> vention relative to the Treatment of Prisoners of War, of
> 12 August 1949, and to comply with the Geneva Conven-
> tion relative to the Protection of Civilian Persons in Time
> of War, of 12 August 1949; [...]
> *Calls upon* all States to take immediate measures to put to
> an end all activities that help to exploit the Territories
> under Portuguese domination and the peoples therein and
> to discourage their nationals and bodies corporate under
> their jurisdiction from entering into any transactions or
> arrangements that strengthen Portugal's domination over,
> and impede the implementation of the Declaration with
> respect to, those Territories. (Resolutions, Sessions XXVI,
> Part VI: 7-12)

And, as the acts of Portugal become graver and more horrible,
the support given by Brazil to those acts becomes more
adamant: this time Brazil voted against.

On the 20th of December of the same year, the General
Assembly passed resolution 2878 (XXVI), again

> *Strongly deploring* the policies of those States which, in
> defiance of the relevant resolutions of the Security
> Council, the General Assembly and the Special Committee
> [...] continue to co-operate with the Governments of
> Portugal and South Africa and with the illegal racist
> minority regime in Southern Rhodesia; [...]
> *Requests* the Special Committee to undertake a special

189

study on the compliance of Member States with the Declaration and with other relevant resolutions on the question of decolonization, particularly those relating to the Territories under Portuguese domination, Namibia and Southern Rhodesia, and to report thereon to the General Assembly at its twenty-seventh session. (Resolutions, Session XXVI, Part I: 63-68)

Once again, Brazil resorted to her usual recourse of abstention. (68) The resolution further

Urges all States and the specialized agencies and other organizations within the United Nations system to provide [...] moral and material assistance to all people struggling for their freedom and independence in the colonial territories. (65)

In 1972, the United Nations General Assembly heard the historic and tragically moving speeches of Amilcar Cabral and Marcelino dos Santos, leaders of the liberation movements of Guinea Bissau and Mozambique respectively. On the strength of these statements and many other considerations, the General Assembly took the landmark step of recognizing the national liberation movements of Angola, Mozambique and Guinea Bissau as the "authentic representatives of the true aspirations of the peoples of those Territories." (Resolutions, Session XXVII, Part VI: 2) It recommended that they be included in all matters pertaining to the Territories, "in an appropriate capacity and in consultation with the Organization of African Unity" (2), pending the accession of the Territories to independence. Almost all the other concepts embodied in the aforementioned resolutions were incorporated, along with more specific wording of the condemnation of

the persistent refusal of the Government of Portugal to comply with the relevant provisions of the aforementioned resolutions of the United Nations, and in particular, the continuation by Portuguese military forces of the indiscriminate bombing of civilians, the wholesale destruction of villages and property and the ruthless use of napalm and chemical substances in Angola, Guinea (Bissau) and Cape Verde and Mozambique, as well as the continued violations of the territorial integrity and sovereignty of independent African States neighboring Angola, Guinea (Bissau) and Cape Verde and Mozambique, which seriously disturb international peace and security. (2)

Brazil, despite her claims to anti-colonialism, voted against this resolution, on November 14, 1972.

About a month later, the General Assembly passed a resolution dealing with the "Activities of foreign economic and other interests which are impeding the implementation of the Declaration on the Granting of Independence to Colonial Countries etc." This resolution, 2979 (XXVII) states that the Assembly,

> *Deeply disturbed* by the increasingly intensified activities of those foreign economic, financial and other interests in the Territories which, contrary to the relevant resolutions of the General Assembly, assist the Governments of South Africa and Portugal [...] and impede the realization by the peoples of the Territories of their legitimate aspirations for self-determination and independence, [...]
> *Condemns* the policies of the colonial Powers and other States which continue to support those foreign economic and other interests engaged in exploiting the natural and human resources of the Territories without regard to the welfare of the indigenous peoples, thus violating the political, economic and social rights and interests of the indigenous people and obstructing the full and speedy implementation of the Declaration in respect of those Territories; [...]
> *Requests* all States to take effective measures to end the supply of funds and other forms of assistance, including military supplies and equipment, to those regimes which use such assistance to repress the peoples of the colonial Territories and their national liberation movements. (Resolutions, Session XXVII, Part VI: 18-19)

Brazil, once again, abstained on this point so essential to the decolonization of the Portuguese-dominated African nations. (20)

On December 12, 1973, resolution 3113 (XXVIII) concerning the "Question of Territories under Portuguese Administration" condemned

> ... the brutal massacre of villagers, the mass destruction of villages and property and the ruthless use of napalm and chemical substances, in order to stifle the legitimate aspirations of those peoples for freedom and independence;

and demanded that the Government of Portugal discontinue its pitiless repression of the inalienable rights of those peoples

> ... including the eviction from their homes and the regrouping of the African populations in *aldeamentos* and the settlement of foreign immigrants in the Territories;

and reiterated the demand that Portugal adhere to the Geneva Convention relative to the treatment of Prisoners of War; it

> ... invites the International Committee of the Red Cross to continue to maintain close contact with the liberation movements, [...] to provide reports on conditions in prisoner of war camps and treatment of prisoners of war detained by Portugal. (Resolutions adopted on the reports of the Fourth Committee, Session XXVIII: 212)

This resolution also contains the points made in the previous sessions on this subject. (210-214) Brazil voted *no* on resolution 3113. On the same day resolution 3117 (XXVIII) on the activities of foreign economic and other interests repeated the concepts of the former resolutions on the same subject which we have looked at. Brazil abstained. A year later, in 1974, when it was clear that the wars of liberation were won, Brazil finally voted in favor of resolution 3299 (XXIX) on the activities of foreign economic and other interests, essentially the same as 3117.

These actions went beyond a simple lack of sympathy or absence of friendship to Africa. They constitute an irreducible position of Brazilian antagonism toward the legitimate aspirations of Africa:

> Nothing more, not one message of sympathy, not one solidarity, not one gesture, not to speak of cooperation, as if the spring of African Power were embarassing to us, as if the other soul that we possess humiliated us, as if we were ashamed of our common identity, as if it were possible to continue this dichotomy between international policy mandated by a Europeanized elite, which worked for the conservation of the status quo, and the people, whose entrance in the arena of decision-making began only now. (Rodrigues 1964: 372)

Rodrigues wrote this passage before 1964, when at least it was theoretically possible to hypothesize "popular participation" in decision-making. From 1964 on, the military implanted fascism, excluding workers, students and marginalized poor, from any and all political activity. A good part of the population was excluded from the country, and languish in exile all over the world.

Once more let us reiterate the obvious: neither before nor after 1964 did the Black people have any opportunity to form an integral or even minimal part of the significant levels of Brazil's society and conventional institutions. Their destiny was, and continues to be, social marginalization, even in the regions where they are an absolute majority of the population, as illustrates the state of Bahia.

The rejection of this aspect of the Brazilian personality mentioned by Rodrigues -- the influence and presence of Black African formation in our culture and population -- is not a characteristic monopolized uniquely by a Europeanized "elite" which dominates the politics of our country. It is also characteristic of some of the most "progressive" theoreticians, the ideologues of the "Brazilian Revolution." Intellectuals of Marxist orientation are among those who most deny the existence of the racial question as a determinant of social problems, maintaining that the problem is one of confrontation between *master* and *slave, oppressed* and *oppressor, rich* and *poor* -- and not one of race or color. They themselves at times constitute the best proof that the situation of Blacks, past and present, results in great part from a *racism* which transcends class conscience. We have a significant example in "revolutionary" historian Caio Prado Jr. He shows clearly his position on the African soul of the Brazilian people when he writes:

> ... European immigration constitutes a factor particularly notable in the stimulation of the cultural models of the Brazilian population. A fact which has as easy and immediate proof the great differentiation verified, in this aspect, between the South and the North of the country, and which is due in great if not principal part, to the incorporation in one case, and the absence in the other, of appreciable demographic contingents which were situated in levels sensitively superior to those of the preexistent mass of the working population of the country. (1966: 130)

For those who are not familiar with the geographical traits of Brazil, this statement needs some translating. It refers to the fact that the Northeastern area -- especially Bahia -- is known for the tremendous wealth and proliferation of African and Afro-Brazilian cultural forms, particularly in its religion, music and dance, and cuisine. The southern areas, especially São Paulo and Rio de Janeiro, are more "advanced" -- i.e., more urbanized, industrialized, commercialized, mechanized, impersonalized and plasticized -- with cultural modes *purely imitative of the U.S. and Europe,* which dominate not only the economy but also the ways of life. More importantly, the South was inundated throughout this century by a massive influx of white European immigrants, many subsidized by the State in order to whiten the population. Caio Prado manifestly considers them "sensitively superior" in stock and culture to the "preexistent mass of the working population" -- African slaves and their descendants. The unabashed white supremacist grounding of this statement is a representative sample of the mind-set of the Brazilian left while preaching "racial democracy" and workers' unity...

This passage reveals a racism complementary to that other, underlying the Law-Decree No 7969, signed by the dictator Getúlio Vargas in 1945, regulating the entrance of immigrants into the country, which was to obey the "... necessity to preserve and develop in the ethnic composition of the population the more convenient characteristics of its European ancestry." (Skidmore 1974: 219) Both, Marxist and dictator, coincide fully in their assumption that African culture is inferior, which, incidentally, reflects the dominant concept held in Brazil about African heritage in the culture and the population of our country. A concept succinctly summed up in the words of Nina Rodrigues, mulatto scientist and influential writer who from the beginning of this century anathematized: "The black race in Brazil shall remain forever as the basis of our inferiority as a people." (1945: 28)

Thus we have an invariable constant: the African, enslaved or "free," is irreducibly an inferior being. The suppression of the slave traffic, in 1850, and the abolition of slavery, in 1888,

194

events which should have furnished opportunities for social integration through salaried labor, became in practice allies to the repressive forces. Afro-Brazilians, whom the ruling classes of white European cast had not allowed to prepare for the system of free market labor, were *rejected* as source of labor in the new system. Caio Prado talks about the "stimulation" of European immigration of workers to "overcome the lack of labor force." (1966: 128) He doesn't explain how there could be an absence of labor force when millions of Blacks recently "freed" could not find means of living or subsistence.

Even before the abolition of slavery, in the year 1882, the Black labor force was "leftover," rejected by the system, whose declared objective was the liquidation of the African and his descendant in Brazil. A statistical survey in that year in the important provinces of São Paulo, Minas Gerais, Bahia, Pernambuco, Ceará and Rio de Janeiro, obtained the following breakdown:

Free Workers 1,433,170
Slave Workers 656,540
Desocupados (Idle) 2,822,583
(Moura 1972: 54)

These figures reveal that the category of the unemployed was larger than that of free workers and slaves together. The term *desocupado* was the pejorative euphemism used for so-called "free Africans," ex-slaves to whom the right to life by free labor was denied. Expelled by the dominant society, their strength having been exhausted in the enrichment of that same society, they were cast into a kind of slow death by hunger and all sorts of destitution. An inexorable extermination without drawing blood: very convenient for the system. It is easy to follow the rhythm of this genocidal process by observing the dimunition of the number of slaves as the 13th of May -- the date of Abolition -- approaches:

Year	Population of Country	Slave Population	Percent Slaves
1850	5,520,000	2,500,000	31
1852	8,429,672	1,500,000	15
1887	13,278,616	723,419	5

(Moura 1972: 52)

Naturally the number of slaves diminishes and that of the "idle" increases. And so we see that nothing really changed for the African: from *legal slavery* he became captive of *de facto* slavery. The white European immigrant filled what Caio Prado calls the "lack of labor force." The old white Brazilian stock of Portuguese-colonial origin and recent white immigrants came together to build the wall of racial discimination against Blacks.

The contempt of the dominant classes of Brazil toward Africa and Africans is a reality that has lasted from colonial times to the present. The eyes of this Brazil, following the gaze of colonizing interests, turned yesterday to Europe as today they are looking to the United States. Consequently, her foreign policy can only reflect this reality, in which the Black is absent, among other reasons because the Ministry of Foreign Relations is, by tradition, one of the strongest bastions of racial discrimination in Brazil: there exists not one Black diplomat, in a country whose population is in its majority Black. Since 1850, with the suppression of the slave traffic, Brazil has turned its back on Africa, from whence had come those who constructed its economy and peopled its territory which had been emptied, in part, by the massacre of the indigenous peoples, still today in full execution.

During the entire process of discussion and voting in the United Nations around the decolonization of Angola, to whom our historical formation and development owe a debt of blood, labor and artistic tradition impossible to evaluate in all its extension, Brazil maintained itself, as we have seen above, as the valuable ally of fascist Portugal. At times it attempted to mask its position by resorting to abstention, at times distributing *official notes,* of which we will reproduce an example here in part: a communication of 1961 in which Itamarati (Brazilian Ministry of Foreign Relations) says about the decolonization of Angola,

> ... the position of our Country results, on the one hand, from the firm anti-colonialist position of the Government, and on the other, from the international commitments and the ties of extremely special nature that unite Brazil and Portugal.   (Rodrigues 1964: 380)

Such special ties could as well be inscribed in the Treaty of Friendship and Consultation as they could be found in the "extremely special" agreement denounced in the U.N. by the delegate from the Congo. Nothing can be said in certainty, for silence, secrecy and conspiracy preside over and envelop the gestures and conjectures of Brazilian diplomats, as if Itamarati functioned as a veritable laboratory of occult acts and sciences.

Here it is appropriate to relate a recent event involving this colonial inheritance of secretiveness that predominates in Itamarati. Researching in the United Nations data with reference to the International Convention on the Elimination of all Forms of Racial Discrimination (General Assembly, December 21, 1965), I went to the respective Committee to see the document submitted by Brazil as justification for her adherence to the Convention. I found only that, even in such a case of general interest, Brazil does not allow her presentation to be divulged -- provoking suspicion that she must have adhered with restrictions which she is publically ashamed of.

All of these events of the foreign policy of Brazil as well as our racial relations inside the country, transform certain declarations by the Brazilian Government into raw material for "white humor." This is what happens with the contents of a letter from President General Ernesto Geisel to the Secretary General of the United Nations on the occasion of the International Day for the Elimination of Racial Discrimination. The President, of good Aryan (German) stock, reinforced the traditional style of Brazilian racism:

> ... I wish to associate myself, in the name of the Brazilian Government and people, to the universal manifestations of repudiation of the practices of Apartheid and of racial discrimination. [...] We Brazilians share the conviction that the rights of the human person are disrespected in those societies where connotations of racial order determine the degree of respect with which individual liberties and guarantees should be observed. We offer, to counter this scheme, which unfortunately endures, the example of a society formed by the spontaneous and harmonious integration of many races: which integration is the very essence of the Brazilian nationality. *(O Estado de São Paulo,* March 22, 1977: 25)

197

Here we are dealing with a document reiterating the traditional historical position of the dominant strata with relation to African descendants: their systematic liquidation through "whitening." It is necessary to insist on this point in Geisel's letter. The "essence of the Brazilian nationality" is its inalterable ideology and practice of genocide.

Brazil linked herself so faithfully to the imperialist policies of Portugal in Africa, most likely believing in the "Eternity" of colonialism as preached by the Portuguese ambassador in Washington, Pedro Teotonio Pereira. He emphatically declared in 1961: "We shall continue in our mission in Africa, believing firmly that there we shall still be when all this dust raised by anti-colonialism has settled to the earth." (Rodrigues 1964: 348) The association is, in fact, an old one. Let us evoke history. Brazil obtained independence in 1822. Angola was accompanying from the other side of the Atlantic her emancipationist movement. And this is when Brazil signs her first treaty with Portugal, where "... she declares to renounce all policies of alliance with Angolan separatist forces." (Clington 1975: 83) And so Brazil remained, up to and after the recent independence of Mozambique, Guinea Bissau and Angola, servile handmaiden to the most retrograde European colonialism, that of Portugal. Servile to the extent of imprisoning and torturing, in the famous military prisons of the current fascist dictatorship, representative of the MPLA Lima Azevedo. This was one of the first acts of the present regime when it seized power in 1964, giving public proof from the start of its willingness to bear the responsibility of seeing to the "special" tasks of Western civilization and its powers.

It is not surprising that Brazil's immigration policies have been marked always by the preoccupation of prohibiting the entrance of Africans and stimulating, facilitating, even financing the entrance of Europeans of good Aryan stock, including most recently the policy of receiving with open arms the racist whites expelled from Kenya, the ex-Belgian Congo (Rodrigues 1964: 285) and from Mozambique and Angola. Brazil proclaimed herself the hideout of racist and genocidal criminals among whom stand out the names of Antonio Tomás and Marcelo Caetano, the president and prime minister of Salazarist Portugal, the last to disgrace the lives of the Portuguese and African people.

The representative of Belgium in the Commission of Information on Non-autonomous Territories of the United Nations had well-founded reasons when he sustained the thesis of "internal colonialism" supposedly protecting but in reality attacking the Indians of Brazil, to whom we can add millions of African Brazilians subject to all forms of aggression and prohibitions due to their ethnic orgins.

The problem of the South Atlantic, its strategic and commercial importance, has been a preoccupation of Brazilian politicians and military men since immediately after the second world war, when Colonel Golbery do Couto e Silva, currently General-in-Chief of the Civil House of President General Geisel -- his closest advisor -- advocated the Atlantic as a "peace route," in search of "cooperation and amity." (Rodrigues 1964: 371) It seems that the old dream of a South Atlantic Treaty Alliance, which would include Portugal, South Africa, Brazil and Argentina, is now on the way to becoming a reality.

In its July 1977 issue, the magazine *Africa* published an article entitled "Pretoria Turns to the Latins," in which it examines the steps being taken by the U.S. to resolve certain strategic and economic problems caused by the historical agony of the racist regime of South Africa, the liberation wars in progress in Zimbabwe and Namibia and the stabilization of the new governments of Mozambique and Angola. The United States, in no position to intervene directly in these affairs, and reluctant to openly ally itself with white supremacy in South Africa, has found the most convenient path in a South Atlantic Treaty Organization, modelled after NATO. In the words of Zbignew Brezezinski, Kissinger-surrogate to Jimmy Carter:

> The Southern Atlantic Alliance offers Washington the tool it needs to protect its perceived interests in a post-Vietnam world. Using local allies to serve as proxies is in line with the "Nixon Doctrine." (*Africa*, July 1977: 71, citing Brzezinski article in *Foreign Affairs*.)

The object of such a treaty is the integration of South Africa into the perimeters of Western (U.S.) defense, and the "local allies" in this case would be Brazil, Argentina, Chile and South Africa.

The article in *Africa* relates that "secret talks have been going on since at least 1969 among these countries." It cites a meeting in the Argentine naval base of Porto-Bergano, immediately after the overthrow by the military of Isabel Perón, between the U.S., Argentina and Brazil, at which naval manoeuvres and coordination were discussed along with the general question of security in the South Atlantic. The newspaper *La Nación* of Buenos Aires, recognized mouthpiece of the military regime, commented on this occasion:

> Only three countries, which by their cultures and their traditions are part of the Western World, have a Geographical situation which enables them to play an important role in the control and the protection of the Southern Atlantic: Argentina, Brazil and South Africa. (*Africa,* July 1977: 71)

Soon after this, a joint Argentine-Brazilian military mission arrived at the naval base of Simonstown in South Africa to plan the logistics of future cooperation. South Africa's weakest military force is her navy. The three South American countries have strong naval power which could be of invaluable assistance to the Pretoria regime.

Africa accentuates the recent inauguration of a Buenos Aires - Pretoria air connection, demonstrating the effort on both sides to beef up commerce between an isolated South Africa and the lucrative markets of South America. It goes on to point out that

> Brazil and Argentina are striving to reduce their marked dependency on their American suppliers by diversifying their uranium sources. As is well known, Pretoria has one of the largest reserves of uranium of the world. Using this important bargaining card, it can negotiate its way into the Latin American market under favorable conditions. (1977: 71)

Last year, Pretoria's naval commander, James Johnson, was present as participant in the Inter-American naval exercises. In Rio de Janeiro in the summer of 1976, the Eighth Inter-American naval conference highlighted the threat of the "bridgehead which the pro-communist countries have acquired because of the friendly government in Angola."

The dangers of such an alliance have been denounced at the United Nations by the former Minister of the Exterior of Angola, José Eduardo dos Santos, who declared that "... it is in effect an offensive military pact against southern Africa and it constitutes a menace to world peace." (1977: 71) And indeed, recent history shows with what efficacy the arms of NATO aided Portugal in her colonial wars against the people of Angola and Mozambique. It is but the latest of futile efforts of the repressive forces of the West against the people of Africa: for, as Samora Machel, leader of the people of Mozambique in combatting the sophisticated technology of NATO and Portugal, underlined in his speech to the Symposium in Honor of Amilcar Cabral held in Conakry on January 31, 1973:

> It was the struggle, the unity of the people in their combat, [...] that not only permitted the people to forge their personality, but also to assert themselves on the international level. And it is this that the bullets shot by the agents of PIDE [Portuguese intelligence] at Amilcar Cabral or the murderous bombs dropped by the airplanes of NATO against the population were never able to impede. (1-2)

South Africa's institutionalized policies of Apartheid, constitute the daily practice of genocide against the majority of Africans in that country by a white minority. This criminal act directly affects all peoples of African origin. To stop its continuation with impunity, to prevent the reinforcement of this destructive force, is a duty of self-defense that imposes itself on all of us as Blacks, as Africans of the Diaspora.

This Congress witnesses a historical epoch in which the Africans of this part of the world, surpassing the phase of lamentation or declamation, are moving in the sense of organizing ourselves to confront the great battle of our future, of our existence with liberty and dignity. Consequently I propose that this Congress direct itself to the governments of the U.S., Argentina and Brazil as well as Chile, transmitting our repulsion and our energetic opposition to the manoeuvres, diplomatic and military, and the conversations, meetings, or any other events that could lead to the concretization of the South Atlantic Treaty Alliance or any other entity under any denomination that attempts to mask the objectives of collaboration with the racist white criminals heading the government of South Africa.

BIBLIOGRAPHY

Clington, Mário de Sousa (1975) *Angola Libre?* Paris: Gallimard.

Machel, Samora (1973) *Falar de Amilcar Cabral é Falar de um Povo.* Intervention by FRELIMO in Symposium in Homage to Amilcar Cabral, Conakry, January 31, 1973. Lisbon: Edições CEC (mimeograph).

Moore, Carlos (1972) *Were Marx and Engels White Racists? - the Prolet-Aryan Outlook of Marx and Engels.* Chicago: Third World Press.

Moura, Clovis (1972) *Rebeliões da Senzala - Quilombos, Insurreições, Guerrilhas.* Rio de Janeiro: Editora Conquista.

Nascimento, Abdias do (1977) *"Racial Democracy" in Brazil: Myth or Reality?* Ibadan: Sketch Publishing Co., Ltd.

Prado, Caio Jr. (1966) *A Revolução Brasileira.* São Paulo: Editora Brasiliense.

"Pretoria Turns to the Latins" (1977) (Special Report), *Africa.* London: Africa Journal Ltd., July (No. 71), pp. 70-71.

Rodrigues, José Honório (1964) *Brasil e África - Outro Horizonte,* 2nd Edition. Rio de Janeiro: Civilização Brasileira.

Rodrigues, Nina (1945) *Os Africanos no Brasil.* São Paulo: Companhia Editora Nacional.

Skidmore, Thomas E. (1974) *Black into White - Race and Nationality in Brazilian Thought.* New York: Oxford University Press.

Sodré, Nelson Werneck (1970) *Formação Economica do Brasil,* 5th Edition. São Paulo: Editora Brasiliense.

United Nations (1974) *Report of the Special Committee on the Situation with Regard to the Implementation of the Declaration on the Granting of Independence to Colonial Countries and Peoples,* Volume II. U.N. Official Records:

Twenty-Fourth Session, Supplement No. 23. New York: United Nations General Assembly.

United Nations General Assembly Round-Up and Resolutions, Sessions XXII-XXIX. New York: United Nations General Assembly.

SELECTED GENERAL BIBLIOGRAPHY

Abimbola, Wande (1976) *Ifa: An Exposition of Ifa Literary Corpus.* Ibadan: Oxford University Press Nigeria.

Andrade, Jorge (1971) "Quatro Tiradentes Baianos," *Realidade.* São Paulo: November, pp. 34-53.

Andrade, Mario (1959) *Danças Dramáticas do Brasil.* São Paulo: Editora Martins.

Asante, Molefi Kete (1978) *Epic in Search of African Kings.* Buffalo: New Horizons, Inc.

-- (1978) *Systematic Nationalism and Language Liberation.* Buffalo: New Horizons, Inc.

Azevedo, Thales de (1975) *Democracia Racial: Ideologia e Realidade.* Petrópolis: Editora Vozes.

Bastide, Roger (1958) *Le Candomblé de Bahia.* Paris: Editions Mouton.

-- (1971) *African Civilizations in the New World* (translated by Peter Green). New York: Harper and Row Publishers.

-- (1973) *Estudos Afro-Brasileiros.* São Paulo: Editora Perspectiva.

Bastide, Roger and Florestan Fernandes (1959) *Brancos e Negros em São Paulo.* São Paulo: Companhia Editora Nacional.

Bastide, Roger et. al. (1968) *Colloque sur l'Art Negre.* Paris: Présence Africaine.

Bomilcar, Alvaro (1916) *O Preconceito de Raça no Brasil.* Rio de Janeiro: Typografia Aurora.

Cabral, Amilcar (1973) *Return to the Source: Selected Speeches of Amilcar Cabral* (edited by Africa Information Service). New York and London: Monthly Review Press and Africa Information Service.

-- (1975) *L'Arme de la Theorie.* Paris: Francoise Maspero.

Cardoso, Fernando Henrique (1977) *Capitalismo e Escravidão no Brasil Meridional.* Rio de Janeiro: Editora Paz e Terra.

Clarke, John Henrik (1974) *Marcus Garvey and the Vision of Africa.* New York: Random House.

Clington, Mario de Sousa (1975) *Angola Libre?* Paris: Gallimard.

Davis, David Brion (1968) *El Problema de la Esclavitud en la Cultura Occidental.* Buenos Aires: Editorial Paidos.

Degler, Carl N. (1971) *Neither Black nor White: Slavery and Race Relations in Brazil and the United States.* New York; MacMillan Publishing Co.

Diop, Cheikh Anta (1974) *The African Origin of Civilization* (translated and edited by Mercer Cook). Westport: Lawrence Hill and Co.

-- (1978) *The Cultural Unity of Black Africa* (translation by authorization of Présence Africaine). Chicago: Third World Press.

Dzidzienyo, Anani (1971) *The Position of Blacks in Brazilian Society.* London: Minority Rights Group, Report no. 7 (mimeograph).

Fanon, Frantz (1963) *Los Condenados de la Tierra* (translated by Julieta Campos). Mexico and Buenos Aires: Fondo de Cultura Economica.

Fernandes, Florestan (1964) *A Integração do Negro na Sociedade de Classes,* 2nd edition, 2 vols. São Paulo: Dominus Editora, Universidade de São Paulo.

Freire, Paulo (1975) *Pedagogia do Oprimido.* Porto: Afrontamento.

Freyre, Gilberto (1966) *Casa Grande e Senzala,* 14th edition, 2 vols. Rio de Janeiro: José Olympio Editora.

-- (1976) "Aspectos da influencia africana no Brasil," *Cultura*. Brasília: Ministério da Educação e Cultura, October - December (Ano VI, no. 23), pp. 6-19.

Gilliam, Angela (1975) *Language Attitudes, Ethnicity and Class in São Paulo and Salvador de Bahia, Brazil*. Dissertation, Union Graduate School, New York (Unpublished)

Ianni, Octavio (1972) *Raças e Classes Sociais no Brasil*, 2nd edition, Rio de Janeiro: Civilização Brasileira.

James, George G. M. (1976) *Stolen Legacy*, 2nd edition. San Francisco: Julian Richardson Associates.

Karenga, Maulana Ron (1975) "Ideology and Struggle: Some Preliminary Notes," *Black Scholar*. Sausalito: January - February (Vol. VII, no. 5), pp. 23-30.

Landes, Ruth (1967) *A Cidade das Mulheres* (translator unknown at this writing). Rio de Janeiro: Civilização Brasileira. (Original in English: The City of Women, 1947.)

Macedo, Sergio D. T. (1974) *Crônica do Negro no Brasil*. Rio de Janeiro: Distribuidora Record de Serviços de Imprensa.

Madhubuti, Haki (Don L. Lee) (1978) *Enemies: the Clash of Races*. Chicago: Third World Press.

Maglangbayan, Shawna (1972) *Garvey, Lumumba, Malcolm: Black Nationalist Separatists*. Chicago: Third World Press.

Mancuso, Flora Edwards (1975) *The Theater of the Black Diaspora: a Comparative Study of Black Drama in Brazil, Cuba and the United States*. PhD. dissertation, Department of Comparative Literature, New York University. (Unpublished)

Mello, A. Silva (1958) *Estudos sobre o Negro*. Rio de Janeiro: José Olympio Editora.

Moore, Carlos (1972) *Were Marx and Engels White Racists? the Prolet-Aryan Outlook of Marx and Engels*. Chicago: Third World Press.

Moura, Clovis (1972) *Rebeliões da Senzala - Quilombos, Insurreições, Guerrilhas.* Rio de Janeiro: Editora Conquista.

-- (1977) *O Negro - de Bom Escravo a Mau Cidadão?* Rio de Janeiro: Editora Conquista.

Nabuco, Joaquim (1949) *O Abolicionismo.* São Paulo: Instituto Progresso Editorial.

Nascimento, Abdias do (1960) *Sortilégio: Mistério Negro.* Rio de Janeiro: Teatro Experimental do Negro.

-- (ed.) (1961) *Dramas para Negros e Prólogo para Brancos.* Rio de Janeiro: Teatro Experimental do Negro.

-- (1966) "Open Letter to the First World Festival of Negro Arts," *Présence Africaine* (English edition). Paris: Second Quarterly (Vol. 30, no. 58), pp. 208-218.

-- (ed) (1966) *Teatro Experimental do Negro - Testemunhos* Rio de Janeiro: Edições GRD.

-- (1967) "The Negro Theater in Brazil" (translated by Gregory Rabassa), *African Forum.* New York: The American Society of African Culture, Spring (Vol. II, no. 4), pp. 35-53.

-- (1968) *O Negro Revoltado.* Rio de Janeiro: Edições GRD.

-- (1976) "Afro-Brazilian Art: a Liberating Spirit" (translated by Elisa Larkin Nascimento), *Black Art: an International Quarterly.* New York: Fall (Vol. I, no. 1), pp. 54-62.

-- (1977) "Afro-Brazilian Theater: a Conspicuous Absence," (translated by Elisa Larkin Nascimento), *Afriscope.* Lagos: January - February (Vol. VII, no. 1), pp. 27-33.

-- (1977) *"Racial Democracy" in Brazil: Myth or Reality?* (translated by Elisa Larkin Nascimento). Ibadan: Sketch Publishing Co.

-- (1978) "African Culture in Brazilian Art," *Journal of Black Studies.* June (Vol. 8, no. 4), pp. 389-422.

Nyerere, Julius K. (1974) *Ujamaa - Essays on Socialism.* London and New York: Oxford University Press.

-- (1974) "Speech to the Congress," *Black Scholar.* Sausalito: July - August (Vol. V, no. 10), pp. 16-22.

Ogunsanya, Ebun Omowunmi (1971) "Residual Yoruba-Portuguese Bilingualism." B.A. Thesis, Harvard University, Cambridge Mass. (Unpublished)

Olinto, Antonio (1967) "The Negro Writer and the Negro Influence in Brazilian Literature," (translated by Gregory Rabassa), *African Forum.* New York: The American Society of African Culture, Spring (Vol. II, no. 4), pp. 5-19.

Pierson, Donald (1942) *Negroes in Brazil.* Carbondale and Edwardsville: Southern Illinois University Press.

Rabassa, Gregory (1965) *O Negro na Ficção Brasileira* (translated by Ana Maria Martins). Rio de Janeiro: Edições Tempo Brasileiro.

Ramos, Arthur (1946) *As Culturas Negras no Novo Mundo.* São Paulo: Companhia Editora Nacional.

Ramos, Guerreiro (1957) *Introdução Crítica à Sociologia Brasileira.* São Paulo: Editiorial Andes.

Ribeiro, René (1956) *Religião e Relações Raciais.* Rio de Janeiro: Ministério da Educação e Cultura.

Rodrigues, José Honório (1964) *Brasil e África: Outro Horizonte,* 2nd Edition, 2 vols. Rio de Janeiro: Civilização Brasileira.

Rodrigues, Nina (1945) *Os Africanos no Brasil.* São Paulo: Companhia Editora Nacional.

Santos, Deoscoredes Maximiliano dos (Mestre Didi) (1961) *Contos Negros da Bahia.* Rio de Janeiro: Edições GRD.

-- (1963) *Contos Nagô.* Rio de Janeiro: Edições GRD.

-- (1976) *Contos Crioulos da Bahia.* Petropolis: Editora Vozes.

Santos, Juana Elbein dos (1977) *Os Nagô e a Morte,* 2nd Edition. Petrópolis: Editora Vozes.

Sayers, Raymond (1956) *The Negro in Brazilian Literature.* New York: Hispanic Institute in the United States.

Seljan, Zora (1967) "Negro Popular Poetry in Brazil" (translated by Gregory Rabassa), *African Forum.* New York: The American Society of African Culture, Spring (Vol. II, no. 4), pp. 54-77.

Sena, Marina de Avellar (1977) *Compra e Venda de Escravos em Minas Gerais.* Belo Horizonte: printed by Editora Littera Maciel Ltda.

Skidmore, Thomas E. (1974) *Black into White: Race and Nationality in Brazilian Thought.* New York: Oxford University Press.

-- (1976) *Preto no Branco: Raça e Nacionalidade no Pensamento Brasileiro* (translated by Raul de Sá Barbosa). Rio de Janeiro: Editora Paz e Terra.

Şoyinka, Wọle (1976) *Myth, Literature and the African World.* London: Cambridge University Press.

Turner, Doris J. (1975) "Symbols in Two Afro-Brazilian Literary Works: *Jubiabá* and *Sortilégio.*" Commissioned by the Latin American Studies Association and the Consortium of Latin American Studies Programs. Delivered at National Seminar on the Teaching of Latin American Studies, University of New Mexico, Albuquerque. (Unpublished)

Viana, Oliveira (1938) *Raça e Assimilação,* 3rd edition. São Paulo: Companhia Editora Nacional.

Viana Filho, Luiz (1946) *O Negro na Bahia.* Rio de Janeiro: José Olympio Editora.

Walters, Ronald (1977) "Marxist-Leninism and the Black Revolution," *Black Books Bulletin.* Chicago: Institute of Positive Education, Fall (Vol. V, no. 3), pp. 12-17, 63.

Williams, Chancellor (1974) *The Destruction of Black Civilization*. Chicago: Third World Press.

Yai, Ọlabiyi Babalọla (1976) "Alguns aspectos da influencia das culturas nigerianas no Brasil em literatura, folclore e linguagem," *Cultura*. Brasília: Ministério da Educação e Cultura, October-December (Ano VI, no. 23), pp. 94-100.

VOCABULARY

Alagados - Shantytowns built on often unsafe swamplands by displaced poor people, mostly Black.

Babalaô (Babalawo) - Priest and diviner, master of the discipline of the literary corpus of Ifa which contains the age-old wisdom of Yoruba oral tradition. In Brazil he has become identified generally as a priest of the *Candomblé*.

Batuque - Periodic dance or celebration permitted among slave "nations" by the colonial authorities. Also, the name of the version of Afro-Brazilian religion practiced in Rio Grande do Sul.

Candomblé - Religion of the Orixas, brought from Africa to Brazil by the Slaves. *Candomblé* is the name of the form practiced in Bahia especially; it is used as a general term here. It is predominantly of Yoruba origin but incorporates elements of other African cultures such as Bantu, Ewe and Fon.

Carnaval - Annual popular celebration, with specially written songs and much dancing in the streets all over Brazil. African culture, especially rhythmn and musical influence in the *samba,* have made it a unique cultural event, extravagant and colorful.

Cortiços - Extremely overcrowded shanties, one-family units often inhabited by 50 people or more, in the slums of urban Brazil.

Escola de Samba (Samba School) - Groups of Black people organized to dance collectively in a kind of contest of Samba during *Carnaval.* Originally spontaneous and popular creativity, they have become commercialized under the control of white business interests and Government tourism.

212

Favelas - Urban slums, of a poverty and deprivation far worse than any ghetto known to the U.S., often perched high on inaccessible hills on the outskirts of the city, populated primarily by Black people. *Favelados* are inhabitants of *favelas.*

Festac '77 - Second World Festival of Black and African Arts and Culture, Lagos 1977.

Filho de Santo - Initiated medium of Candomblé, priest or priestess of one Orixa.

Gantois - Area of Salvador City, Bahia, where one of the most famous *terreiros* of *Candomblé,* presided over by the Mãe Menininha, is located. She is one of the most important religious figures of African culture in Brazil.

Gêge - Brazilian colonial term for Ewe culture.

Invasões - Squatter settlements of displaced people of extreme poverty.

Latifundio - Huge estate of land, originally plantations but today often unproductive, owned by the aristocratic land-owners called *latifundiarios.*

Macumba - The form of Afro-Brazilian religion, essentially like *Candomblé* but with a greater Bantu emphasis, prevalent in the southern urban areas of Brazil like São Paulo and Rio de Janeiro.

Mãe-de-Santo - High priestess of the Candomblé.

Orixa (Orisha) - Deity of the *Candomblé,* derived from Yoruba religion, with some Brazilian variations in name and character.

Pegi - Shrine, within a *terreiro,* dedicated to one divinity.

Ponto - Ritual song or design to invoke the Orixas.

Pai-de-Santo - High priest of the *Candomblé.*

Quilombo - Society of escaped or rebellious slaves, similar to Maroon Societies of the Caribbean or the *palenque* or *cimarrón* of so-called Spanish America.

Quimbanda - Form of Afro-Brazilian religion identified as a sub-division of Umbanda, found especially in urban areas, most intensely in *favelas.* Certain persons characterized it as a degraded ritual of evil spirit.

Terreiro - Sacred place of worship of the *Candomblé:* temple.

Umbanda - The most eclectic and dynamic form of Afro-Brazilian worship, including elements of Kardecist spiritism, Brazilian Indian, Catholic, Hindu and oriental religions.

Xangô - Orixa of fire and lightning. Also Black religion of Recife.

Note

Those who are familiar with Nigerian Yoruba culture or language will note variations from the usual spelling of Yoruba divinities' names and other Yoruba words. We have chosen to use the Brazilian forms, because we feel it desirable to preserve the distinctly Brazilian character which nevertheless maintains its essential continuity with the African origin. Thus Orişa or Orisha is *Orixa* in Brazilian, Shango is *Xangô,* Oshun becomes *Oxum,* Eshu *Exu;*Ogun is *Ogum,* and Oya *Iansan,* for example.

Books from the Majority Press

THE NEW MARCUS GARVEY LIBRARY

Literary Garveyism: Garvey, Black Arts and the Harlem Renaissance. Tony Martin. $19.95 (cloth), $8.95 (paper).

The Poetical Works of Marcus Garvey.
Tony Martin, Ed. $17.95 (cloth), $7.95 (paper).

Marcus Garvey, Hero: A First Biography.
Tony Martin. $19.95 (cloth), $7.95 (paper).

The Pan-African Connection.
Tony Martin. $22.95 (cloth), $7.95 (paper).

Message to the People: the Course of African Philosophy.
Marcus Garvey. Ed. by Tony Martin. $22.95 (cloth), $8.95 (paper).

Race First: the Ideological and Organizational Struggles of Marcus Garvey and the Universal Negro Improvement Association.
Tony Martin. $29.95 (cloth), $10.95 (paper).

The Philosophy and Opinions of Marcus Garvey.
Amy Jacques Garvey, Ed. $10.95 (paper).

Amy Ashwood Garvey: Pan-Africanist, Feminist and Wife No. 1.
Tony Martin. Forthcoming 1989.

African Fundamentalism: A Literary and Cultural Anthology of Garvey's Harlem Renaissance. Tony Martin, Ed. $12.95 (paper). Spring 1989.

THE BLACK WORLD

Brazil: Mixture or Massacre? Essays in the Genocide of a Black People. Abdias do Nascimento. $9.95 (paper).

Studies in the African Diaspora: A Memorial to James R. Hooker (1929-1976). John P. Henderson and Harry A. Reed, Eds. $39.95 (cloth).

In Nobody's Backyard: the Grenada Revolution in its Own Words. Vol. I, the Revolution at Home.
Tony Martin, Ed. $22.95 (cloth), $7.95 (paper).

In Nobody's Backyard: the Grenada Revolution in its Own Words. Vol. II, Facing the World.
Tony Martin, Ed., $22.95 (cloth), $7.95 (paper).

Order from The Majority Press, P.O. Box 538, Dover, MA 02030, U.S.A. Mass. residents add 5% sales tax.